ZENBU
ZEN

ZENBU ZEN

FINDING FOOD, CULTURE & BALANCE IN KYOTO

JANE LAWSON

MURDOCH BOOKS

genjitsuka
THE REALISATION
10

shiwasu / juunigatsu
DECEMBER
the 12th month
20

mutsuki / ichigatsu
JANUARY
the 1st month
108

kisaragi / nigatsu
FEBRUARY
the 2nd month
195

yayoi / sangatsu & uzuki / shigatsu
MARCH & APRIL
the 3rd & 4th months
237

DEDICATION
271

THANK YOU
274

GLOSSARY
278

INDEX
282

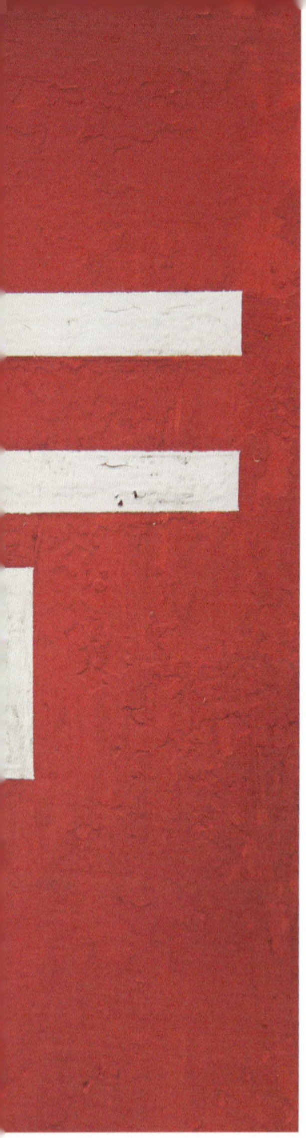

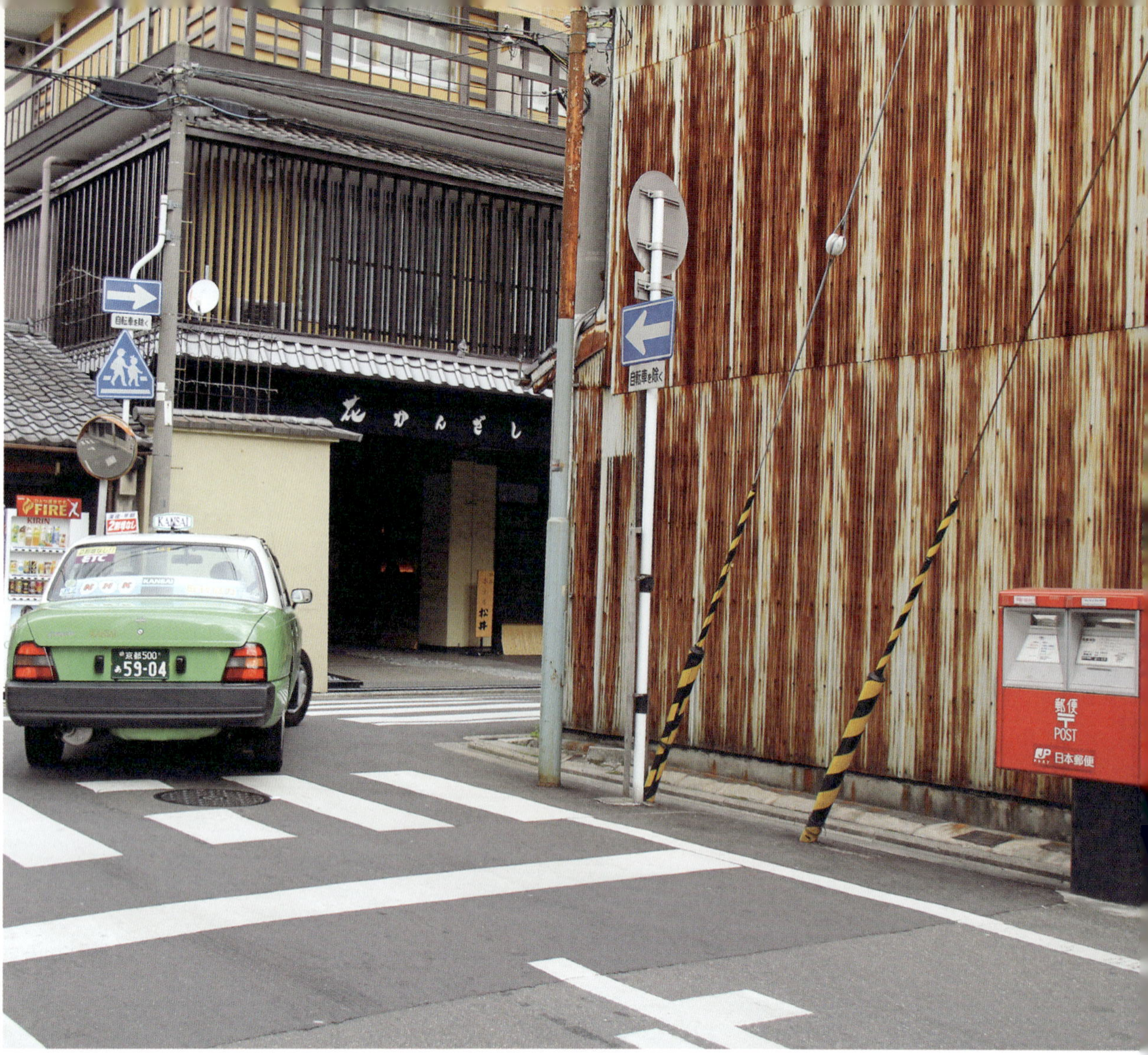
FIRE
59-04
POST
日本郵便

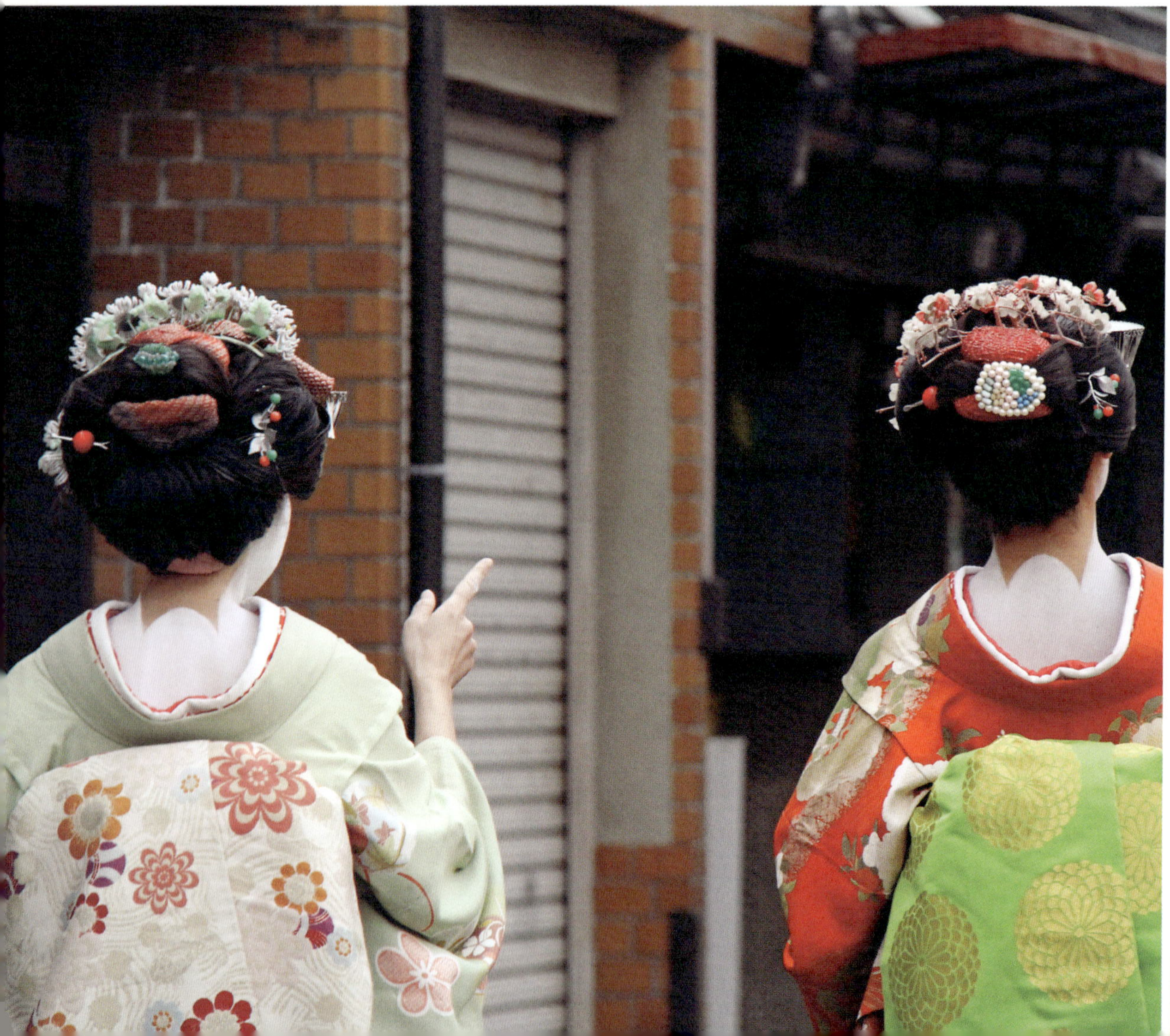

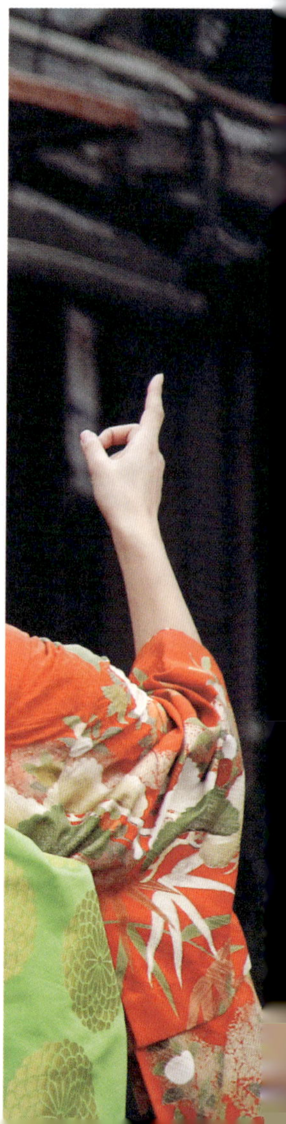

Life constantly presents us with difficult challenges. During those times I tell myself 'Zenbu Zen' – that ultimately everything is Zen, and it will all be okay in the long run. The ups, the downs and the in-betweens are all part of the glorious ride.

In Japan, there is the utmost respect for those who may be by one's side seeking the same journey — so much so that although you may not be alone, you can feel as though there is no one else in existence for that brief moment.

genjitsuka

THE REALISATION

CHAPTER 1

stress

The mere mention of the word tugs at my adrenal glands in a dismal reminder of a time not so long ago. Although far enough distanced from its clutches, I still find it essential during moments of provocation to diffuse my body's learnt responses. A propensity towards the release of acrid fire into the pit of my stomach — which would rapidly coil itself around my internals before attempting to erupt through my chest cavity — has thankfully been disengaged. Nevertheless, the residual wounds remain a touch tender.

This global affliction is not a new one. But you would have to have been trapped beneath a boulder on an isolated islet to not notice its rise in recent years. People incessantly complain about 'their load' in some form or another. And statistics scream out the potential long-term damage to both our physical and mental health. Yet some of us simply can't stop ourselves from walking up to it and vigorously shaking hands in invitation. Ridiculously, we wear 'stress' like a badge of honour, as a measure of our success: the perception being that if you're not constantly 'under the pump', you simply aren't 'cutting it'.

The beast has become so ingrained in our social makeup that those who thrive on it are tragically in the majority. In order to assimilate, all too many folk have disregarded, possibly even chortled defiantly, at any suggestion of 'workaholism' from those who have cleverly managed to scrape together some semblance of that work–life balance stuff. When chronically pressured or in a constant state of 'fight or flight', the resulting adrenaline pumping through one's system becomes addictive, as it allows those affected to live in a delusional state of invincibility until, of course, their batteries are seriously depleted, and they collapse in a rather unkempt heap.

But exactly how does one end up in such a predicament? I was rapturous when I was appointed publisher of a prestigious book list and excitedly threw myself into the role. I proudly waved the company and author flags as high as my arms would extend. I unrelentingly, and somewhat unwittingly, pushed my mind and body to their outermost limits because, quite frankly, it gave me a sensational buzz and sense of *faux* energy, which I foolishly believed would last forever.

Days quickly turned to months of too many back-to-back all-day meetings, after which I'd sit to stop my head from spinning just long enough to read the constant barrage of emails, manuscripts and proposals. Next I'd be wrangling with the legalities and nuances of author contracts, haggling with agents and continuously churning out 'unique' concepts for a non-authored list. On top of this was the considerable task of scouring for new 'talent' and managing author relationships. There was regular interstate travel, textbook office politics, and more work-related socialising (a.k.a. networking) than one human body should ever be subjected to. Suddenly, my life started to look a tad unbalanced.

Wining and dining, dutifully attending food and wine festivals, book launches, food-media-related events and publicity tours may sound like fun (and yes, I can hear that tiny violin playing), but it is also exhausting and an excellent way to fast-track a heart attack; I may as well have been mainlining cholesterol.

In some ways, it was my dream job — a highly creative role working with many frighteningly talented, inspiring beings. But the sum of all parts led my mind, body and soul to suffer in a rather serious way: the common term for my condition being 'burnout'.

I stopped exercising, eating properly, seeing my family or being involved in any genuine form of social life and was literally forgetting to breathe. I was 'over-adrenalised', according to my doctor, and wasn't sleeping. Anxiety reared its ugly mug for the first time in my life. I suffered panic attacks most nights, right at that crucial point halfway between consciousness and sleep — a feeling of impending doom grabbing me by the throat and choking me awake. There I would lie in fear, with my heartbeat pounding in my eardrums against the still of the night, wondering, wide-eyed, what the hell was going on with me?

My skin broke out in inflamed, angry welts on my cheeks and jaw — apparently a result of too much cortisol, the stress hormone — and a fine sprinkling of spots covered my pallid décolletage. A haywire immune system forced my body into a highly allergic state — the fury of which was demonstrated by a horrendous, hacking cough that sounded like I was choking. A raging, itchy dermatological rash crawled around my armpits, fluid built up in my ears, causing them to ache relentlessly, and I suffered intermittent vertigo. I was pasty and dangerously flabby, with red, scratchy eyes, and I was highly irritable, as though in a constant state of heightened PMT. Not a pretty picture.

Friends and family were clearly concerned, and those who didn't know me well enough to understand this was 'not the normal Jane' fell by the wayside. My priorities were notably warped, but I didn't have the energy to argue or defend my inability to attend an event or chat on the phone; I felt drained of every last drop of my essence and my nerves were shot. Flat and scared, with much of the joy siphoned from my life, I recall likening myself to a half-stubbed-out cigarette on a dirty pavement, its dying embers pathetically sucking on any available oxygen just to keep alight. My brain felt as though it had been deep-fried, my memory suffered considerably and my creativity was at an all-time low. I didn't feel of much use to anyone. Like many misguided fools before me, I truly believed I could keep pushing myself, spurred on by overzealous adrenal trickery. But my energy was spent.

While the workplace would seem an easy target at which to aim accountability, I came to accept that I was the only person responsible for my continued self-destructive behaviour and ignorance.

Countless tests, lotions, potions and pills bore little to no improvement on my condition and, collectively, my doctor, naturopath and shrink prescribed an imperative 'time out'. After much consideration and soul-searching, I decided it was time to resign from life as it was. There was no option but to make urgent and vital change — starting with an escape plan.

*

For reasons unknown, Japan has always felt like a second home, so it was a logical choice for my retreat. I needed to be far away from my everyday routine, yet I craved the secure swaddling of the familiar — somewhere where I felt comfortable and safe.

During my introduction to Japan, as a 15-year-old on holiday with my family, I was jolted alive by an immediate and intense connection to this ancient land. I have since spent a good portion of 25 years' worth of annual leave traversing the length and breadth of its complex and wondrous islands.

At the grand age of 20, I moved to Tokyo for what should have been a year, but was downgraded to three months when the exotic allure of working in a foreign land wore rice-paper thin. During the 1980s 'bubble' it was viewed as a status symbol for a Japanese company to employ a Westerner — regardless of whether there was any need to do so. I was the token blonde-haired, blue-eyed Aussie mascot and my office 'job', a term I use loosely, entailed sitting silently at the front desk ready to bow, in respectful welcome, to any client who might dare walk through the door. During one busy week, there were a total of three guests.

After committing office *seppuku* (hara-kiri), by hiding a book in my desk drawer to alleviate the boredom, I continued to behave in a culturally unacceptable manner by pleading for more work. This resulted in many hushed and huddled discussions; my colleagues were both alarmed and confused by my *gaijin* (foreigner) ways. When the occasional trip to the post office didn't quell my frustrations, I was awarded the salubrious task of plucking dead leaves from the office pot plants. While it beat doing nothing, it wasn't enough to distract me from my increasing homesickness so, with mixed feelings, I trudged back to my natural habitat — returning only at a safe distance, as an over-enthusiastic tourist, for the next two decades.

So there I was, almost 20 years to the day, finding myself desirous to live life *à la Japonaise* once more. One thing was certain, the frantic pace and buzz of electrical Tokyo held no appeal; in fact, seeking that kind of kick would have been like putting a gun to my head. It was Kyoto, the one-time capital and cultural and spiritual epicentre, that my internal GPS was programmed for.

Almost 128 million people call relatively tiny Japan home; Australia, twenty times its size, houses a mere 22.5 million. Japan is also particularly mountainous, rendering much of the land uninhabitable. Based on those numbers, it is not the first place most people consider for peaceful rehabilitation. However, I have always been intrigued by the Japanese people's seemingly innate ability to quieten their minds — particularly within the confines of big-city madness. Though difficult to imagine how it might occur, it is nevertheless fairly predictable that the Japanese might choose to recharge their batteries by being alone. In fact, they schedule regular interjections of mindfulness into their daily lives. Contemplating life, nature or beauty in any form could be considered a national pastime and it is common to witness individuals sitting meditatively by a river or Zen rock garden, or stopping in their tracks to admire everything from a decorative cabbage to gnarly moss-covered tree roots.

The soothing, ceremonial preparation of tea is almost as popular today as it was during the time of the samurai, who found the subtle art of *sado* (also *chado* — 'the way of tea') an excellent counterbalance to the atrocities of the battlefield. The ceremony is a slow, exquisite art in itself. But the joy of slowly sipping the earthiness of freshly whisked matcha at an authentic teahouse while inhaling the faint, hay-like scent of tatami flooring is strangely blissful. Leaning on a bamboo bridge over a pond full of meandering koi is as nurturing to the human soul as a fish dinner is to one's growling stomach. Strolling through a Shinto shrine's garden, tiptoeing through the dappled orange glow of maple-filtered sunlight, or picnicking under a canopy of pale pink *sakura* (cherry blossom) puftaloons are immeasurable pleasures that both delight and calm.

Self-reflection is inevitable in such surroundings, where there is little risk of sudden loud noise or chatter. In Japan, there is the utmost respect for those who may be by one's side seeking the same journey — so much so that although you may not be alone, you can feel as though there is no one else in existence for that brief moment.

In Kyoto, one tends to frequently stumble across unfathomably serene and beautiful spaces. One minute you may find yourself in the midst of a colourful street festival, and at the next turn you are witnessing an achingly beautiful but sombre ceremonial ritual.

The Japanese believe that the year is divided evenly, according to the lunisolar (moon-phase) calendar, into 24 *sekki* (small seasons) that mark subtle changes within the four main seasons. These 24 smaller seasons are all celebrated in some way, shape or form. The entire population's innate design consciousness directly connects with each season, and everyday aesthetics, such as the patterns and colours of traditional costumes, ceramics and street ornaments, are all an ode to a specific period.

Something that is very close to my heart and also in line with the seasons is, of course, food. While eating seasonally is not a new concept, the Japanese observe nature's bounty like no other nation. A stint for a particular vegetable may be as short as a few days, but there's no doubt it will be in-store for purchase by astute shoppers. Cherishing each season, large or small, results in a varied, delicious and predominantly healthy cuisine that is also highly visually appealing.

I knew time spent in Kyoto would be medicine for both body and soul and an opportunity to get reacquainted with myself, so there was no option but to swap my daydreams for reality. My focus would naturally be on culinary culture, but as part of that I was hoping to gain some insight into the basic philosophy of a race who, while not considering themselves entirely religious, are nevertheless heavily influenced by both Buddhist and Shinto practices, and therefore possess a strong respect for nature and its impermanence.

Naturally, I questioned what sane single person with a hefty mortgage and associated costs would be 'stupid' enough to resign from financial security and run off to live a little of the Zen life. I wisely lectured myself to breathe and trust my instincts and, in the interim months, kept myself buoyed with happy cinematic memories. Beckoned by Kyoto's siren call, I envisioned myself wandering aimlessly along cobbled laneways; following the blossom-lined Tetsugaku No Michi ('The Philosopher's Path'); lazily strolling through the cool, green of Arashiyama's bamboo forest on a humid day; and shuffling barefoot over the impossibly smooth floor of an incense-filled ancient temple while the soothing chants of Buddhist monks hummed low in the background …

Kyoto is home to over 1600 Buddhist temples, making it a very fine town in which to seek a little of the Zen life. Peaceful, calm, sometimes eerily beautiful — each temple has a unique atmosphere, an almost human quality. Although I'm not religious, I love to slowly wander temple precincts, if only to inhale the aroma of their chosen incense and slide my feet over the wooden floors, silken with age.

shiwasu/ juunigatsu

DECEMBER | THE 12TH MONTH

CHAPTER 2

THE 12TH MONTH

According to the old calendar, shiwasu means 'priest run', the month in which even the head priest runs around on end-of-year business. There are many events at this time of the year in order to 'close' the past year and prepare for the new.

december

shiwasu / juunigatsu

Tsugi wa Kyoto desu — next stop Kyoto. If you'd met me on the flight over to Japan, you would have been forgiven for thinking I had never been on a plane. Apart from the obvious signs of age, I could have been that 20-year-old leaving the country on her own for the first time — giddy with both anticipation and trepidation.

I hoped to return from Japan with the skeleton of a book under my wing, but negative thoughts pervaded my headspace. I purposefully shook myself out of the pretzel I had wrapped myself into and kindly requested my self-confidence to make an appearance. I was committed to the quest and wished to continue to freefall into the wonder of the unknown. At the end of the day, if all else failed, I was up for an exquisite 'time out' in a place I adored.

When I arrived on Japanese soil, I was efficiently ushered onto my shuttle bus, where I settled in to enjoy the 90-minute ride to my new home. As I gazed out at the flickering Osaka neon, I pondered the fine line between running away from or towards something; I was sure to discover my direction soon enough.

While waiting for delivery of my keys, I examined the common areas of the building. It was pin-drop quiet. In fact, had I not heard someone furiously scrubbing a bathroom, I'd have questioned whether anyone lived there! The walls were painted a sickly bluish-green and the vinyl flooring was shaded to match. Even though the 'mansion' was spotlessly clean, it appeared a little crusty. The accompanying fumes of hospice-grade disinfectant mingled with musty cooking odours did little to endear me to my new abode, which I'd also noted was nestled between several dubious-looking 'love hotels'. However, once I was standing in the *genkan* (entrance) to Apartment No. 402, I knew I was in the right place: I could just make out the neighbouring temple and the faint outline of Higashiyama, the Eastern mountain range, in the moonlight.

My landlady, Myong Hee, an incredibly stylish Korean artist, oozed warmth, intellect and intrigue and seemed to levitate over the floorboards as she introduced me, in perfect English, to my new surroundings. Although I planned to dramatically improve my Japanese, it was comforting to know that I could converse in my native

tongue should the need arise. It was late, so we just covered the important stuff, like which button heated the toilet seat.

*

I was welcomed to the first morning of my new life by a chorus of sweetly chirping birds. Doing my best rendition of a Disney princess, I flew out of bed and drew open the curtains in anticipation of the view I had been promised via the web. I wasn't disappointed. Manganji Temple, directly in my line of vision, seemed to watch over me protectively, like a wise old monk, weathered but strong in mind. It looked serious and foreboding, yet there was peace in its stillness.

Higashiyama was dotted with a few remaining autumn-hued trees, illuminated by a radiantly clear sky. The apartment was flooded with light and I finally relaxed, safe in the knowledge this was where I was meant to be.

Ravenous, and without a crumb of food in the place, I quickly dressed and headed for the tiny supermarket just a three-minute walk away. Although small, it was crammed to the rafters and I excitedly pounced on some fresh yuzu and *sudachi* (Japanese citrus varieties) and fragrant strawberries. I grabbed some butter and yoghurt courtesy of Hokkaido in northern Japan (home to dairy cattle and an unfathomable amount of powder snow) and couldn't resist a packet of condensed milk doughnuts and a jar of *mikan* (mandarin) marmalade. I had made a pledge to only eat miso soup, rice and eggs for breakfast, but one must ease into these things …

I spied Kyoto's famous red carrots — an essential, if only for the colour — and added some crunchy *renkon* (lotus root), a threesome of tall, slender leeks, a packet of pickled daikon and some regal-looking *myoga* (native ginger buds) to my basket.

Catching my eye were two small packages containing tiny purplish shiso flowers and a tangle of deep magenta spriglets called *tade* (peppery leaves with antibacterial properties that are often added to soy sauce for sashimi). They were included in my stash along with some taut-headed shimeji mushrooms, perfectly upstanding peppery *kaiware* (daikon sprouts) and fresh, fat *hotate* (scallops).

Some Japanese supermarkets, particularly those in *depachika* (department store food halls), sell freshly prepared, excellent-quality cooked dishes that are completely superior to what is commonly available in Western supermarkets, so I felt justified in collecting some *konnyaku gobo* (burdock root with *konnyaku* — a starchy, nutritious, jelly-like substance) and *wakatake nimono* (fresh bamboo shoots cooked with wakame seaweed; see page 35).

I selected an elegant bottle of sake, as it was clearly the appropriate beverage for celebrating my new life, and flicked a small packet of dried yuzu rind with pepper into the mix; it would prove to be a strangely addictive bar snack. As my matchbox-sized kitchen was lacking a *suribachi* (ribbed Japanese mortar and wooden pestle), I also grabbed some pre-crushed sesame seeds to add to sauces and dressings.

My salivary glands went into overdrive as I continued along the aisles. I fumbled with a punnet of wobbly, freshly made tofu and collected Japanese pantry essentials of mirin, rice vinegar, sake, shoyu (soy sauce), miso, rice and nori.

dashi

Finally, I stood before the shelf housing the two most crucial ingredients in any Japanese kitchen: the seemingly humble kombu (dried kelp) and *katsuobushi* (shaved dried, smoked bonito). Once home, I bathed them gently in simmering water, transforming them into the cornerstone of Japanese cuisine: dashi or, more correctly, *katsuo dashi*.

Dashi is the single most important element required to cook authentic Japanese cuisine. Almost every dish has a foundation of dashi, in one of its guises, forming the base for soups, *nabe* (hotpots or stews), sauces or dressings; it is sometimes even used instead of water for blanching and simmering vegetables.

Katsuobushi are smoked dried fish shavings made from *katsuo* (bonito or skipjack tuna); a similar product is sometimes made from other oily fish such as *maguro* (another tuna species) and mackerel. They look and smell a little like fish food flakes, but don't be put off! Add dried kombu (kelp), water and heat and you are on the road to discovering the nuances of Japanese cuisine.

Three basic ingredients — *katsuobushi*, kombu and water — are used to make both an initial stock (ichiban dashi, or no. 1 dashi), which should be clear and taste fresh, slightly salty and subtly of the sea, making it perfect for elegant clear soups and sauces, and a secondary stock (niban dashi, or no. 2 dashi), which recycles the initial ingredients to make a fishier, earthy-flavoured stock suitable for more robust dishes such as *nabe*, thick, rich soups, and dressings where a deeper, more complex flavour is desired. This secondary cooking also renders the stock cloudy, so it is also used in dishes where a clear stock is not necessary for presentation.

In Japan, *katsuobushi* is available in different grades, the highest of which contains an edible mould. Whole elongated pieces of the dried fish, resembling weather-smoothed driftwood, can be shaved to order by a *katsuobushi* specialist. Kombu varies depending on the water of the region in which it is grown, so depending on a cook's selection of these ingredients, and the quantities in which they are used, the flavour profile of dashi varies.

ichiban dashi
no. 1 dashi
MAKES 2 LITRES (70 FL OZ/8 CUPS)

Like a stock in any cuisine, the base recipe will vary and evolve through time, so a cook in the Kansai region (Kyoto/Osaka/Kobe) may possess a rather different method and opinion on the matter than their cousin in Kanto (Tokyo area). This contemporary version is based on tips from friends in Kyoto, and this particular method and temperature guide is believed to extract the maximum amount of all-important *umami*.

1 strip of kombu (dried kelp), about 6 x 20 cm (2½ x 8 inches), weighing 15–20 g (½–¾ oz); note that thinner kombu will weigh a little less — look for the thicker variety
2 large handfuls, about 40 g (1½ oz), *katsuobushi* — use the best grade available, and/or combine two or more varieties for your preferred depth of flavour

Use moistened hands or a clean, damp cloth to dab off any grit from the kombu, but try not to remove too much of any powdery white substance on the surface.

Place the kombu in a large pot and pour in 2 litres (70 fl oz/8 cups) cold water. (If the water where you live is not of good quality, use filtered water — the Japanese have very good-quality mountain water, which helps assure clean-flavoured stocks and sauces. It is also the reason the Japanese believe they produce the finest rice in the world — and also, therefore, wonderful sake!)

Allow the kombu to sit for 30 minutes, then place the pot over medium–low heat. Slowly bring the water to 60–65°C (140–150°F), using a cook's thermometer to check. If you don't have a thermometer, look for a point where a little steam is rising, but there are only the most minuscule bubbles forming like pinpricks on the bottom of the pan — none should break the surface of the water.

Retain this temperature for 30–40 minutes to release the *umami* from the kombu, then remove the kombu and set aside for use in niban dashi (no. 2 dashi, page 29).

Increase the water temperature to about 80°C (175°F), which will allow it to just begin to simmer, but do not allow the water to boil. If you don't have a thermometer, just ensure the water is gently simmering, then turn off the heat.

Evenly sprinkle the *katsuobushi* over the surface and allow them to leisurely 'swim' into the pot until they are just soaked through — this should take just under a minute. Strain the liquid through a cloth-lined sieve. Retain the solids for use in niban dashi (page 29).

Use ichiban dashi for elegant dishes calling for clean, sharp-flavoured dashi, such as clear soups, sauces or dressings, and as indicated in individual recipes.

Note: All the dashi recipes on pages 26 and 29 can be easily halved or doubled, and freeze well for up to 2 months, which is convenient when only small portions are called for. If you are cooking Japanese food regularly, you can make a pot or two each week and store the dashi in the fridge for up to 2 days to use as required in individual recipes.

Dashi is an incredible source of *umami*, the so-called 'fifth taste' — a culinary topic that has gained much attention in recent years.

For added variety, tiny dried sardines and other fish are sometimes used in place of, or combined with, *katsuobushi*. The choices available are a little restricted outside Japan, but your Japanese grocery specialist should at least have a few options, so just try them all to find the flavour most suited to your taste.

niban dashi
no. 2 dashi
MAKES 2 LITRES (70 FL OZ/8 CUPS)

reserved kombu and *katsuobushi* from ichiban dashi (no. 1 dashi, page 26)
a small handful of extra *katsuobushi* (optional, for added flavour)

Place the reserved kombu and the strained *katsuobushi* from the ichiban dashi in a large pot. Add 2 litres (70 fl oz/8 cups) good-quality or filtered cold water and the extra *katsuobushi*, if using.

Bring to a simmer and cook for 10–15 minutes. The broth will become slightly cloudy.

Strain into a cloth-lined sieve, then gently squeeze the cloth to extract the excess liquid from the solids. Discard the solids — or rinse the kombu well and allow to dry before using in *tsukudani* (pages 113–115) or *kakiage* (page 165).

Use niban dashi for full-flavoured soups, hotpots, stews, sauces or dressings, or as called for in recipes.

shiitake dashi
shiitake mushroom dashi
MAKES ABOUT 1 LITRE (35 FL OZ/4 CUPS)

6 medium dried shiitake mushrooms

Put the mushrooms in a saucepan with 1 litre (35 fl oz/4 cups) good-quality or filtered cold water and leave to soak for 8 hours.

Place the pan over high heat, bring the liquid almost to the boil, then turn off and remove the mushrooms.

The mushrooms can be used in other recipes where rehydrated shiitake are called for, or you can make them into *tsukudani* (pages 113–115) using the method for *kombu no tsukudani* on page 114.

The dashi is now ready to use in individual recipes.

kombu dashi
dried kelp dashi
MAKES 2 LITRES (70 FL OZ/8 CUPS)

Regular dashi is not suitable for *shojin ryori* (Buddhist vegetarian cuisine), so instead either kombu dashi or shiitake dashi are commonly used, depending on the particular dish's requirements or what other ingredients will be used in the meal.

Shiitake dashi is used when a deeper, earthier flavour is required, and sometimes *kampyo* (dried gourd) and *daizu* (dried beans) are added to make *shojin dashijiru* (shojin dashi, relating back to early Zen Buddhism) for a more complex flavour.

Kombu dashi is used for lighter, fresher-tasting vegetarian dishes, and is also preferred over regular dashi for cooking certain fish and seafood dishes, so as not to mask the delicate flavours.

1 strip of kombu (dried kelp), about 6 x 20 cm (2½ x 8 inches), weighing 15–20 g (½–¾ oz)

Use moistened hands or a clean, damp cloth to dab off any grit from the kombu, but try not to remove too much of any powdery white substance on the surface. Place the kombu in a large pot filled with 2 litres (70 fl oz/8 cups) good-quality or filtered cold water. Sit for 1 hour.

Place over low heat and slowly bring the water temperature to 60–65°C (140–150°F), using a cook's thermometer to check. If you don't have a thermometer, look for a point where a little steam is rising, but there are only the most minuscule bubbles forming like pinpricks on the bottom of the pan — none should break the surface of the water. Keep the water at this temperature for 40 minutes.

Remove from the heat and discard the kombu — or allow to dry and use in *tsukudani* (pages 113–115), or thinly shredded in *kakiage* (page 165).

The dashi is now ready to use in individual recipes.

As my dashi was cooling, I received a visit from Myong Hee, who was so lovely and forthcoming with useful information that I couldn't contain my happiness at having randomly found her through an apartment rental website during my darkest hour. My eyes welled with tears and she instantly enveloped me in a warm hug, slipping me an invitation as she released her hold. It was for her art exhibition the following Sunday and she suggested we breakfast beforehand at the Museum of Modern Art, which was just a few minutes' walk from my apartment. It was all so very civilised and I was certain I was about to fall in love with my new life.

As she left, she turned and said: 'Just one more thing … you are my friend while you are here … I think that is best.' She felt sure I was a 'wonderful person' and was pleased to see me already so happy at Villa Heiwa. I happily accepted her sentiments.

Armed with a freshly scrawled 'mud map', I trotted out for an afternoon stroll in the hope of acquainting myself with the neighbourhood. It was quiet, peaceful and attractive. Past the Heian Jingu (one of Kyoto's largest Shinto shrines), under its giant vermilion gate and across the Nijo Bashi (Nijo Bridge), I came upon a small, 'samurai-movie-set-perfect' shop brimming with fresh-cooked, palm-sized round *senbei* (rice crackers). The familiar scent of caramelised shoyu invited me in to take a closer look. I greedily filled a small bamboo tray with a selection of savoury *senbei* flavoured with shoyu, miso, sesame, bonito, garlic and spicy *karashi* (Japanese mustard). The *nure* (damp) *senbei*, with chewy centres and crusty exteriors, were delicious, despite their unappealing moniker. I avoided the modern versions with coffee and maple glazes, but couldn't resist one curious cracker: hand-iced with a Christmas tree. It later took pride of place in the *tokonoma* (spiritual altar) in my apartment, an appropriate homage to the season.

Heavy rain and a dramatic drop in temperature had me diving into a cab for the short distance home. I was desperate to get into the aromatic fresh citrus called yuzu, so a squeeze of juice and a healthy slither of zest were ritualistically added to a tumbler of sake along with a few shiso flowers, which I rolled between my hands to release the subtle fragrance. Although served chilled, the heavenly nectar warmed me from the inside out — a necessary precaution as it dropped to −1°C (30°F) overnight.

Appetite stimulated by the aperitif and a *senbei* or three, I grabbed some chopsticks in my right hand, cracked open the *wakatake nimono* (fresh bamboo shoots cooked with wakame seaweed; see page 35) and nibbled away while my left hand deftly plucked some scallops from the fridge to be quickly seared with some soy butter sauce (page 34).

*

31　shiwasu / juunigatsu – december / the 12th month

senbei

rice crackers
MAKES 12 LARGE RICE CRACKERS

145 g (5 oz/1 cup) *mochiko* (glutinous rice flour)
1 teaspoon fine sea salt
¼ teaspoon bicarbonate of soda (baking soda)
100 ml (3½ fl oz) warm dashi or water
1½ tablespoons vegetable oil
2 teaspoons sesame oil
3 teaspoons black or white sesame seeds (optional)

GLAZE
3 teaspoons mirin
1½ teaspoons caster (superfine) sugar
3 teaspoons usukuchi shoyu (light Japanese soy)

Preheat the oven to 180°C (350°F/Gas 4). Line two baking trays and a bamboo steamer with baking paper.

Put the rice flour in a bowl and make a well in the centre. Dissolve the salt and bicarbonate of soda in the warm dashi. Add the vegetable and sesame oils to the well and start to mix, then gradually mix in the dashi mixture. Continue to mix until you have a thick, quite soft paste like kids' modelling dough — note that depending on the level of humidity in the air, you may not need to add all the dashi. The dough will be a little oily.

Knead for a few minutes just to bring the dough together. Break off 12 even pieces about the size of a walnut and roll them into smooth balls between your hands. Place in the lined bamboo steamer and steam for 12 minutes over a pot of boiling water — this will soften the texture and make the dough more pliable.

Remove from the heat. When cool enough to handle, place each ball between two pieces of baking paper, then use a rolling pin to press and roll out each ball into a disc about 9 cm (3½ inches) in diameter and 2–3 mm (1/16–1/8 inch) thick. If using the sesame seeds, slightly flatten the balls with your hands first, sprinkle each with ¼ teaspoon of seeds, pat them lightly onto the dough, then continue to roll the discs out between the baking paper sheets with the rolling pin — the seeds will be incorporated into the dough.

Place the discs on the lined baking trays and bake for 30 minutes, or until deeply golden and crisp. (You can also deep-fry the crackers at 190°C/375°F for 2–3 minutes. They will be crisp on the outside, chewy in the centre and notably different in texture from the firm crunch of the baked version.)

Meanwhile, make the glaze. Place the mirin and sugar in a small saucepan and bring to the boil over high heat. Cook for 1 minute, then stir in the shoyu and cook for a further few seconds. The mixture should be glazy but still runny.

When the crackers come out of the oven, place them on a wire rack, then lightly brush each side with the glaze.

Eat immediately, or place back onto the wire rack and allow to dry completely. Store in an airtight container for up to 2 weeks — if they last that long!

Variations: Once the rice crackers are glazed, immediately wrap a strip of nori around them, or sprinkle with one of the following: *shichimi togarashi* (seven-flavour spice mix), crystallised sugar, ground sansho or your choice of spice. You can omit the glaze altogether if you like.

Before kneading the raw dough, you can also add some Japanese curry powder, *aonori* (seaweed), ground ginger or ginger juice, miso or other ingredients for extra flavour.

hotate batayaki

seared scallops with butter and shoyu
SERVES 2 AS A MAIN COURSE, OR 4–6 AS PART OF
A MULTI-DISH MEAL

Don't bother trying to make this dish when scallops are out of season — and only use the best-quality seafood, as the results cannot be compared. Cheaper scallops are full of water and the sauce will not glaze properly.

3 teaspoons usukuchi shoyu (light Japanese soy)
2 teaspoons sake
2 teaspoons mirin
½ teaspoon *kurosato* (Japanese black sugar) or dark brown sugar
3 teaspoons fresh yuzu juice; if fresh is not available, use the bottled juice or fresh lemon juice
2 teaspoons vegetable oil
12 large, evenly sized, best-quality queen scallops, without the roe, muscle removed
10 g (¼ oz) butter
½ teaspoon finely grated yuzu zest or lemon zest

Combine the shoyu, sake, mirin, sugar and 2 teaspoons of the yuzu juice. Set aside.

Heat a large, heavy-based frying pan over high heat — the pan needs to be very hot to sear the scallops properly. Do not use a non-stick pan, and ensure it is large enough that the scallops will not be crowded.

Pat the scallops with kitchen paper to remove any excess moisture. Season the scallops lightly with freshly cracked black pepper. Add the oil to the hot pan. When the oil sizzles, add the scallops and cook for about 1 minute, or until golden underneath, then turn them over and cook for a further 1 minute. Remove then pan from the heat; remove the scallops from the pan and set aside.

Splash the shoyu mixture into the pan and add the butter. Shake and swirl the pan over the heat for 30 seconds to 1 minute, or until the sauce just starts to become glazy.

Return the scallops to the pan and cook for a further 30 seconds, while you swirl them in the glaze. The scallops should look like they are coated in a light teriyaki-style glaze and be just cooked through.

Remove from the heat, then transfer to a serving plate or individual plates. Sprinkle with the remaining yuzu juice and the zest and serve immediately.

wakatake nimono

simmered bamboo shoots and wakame

SERVES 4–6 AS PART OF A MULTI-DISH MEAL

This healthful and curiously harmonious dish is fragrant with both earth and sea. It can also be drained and served cold as a side dish or salad.

300 g (10½ oz) cooked bamboo shoots; if using frozen shoots, thaw them first
750 ml (26 fl oz/3 cups) ichiban dashi (page 26) or niban dashi (page 29)
80 ml (2½ fl oz/⅓ cup) sake
60 ml (2 fl oz/¼ cup) mirin
2 teaspoons caster (superfine) sugar
2 tablespoons usukuchi shoyu (light Japanese soy)
2 tablespoons dried wakame (seaweed) pieces

Cut the bamboo shoots into slim wedges, 1 cm (½ inch) at the widest point.

Put the bamboo shoots and dashi in a saucepan and bring to the boil over high heat. Reduce the heat to low, add the sake and mirin and simmer for 10 minutes. Stir in the sugar and shoyu and cook for a further 5 minutes.

Meanwhile, soak the wakame in cold water for 1 minute, or until slightly rehydrated. Add to the pan and cook for 1 minute, or until heated through but not slimy.

Serve warm in a bowl, with a little of the broth poured over if desired.

zenbu zen 36

Although almost encircled by mountains, the ancient low-rise city of Kyoto is set on a flat grid – perfect for navigating or sightseeing by bicycle. I enjoy getting lost in the backstreets of Kyoto, but if you are sticking to the main city roads, you won't lose your way if you simply look up and locate the mountain ranges: Higashiyama to the east, Kitayama to the north and Arashiyama to the north-west. If you can't see distant mountains, you are likely facing south.

The next morning, I found myself en route to the supermarket to purchase atmospherics of incense and candles, and the rather more practical item of toilet paper — all three essential to the development of my sense of 'living' as opposed to holidaying. I slowly zigzagged between a handful of closely situated temples and shrines. At each, fingers of cool, sacred air softly stroked my face as if to assure me I was safe now. The last of the season's silky camellias were radiant in the pale sunlight, and shiny baubles decorated doorways and sculptured Japanese shrubbery, which brought a smile to my face and a stab of family-centric guilt to my chest when I flashed forward to Christmas Day.

An open-air pickle stand outside the Kumano Jinja shrine caught my eye: it was overflowing with salty umeboshi plums, limp bundles of cabbage, and pungent garlic and cheesy-flavoured cucumber *miso zuke* (see page 158). I sampled a strip of paste from a fruit unidentifiable by the picture on its hand-drawn signage and enquired of its name: the vendor grunted unhelpfully and pointed back towards the sketch. Startled by this uncharacteristic behaviour, and miffed at this pinprick to my bliss bubble, I propelled myself through the gates of the shrine.

Kumano Jinja is dedicated to strong marriages, ease in childbirth, good health and long life. The latter two would do me for now; I wasn't greedy. Reflective, I stood for some time, admiring the graceful curve of the thatched roof and the wooden votives covered with handwritten wishes or emblazoned with ebony crows. I had encountered several of these black scavengers, the size of small dogs, since arriving and they irked me. I'd dreamt of these ominous beasts in the past, just prior to significant and often sad events — including my father's untimely death 11 years earlier — and I felt unnervingly superstitious. Curious to know more, I quickly scanned a signpost in English explaining that Kumano Jinja celebrates Shinkosai ('Happiness of the God' festival) on 29 April each year: the anniversary of my father's death. A small shiver scampered up my spine. In the back of my mind, I knew this trip would touch on my losing him and possibly help to facilitate the final, somewhat prolonged, stage of grieving. But I wasn't prepared for it to bubble up so soon.

I wandered on, feeling bewildered and pensive, like I had brushed against something mystical; it would turn out to be the first of many similar occurrences in spirit-dense Kyoto. Soon enough, however, I was once again happily noticing the beautifully rustic traditional homes and *machiya* (townhouses originally owned by merchants), *sento* (bath-houses), modern office buildings and chic art galleries. Dotted between were tiny patisseries, charcuteries, second-hand bookstores, *combini* (convenience stores) and ultra-cute cafés. A large, sturdy citrus tree heaving with fruit lurched outside one weathered dwelling in ode to the winter, while a small kiwi fruit tree bore just a few wrinkled orbs, suggesting some early morning frosts had signalled the end of their days.

As I turned south onto Kawabata Dori (Kawabata Street), parallel to the Kamogawa (Kamo River), which separates eastern Kyoto from the rest of the city, something urged me to make a 180-degree turn towards Kitayama, the northern mountain range. Through weeping willows and near-naked maple trees, the light on the mountains was otherworldly. Several independent passersby also drew to a stop, cautiously glancing towards each other, as if to confirm they weren't hallucinating. It was so breathtaking: a layer cake of sky blue, snow-cloud silver and rolling mountain green was iced with swirls of pale pink cloud and sprinkled with magenta and gold. I loitered, breathing it all in, as I knew all too soon this scene would again transform with the increasingly cold days.

I continued on, my camera recording the remnants of the season, with a fat smile plastered on my face. I was happy, really happy, and I hadn't felt like that in a long time. Although I was not alone on the path beside Kyoto's fluid spine, it was incredibly peaceful. Apart from the occasional dinging of a bicycle bell alerting me when to move to the side, I was otherwise only aware of sweet birdcalls and the tranquil murmurs of the Kamogawa.

There were new textures and patterns at every turn and I wanted to transport it all home with me: from the roof tiles to wooden slats, manhole covers and stone walls, to the fine variegated points of a dark red *momiji* (Japanese maple) leaf, and even the desiccated shell of a once-robust flower. But memory and photographs would have to do. I made a mental note of my materialistic desire to covet such things and understood I had a way to go before I could just appreciate them for what and where they were in the world. I then made a conscious decision to 'let go' of the wanting, which seemed so very desperate.

Nearby Kiyamachi Dori was relatively people-free during the morning, being more of an afternoon and evening playground. I took the opportunity to duck under several gorgeously designed *noren* (split curtains that act as decorative signage), and along a few of the narrow laneways that lead to the fine-dining riverside restaurants. These catwalks of the restaurant world can be incredibly beautiful: some are paved with stones (often freshly watered to depict cleanliness, purity and, in summer months, coolness); others are made of polished concrete or timber slats. The walls are often lined with thin bamboo fencing or other organic materials and may include inviting displays of *ikebana* (flower arrangement), stone lanterns or water features. The degree of refinement ensures you understand the commitment you have made to dine at certain establishments — which is likely a combination of time, respect and serious yen.

Before long, I was joined by the hungry hordes on their way to luncheon appointments. The midday meal starts early in Japan — about 11.30 am — and you risk missing out on a spot if you leave it too late. Deeply distracted, I had inadvertently let time escape me so that everywhere that appealed was already at capacity. I headed south down Kawaramachi Dori to the somewhat dingy, ageing Sanjo Arcade and found a restaurant specialising in a range of *katsu* (crumbed fried cutlets). A placard at the entrance was stamped with approval from the Kyoto Restaurant Association, so I tentatively peeled open the *noren* and was surprised and delighted to find a gorgeous wooden walkway: it transported me out of the cold into a very cosy restaurant far from the hustle and bustle. Smooth honeyed wooden walls and furniture and low lighting from paper lanterns set the mood and I opted to sit at the large communal table. There were a few curious glances at the sole *gaijin*, but mostly everyone was too busy with their meals. I soon found out why.

I ordered the *rosu katsu* (pork sirloin cutlet) and *yuba korokke* (a soy milk-skin croquette) set course menu. The pork was sensational: juicy, flavoursome and texturally orgasmic. It was accompanied by three things in bottomless supply: *miso shiru* (miso soup, page 46), based on a respectable dashi using a unique house blend of

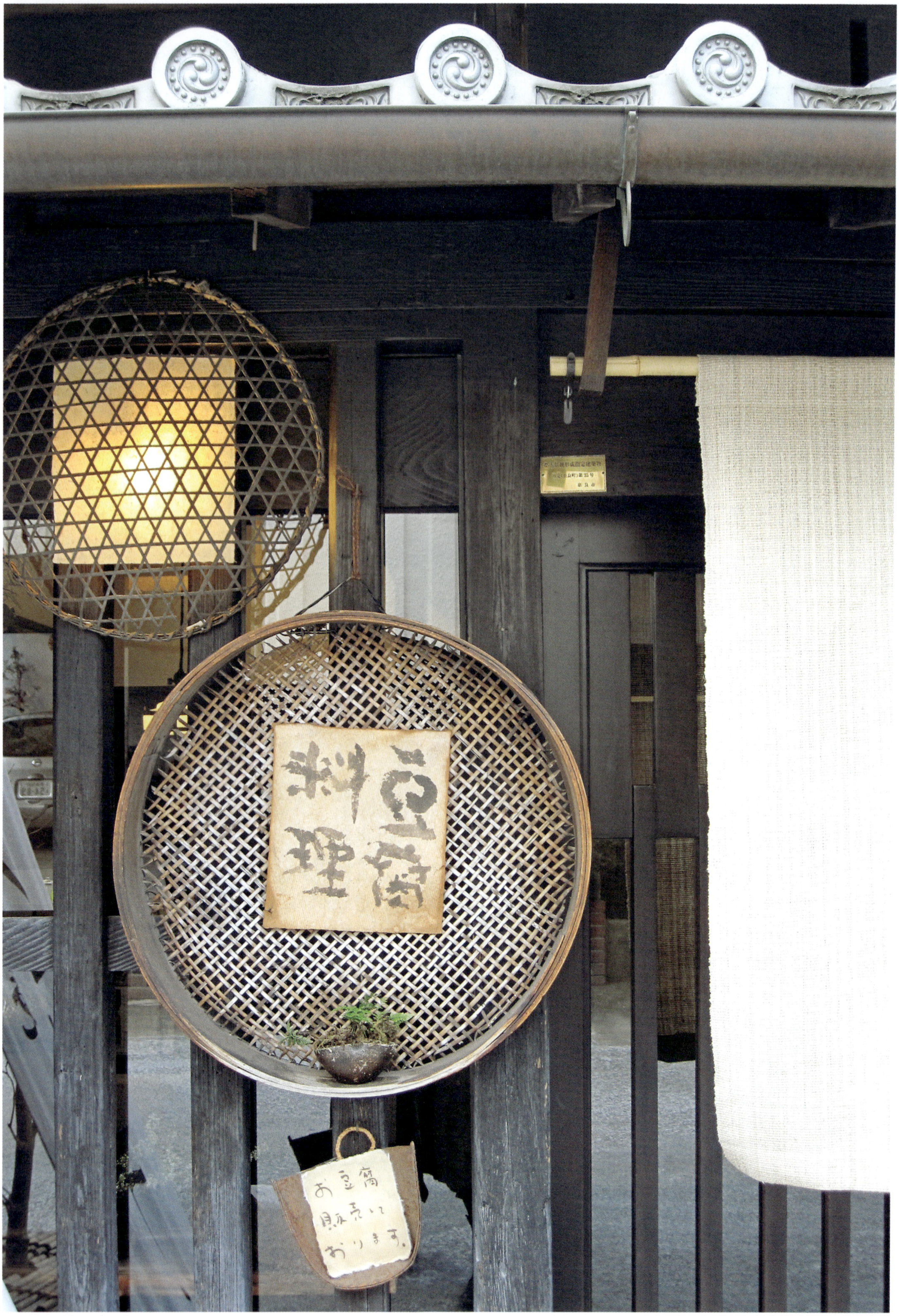
豆腐料理
お豆腐販売しております。

dried fish species; rice cooked with rolled barley; and some finely shredded raw cabbage to aid digestion of the main dish.

On each table were several small pots — one containing a soy and yuzu dressing (see right) for drizzling over the cabbage, and two thick sauces. I ground my toasted sesame seeds in the small *suribachi* (ribbed Japanese mortar and wooden pestle) provided, before ladling in a little of each, designing my own signature dip.

Also on the table were cucumber pickles, aromatic with shiso and acting as *hashi yasumi* (literally a 'holiday for your chopstick') to cleanse the palate. The cheerful waitress was clearly amused by the fact I understood the drill and, as is commonplace, praised me on my language skills — *'Nihongo joozu desu ne'* ('Your Japanese is great!') — even though my Japanese was seriously poor.

She poured me another cup of *houjicha* (roasted green tea) and, as I sipped, a sensation of calm spread through my body.

*

kyabetsu to yuzu-ae

cabbage with yuzu dressing

SERVES 4–6 AS PART OF A MULTI-DISH MEAL

Great with any fried foods to aid digestion and cleanse the palate.

300 g (10½ oz) cabbage

YUZU DRESSING

60 ml (2 fl oz/¼ cup) fresh or bottled yuzu juice or lemon juice

1½ tablespoons usukuchi shoyu (light Japanese soy)

1 tablespoon mirin

2 teaspoons rice vinegar

1 tablespoon sesame oil

1 teaspoon caster (superfine) sugar

Combine all the dressing ingredients in a small bowl or a small jug or beaker and stir until the sugar has dissolved.

Remove the core from the cabbage. Very, very finely shred the cabbage using a mandoline or very sharp fine knife.

Serve the cabbage in light, airy mounds and stir the dressing before drizzling over the top.

tonkatsu

fried crumbed pork cutlets
SERVES 4

The Japanese, in a never-ending quest to better the world in most things, have managed to breed a nation of super fryers, and fried food is eaten more commonly than one might assume — always in combination with other ingredients that help digest the oil and cut through the richness. This is one of the most satisfying dishes to eat in the middle of winter — dressed with a sharp, sweetish brown sauce, every mouthful sings the kind of harmony that keeps you going back for more. *Tonkatsu* is also served as *miso katsu* in some parts of Japan, and as *katsu kare* (*katsu* with curry sauce) in almost every city across the country.

When pork sirloin is used, the dish is known as *rosu katsu*; when pork fillet is used it is called *hire katsu*. In Japan you usually have the choice of ordering either or a combination of these two cuts.

TONKATSU SAUCE
2 tablespoons very finely chopped brown onion
½ carrot, finely chopped
½ celery stalk, finely chopped
½ apple, finely chopped or grated
70 ml (2¼ fl oz) tomato sauce (ketchup)
50–60 ml (1¾–2 fl oz) worcestershire sauce (preferably Japanese-style)
60 ml (2 fl oz/¼ cup) rice vinegar, plus 1 teaspoon extra
2 tablespoons mirin, plus 1 teaspoon extra
2 tablespoons sake, plus 1 teaspoon extra
2½ tablespoons shoyu, plus 1½ teaspoons extra
¼ teaspoon ground allspice
a pinch of ground cinnamon
a small pinch of ground cloves
2½ tablespoons *kurosato* (Japanese black sugar) or dark brown sugar
1 teaspoon finely grated fresh ginger
1 small garlic clove, bruised
½ teaspoon *karashi* (Japanese mustard) or hot English mustard

KATSU
4 best-quality pork loin cutlets, each about 2.5–3 cm (1–1¼ inches) thick and weighing 200 g (7 oz), on the bone
1 tablespoon saikyo miso (sweet, white Kyoto-style miso) or white miso
plain (all-purpose) flour, seasoned with sea salt and freshly ground black pepper, for coating
2 eggs, lightly beaten
panko (Japanese breadcrumbs), for coating (see Note)
vegetable oil, for deep-frying
4 tablespoons freshly toasted sesame seeds, to serve
karashi (Japanese mustard) or hot English mustard, to serve (optional)

Combine all the tonkatsu sauce ingredients (except the extra vinegar, mirin, sake and shoyu) in a saucepan with 80 ml (2½ fl oz/⅓ cup) water. Place over medium heat, stirring occasionally until the mixture boils. Reduce the heat to a simmer and cook for 1 hour, or until the vegetables are very tender.

Remove from the heat, discard the garlic clove and process with a hand-held stick blender until smooth. Pass the sauce through a sieve into a bowl and stir in the extra vinegar, mirin, sake and shoyu to season. Pour into a jug or a deep container with a small ladle ready for serving —

in Japan the sauce is served in ceramic pots with a small, deep bamboo ladle.

To prepare the katsu, carefully cut the meat from the bone using a sharp knife. Cut small nicks all the way around the edge of the pork, at 1.5 cm (5/8 inch) intervals, so the meat doesn't curl up too much when it cooks. Bash the cutlets with a meat mallet or rolling pin until they are about 1.5 cm (5/8 inch) thick. Smear the miso evenly over the pork.

Place the flour, egg and breadcrumbs in three separate dishes. Dip the cutlets into the flour, then the egg, allowing any excess to drip back into the dish. Then coat the cutlets well with the breadcrumbs, pressing them down to help them adhere. Refrigerate for 30 minutes to help the coating set.

Fill a deep-fryer or large deep saucepan with oil and heat to 170°C (325°F), or until a cube of bread dropped into the oil browns in 20 seconds. Line a wire rack with kitchen paper. Cook the cutlets, one at a time, for 5 minutes each, or until the crumbs are golden and the pork is just cooked through.

Drain the cutlets on the kitchen paper and allow to rest for a few minutes before serving. The cutlets are best served immediately, but you can keep them warm in a low oven until you have finished frying them all.

To serve, use a sharp knife to slice each cutlet into 1.5 cm (5/8 inch) strips, then slide a long palette knife underneath and transfer the strips to a plate in one movement. Serve with a little cabbage and yuzu dressing (page 41), a bowl of rice, miso soup (page 46), sesame seeds and mustard if desired, and of course the tonkatsu sauce for dipping.

If you can find four individual *suribachi* (ribbed Japanese mortar and wooden pestles), you can allow each diner to grind their own sesame seeds to add to the sauce, as you would in Japan. Put a tablespoon of sesame seeds in each suribachi, grind them as finely as you like, then stir in the amount of tonkatsu sauce you wish to use — more sauce can be added later as desired. The other option is to grind all the sesame seeds beforehand, stir the sauce through, then divide among small bowls for each diner to dip their katsu into.

Note: Panko is readily available in supermarkets, but you can prepare your own by making large breadcrumbs from white crusty bread. Pulse the bread in a food processor, then spread the crumbs out on trays lined with kitchen paper and allow to dry for 24 hours, or until crisp.

Variation: Instead of the tonkatsu sauce, you can use a mixture of grated daikon, ginger, soy and yuzu or lemon juice for dipping instead.

Tip: If you are short on time you can also buy tonkatsu sauce from Asian grocery stores. It is honestly pretty good flavour-wise, but, as with most things, I prefer to make my own — that way I know what's in it and that it's as additive-free as possible. It's a bit like making your own barbecue sauce instead of buying the bottled stuff!

zenbu zen 44

The origins of this dish are not entirely clear, but most fried Japanese foods — the best-known example being tempura — are commonly attributed to the Portuguese who sailed into Japan's ports in the eighteenth century. Total comfort food for pork lovers — the meat from Japanese pigs is full-flavoured, sweet and succulent, and deep-frying it encased in golden crumbs brings out the very best in this divine swine.

miso shiru

miso soup
SERVES 4–6

This is the most basic form of *miso shiru* for accompanying meals, but you can add any number of additional garnishes, such as the commonly served cubes of silken tofu, wakame seaweed, tiny clams, or tiny enoki, shimeji or nameko mushrooms.

For a more substantial soup, try packing it full of diced vegetables such as cabbage, potato, carrot, celery, daikon, bamboo shoots, leeks, sweet potato, shiitake or other larger mushrooms, or any seasonal vegetable of your choice, and simmering until tender — each ingredient adding a new flavour layer.

In winter I sometimes add grated fresh ginger and/or garlic and a splash of mirin and soy. It is a wonderfully restorative soup — flavoursome but light and healthy.

1 litre (35 fl oz/4 cups) niban dashi (page 29)
3 tablespoons saikyo miso (sweet luxurious miso loved by Kyoto-ites and myself!)
2–3 tablespoons aka miso (red miso)
2 spring onions (scallions), green part only, finely sliced (optional)

Place the dashi in a saucepan over medium–high heat and bring it almost to the boil. Combine a little of the hot liquid with the miso in a small bowl or cup and whisk until smooth, then stir the mixture into the pan and allow to come to a simmer.

Ladle the soup into small bowls and serve sprinkled with the spring onion, if desired.

Note: Use a mixture of miso pastes to fine-tune the flavour to your liking. If miso is new to you, go to the refrigerated section in your Japanese grocery store or health food shop and look for saikyo (sweet, smooth, high-grade white miso), shiro (basic white, mild miso) and aka (red miso, which is a little salty with a deeper flavour) to get you started. Other varieties are also usually available, including mugi (chunky miso with barley) and hatcho (dark brown, rich, salty and slightly sweet) — each with their own distinctive character.

47 shiwasu / juunigatsu – december / the 12th month

Happily fed and watered, and a mere 1400 yen lighter, I entered a nearby store dedicated to chopsticks: hundreds of them in different colours, patterns and even textures. I can certainly testify that chopsticks with a little grip make eating slippery noodles a less arduous chore. A sign in English read 'Chopstick Taboos' and listed 15 rules of use. Be advised you must not skewer, point or cross chopsticks with another's. Don't stand them in your bowl or lick them. Don't pillage from another's plate, pass food to a waiting pair of chopsticks, rest them on your bowl (that's what chopstick rests are for), or indeed use them to pull a dish towards you. No shovelling, drumming, searching or hovering with impatience. Guilty of breaking at least five of these commandments and gorging on deep-fried goodness, I then sprinted homewards.

*

Having slept eight hours straight for the first time in seven months, I woke up feeling particularly refreshed: I was on top of the world. Breakfast was one perfect egg with an almost fluorescent yolk, some tiny slivers of Japanese bacon cut super-thin so that they crisped up in blinking time, and a few small scoops of bamboo with wakame (page 35) and *daizu no gomoku-ni* (simmered soy beans and vegetables; page 199), plus a few daikon pickles for good measure. Possibly a poor attempt at a Japanese-style breakfast, but it was one step closer to being appropriately *haafu*, a word used to describe children born to mixed-race couples. Although once considered derogatory, the word was now, according to some young Japanese friends, deemed acceptable due to the fact it had become 'cool' to be *haafu*.

On a mission to purchase dessert for dinner with friends, I perused the basement of the Takashimaya Department Store, which boasts an incredible food hall. Those who wax lyrical over Harrods in London, which is indeed fantastic for its grandeur, need to get themselves to Japan. A good Japanese food hall will blow your mind and your wallet, as there are many items that are impossible to resist. Even the array of European offerings — perfectly executed patisserie treats by the buttery truckload, meaty small goods, funky cheeses, fresh foie gras and excellent French wines at very reasonable prices — are enough to make you drop to your knees and sing 'Hallelujah!' But the everyday and specialty Japanese foods are something else again! *Wagashi* (tea ceremony sweets) are sculptural morsels displayed like rare jewels. There are tofu-based products that take up an entire wall; wagyu with a marble score so high it could prompt vertigo; and local pork sweet enough to make ice cream out of (and I'm pretty certain that has been done). The seafood is so fresh it still smells and moves like the ocean, and there's a never-ending parade of glorious vegetables.

Dizzy with mirth and gluttony, I left, mission accomplished, with a marron (chestnut) mille-feuille adorned with a perfect red maple leaf. I was ecstatic to be experiencing the tail end of autumn specialties, knowing they would soon be replaced with winter fare.

*

As I went about the apartment performing my morning ritual, I became aware that I hadn't yet seen my face since I'd woken up. At home, there is no choice but to focus on my imperfections on a daily basis via the full-length mirror in my bedroom or the mirrored bathroom cabinet. In my Kyoto apartment I had to open a cupboard for a semi-full body check and turn behind me, from the sink in the bathroom to a small shaving mirror hanging on a hook, just to see my face. As a result, I seemed to be becoming less focused on searching for possible flaws.

The Philosopher's Path felt like an appropriate destination for continuing this chain of thought. I strode out confident of the direction and feeling smug about already knowing my way around this part of town. Except that I didn't ... and I ended up much further away from my planned destination. After bumbling around for more than an hour, I grabbed a taxi to Nanzenji Temple, at the eastern end of the path, famed for its peaceful Zen garden.

A huge urn full of sand, containing a forest of burning incense, stood out the front as an offering before prayer. I removed my boots while stepping backwards onto higher ground and popped my offending footwear into standard-issue protective plastic bags so as not to make this sacred space 'unclean'.

Although the gates to the temple grounds are majestic, the immediate entrance to the garden was rather unimpressive and I began to wonder if I would be disappointed. I padded across the cool, slightly yielding tatami — a grounding sensation I will never take for granted — and turned the corner into a blissful scene at the end of a dimly lit, dark wooded corridor that had me instantly awash with relaxation. I sat cross-legged on the sun-warmed viewing deck with my eyes closed while a few others sat in silence, contemplating the rock formations of the Zen garden. The harmonious sounds of the *shakahachi* (Japanese flute) added to the loveliness.

I opened my eyes to a garden meditative and serene. Fine stone gravel was raked in a pattern representing the ebb and flow of water around the shoreline of the rock 'islands'. I took a few full, deep breaths, holding back tears of joy. After some time, I slowly stood and tiptoed along the squeaking floorboards past inner rooms with enticing names such as Musk and Tiger, before arriving at a second garden with calming water features and sprawling moss. I suddenly became aware that my phone was not ringing off the hook and I felt liberated. I didn't need to rush off anywhere, so I luxuriously perused each nook and cranny. When I eventually strolled towards the exit I smiled knowingly at those walking towards me about to share the experience — as though it was our little secret.

A few wooden signposts indicated the route of The Philosopher's Path. I followed the twisting road past private homes and small temples and came across a restaurant specialising in *yudofu* (page 52). A sign in English read, 'We have only tofu course', and 'Sorry but we can't accept credit card — only cash!' For all of Japan's technological advances, many of the country's venues still prefer cash to credit cards. Feeling decidedly cleansed from my temple experience, the 'only tofu course' sounded fitting. I was welcomed in via a low wooden gate, along a cobblestoned path, past a bamboo and brush fence to the shoe-removal area. The staff slid back the doors and gracefully waved me inside.

There were no chairs — only *zabuton* (flat square cushions) that sat directly on the tatami next to tabletops raised some 20 cm (8 inches) from the ground. Ideally, as a female, I should have knelt with my legs tucked under me, but I cannot perform that kind of contortion for long for fear of never again regaining full use of my legs. After

At age 20, in a surreal moment as I flew over the summit of Fuji-san towards my new life in Tokyo, I saw the most incredibly radiant red orb. The 'land of the rising sun' had sealed our fate in a symbolic blood oath. Red and white — the colours of the national flag — is seen throughout Japan in daily life, but its use is also prolific during culturally significant events. Red represents energy and protects against demons.

a short period of polite discomfort, I shifted to the more masculine pose of crossed legs, which is considered acceptable these days — unless you are wearing a skirt!

I was hastily presented with a warm *oshibori* (damp towelling square, offered cool in summer) to cleanse my hands before eating. Again, if I was a bloke I could get away with wiping my face or cleaning the wax out of my ears, but I respectfully refrained. Dish by dish, a small feast was presented: *gomadofu* (sesame 'tofu', the colour of milk chocolate from the deeply roasted sesame seeds, the consistency of a chilled brûlée; page 252) came adorned with a little fresh grated wasabi to cut through the richness. The flavours exploded in my mouth as I wolfed it down. Small squares of *yakidofu no kinome dengaku* grilled on sticks (see page 53) arrived and I was instructed to 'eat now'. I did as I was told. The miso topping was green from finely pounded fresh *kinome* (the slightly astringent leaf of the numbing Japanese sansho plant) and tasted pleasantly peppery, with a hint of citrus.

An oddly textured cold yam soup was less appealing and I can only describe it as thick, gelatinous snot-like foam with hints of the sea. This would be the first of many disagreeable early encounters with slimy *nagaimo* (a yam variety), which is extremely popular during winter.

The burner for the *yudofu* (page 52) was lit and the hotpot set to simmer gently. When the tofu was warmed through, I used a wire mesh scoop to transfer a couple of squares into my small bowl, then poured a little of the accompanying sauce over the top before sprinkling it with chopped spring onions and *shichimi togarashi* (seven-flavour spice mix). It was delicate, yet wholesome and moreish.

A dish of perfectly crisp, waif-like tempura arrived with a small dish of salt and ground, dried shiso, rather than the better-known soy- and dashi-based dipping sauce, which is considered crass in parts of the Kansai region as it can drown out the natural flavour of food. As is tradition in marking the end of a meal, rice, pickles and tea were served.

When I had stopped adoring my meal, I looked up from my table to see the light shining through a large red paper parasol. It was spectacular and I felt my edges soften just a little bit more.

*

shiwasu / juunigatsu – december / the 12th month

yudofu

simmered tofu

SERVES 2–3 AS A MAIN COURSE WITH SIDES, OR 6 AS PART OF A MULTI-DISH MEAL

Kyoto-ites appreciate tofu in all its forms far more than anywhere else in Japan. This simple way of serving silken tofu highlights its subtle flavour and texture, and is particularly enjoyable on a winter's day. Warming, nutritious, but oh so delicate and light.

15 cm (6 inch) length of kombu (dried kelp)
½ teaspoon salt
250 ml (9 fl oz/1 cup) niban dashi (page 29)
60 ml (2 fl oz/¼ cup) shoyu
2 teaspoons mirin
2 tablespoons shaved *katsuobushi* (shaved dried, smoked bonito)
1 large block of silken firm tofu, 600–800 g (1 lb 5 oz–1 lb 12 oz), cut into 6 even pieces
thinly sliced spring onions (scallions), to serve
shichimi togarashi (seven-flavour spice mix), to serve

Remove any grit from the kombu with a damp cloth and place it in the bottom of a *donabe* if you have one, or a large flameproof casserole dish. Dissolve the salt in 1.25 litres (44 fl oz/5 cups) water, then pour it into the *donabe*. Leave to sit for 1 hour.

Combine the dashi, shoyu, mirin and *katsuobushi* in a non-metallic bowl. Set aside until just before serving, then strain into a small jug or bowl with pouring lip.

Sit the *donabe* or casserole dish on your stove — or, if at all possible, a portable gas burner or electric hotplate that you can place in the centre of the dining table. Set the heat to medium–high and bring the liquid just to the boil. Reduce the heat to a simmer and carefully add the tofu pieces. When the water returns to a simmer, cook the tofu for 2–3 minutes, or until just heated through. Turn off the heat. It is important to warm the tofu at a low heat to retain its silky texture.

Allow guests to serve themselves by lifting the tofu out of the pot with a flat wire mesh ladle, slotted spoon or slotted spatula, and transferring it into small individual bowls. They should then pour over a little of the dashi sauce and season as desired with spring onion and *shichimi togarashi*.

yakidofu no kinome dengaku

grilled tofu with sansho miso
MAKES 6

As legend goes, Dengaku was the name of a monk who performed for the imperial courts by dancing on a pogo stick.

4 tablespoons of your choice of miso — I like to mix 3 parts saikyo miso (sweet white miso) with 1 part aka miso (red miso) or mugi (barley) miso
2 tablespoons sake
1½ tablespoons mirin
3 teaspoons caster (superfine) sugar
1 small egg yolk
12 fresh *kinome* sprigs (see Note)
300 g (10½ oz) block of firm tofu, cut into 6 even rectangular slices about 1.5 cm (⅝ inch) thick

Soak six flat bamboo skewers or 12 thin bamboo skewers in water for 1 hour.

Put the miso, sake, mirin, sugar and egg yolk in a small saucepan and mash together until lump-free. Place over very low heat and stir. The mixture will thin down at first as the miso dissolves, but keep stirring for a few minutes until it thickens and becomes spreadable — which will happen as the egg starts to cook. Immediately remove from the heat and allow to cool completely.

Pick the *kinome* leaves from the sprigs and place in a sieve. Pour over boiling water to soften them, then immediately pour cold water over to refresh them. Drain well. Using a *suribachi* (ribbed Japanese mortar and wooden pestle), grind the leaves until the mixture is as smooth as possible, then add to the miso mixture. Stir to combine well.

Insert a flat bamboo skewer (or two thin skewers) into one short end of each piece of tofu, leaving about 2 cm (¾ inch) sticking out to form a handle — it should look a bit like an iceblock (popsicle/ice lolly) on a stick.

Preheat the grill (broiler) to medium–high. Line a baking tray with foil. Space the tofu sticks on the tray and place under the grill for 2 minutes, or until hot to touch. Turn the sticks over and divide the miso mixture over the tops of the tofu blocks, spreading it out evenly with a spatula — but don't go right to the edge as it will spread out as it heats.

Grill (broil) for another 4 minutes, or until golden. Serve immediately.

Note: As fresh *kinome* (sansho leaves) may be difficult to find, you can substitute with a large handful of *mitsuba* (Japanese trefoil) or flat-leaf (Italian) parsley leaves, mixed with a large pinch of ground sansho pepper, which comes from the same plant as the *kinome*.

Variation: Cut slender eggplant (aubergine) into discs about 1.5 cm (⅝ inch) thick, then fry or grill (broil) until tender. Thread 2–3 discs onto individual skewers, spread the miso mixture over, and replace the *kinome* with chopped toasted walnuts if desired. Grill until golden and serve sprinkled with chopped *kinome* or toasted sesame seeds.

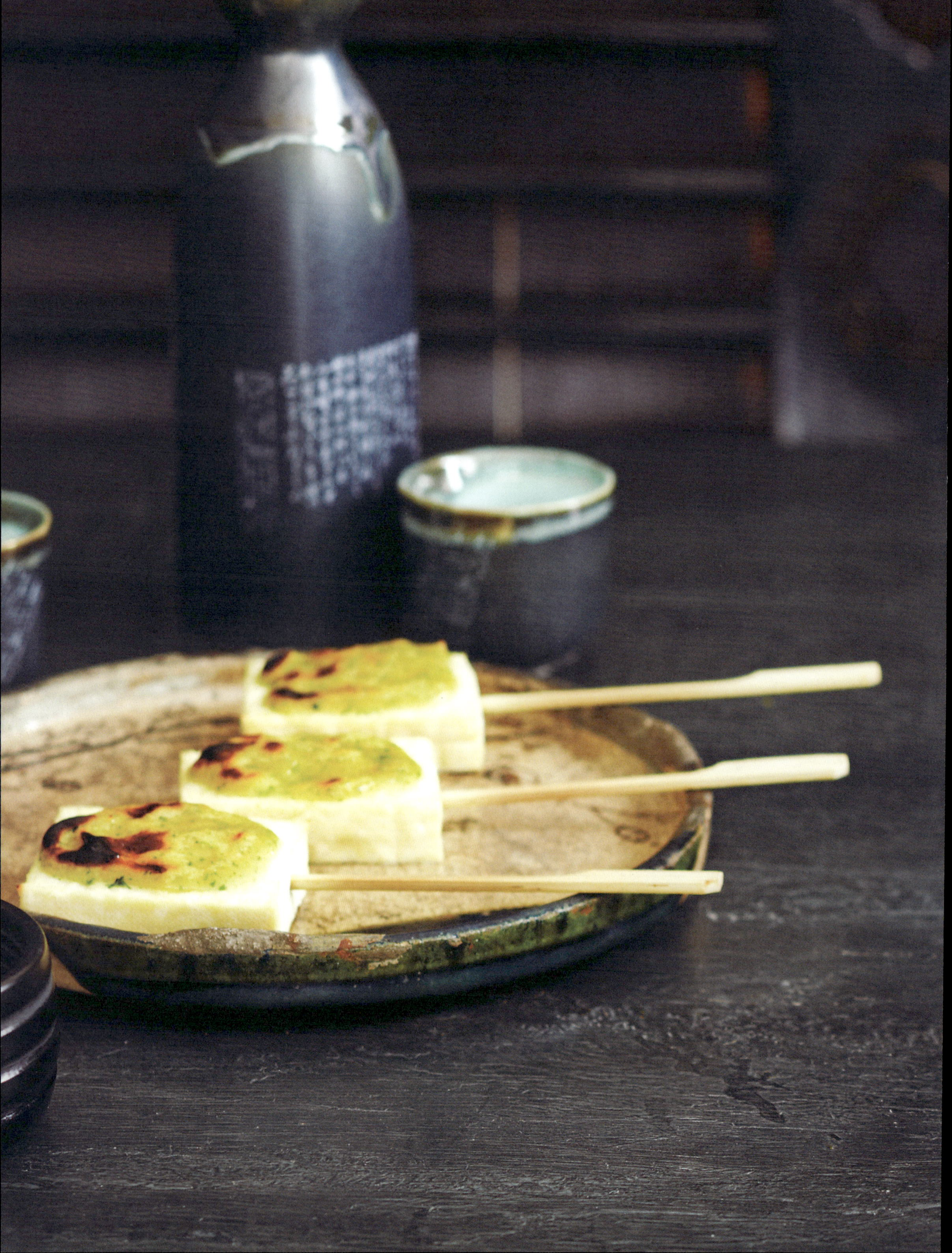

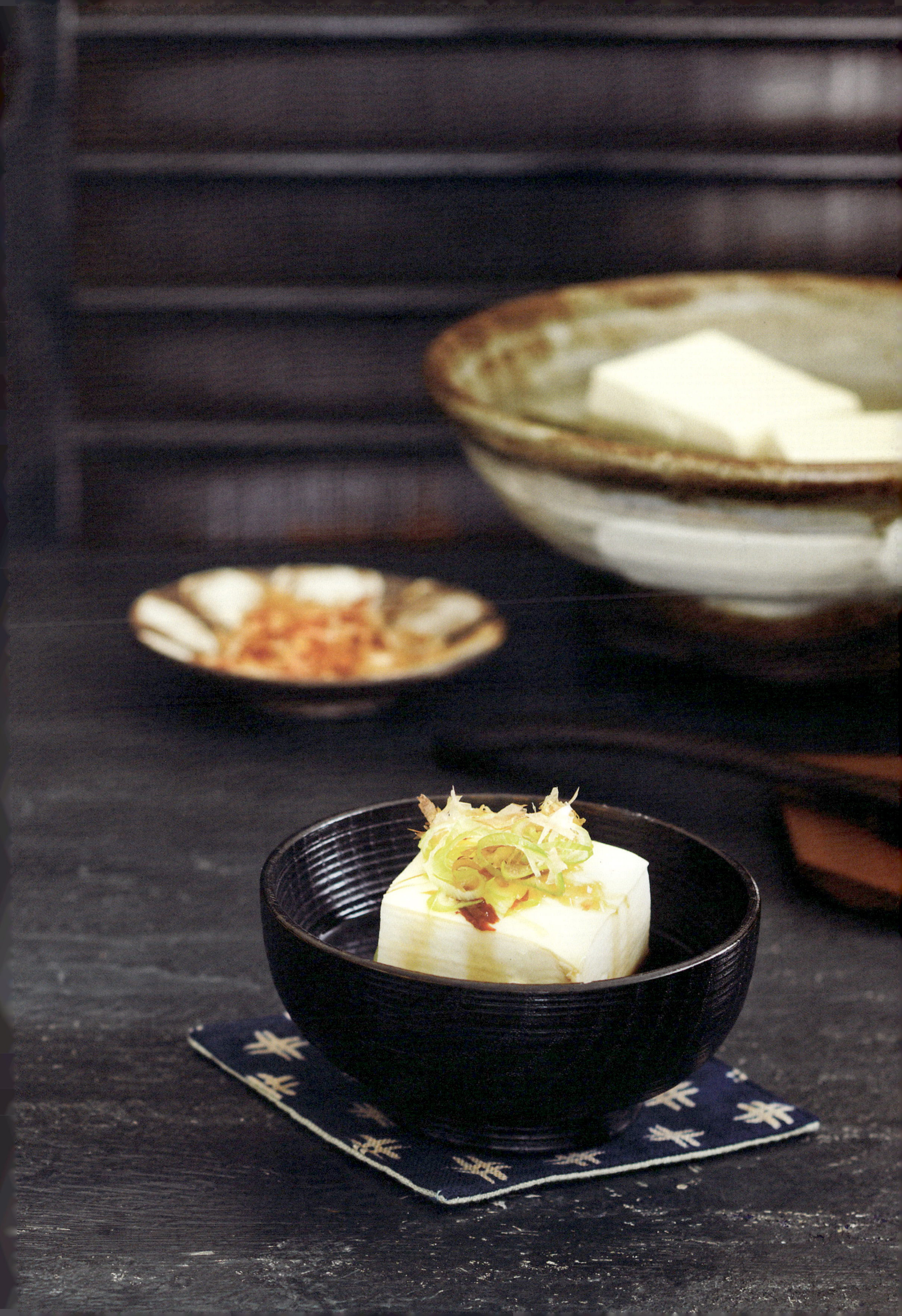

The trees lining the stream alongside The Philosopher's Path were relatively bare and incomparable with the beauty of springtime's overflowing weeping *sakura* (cherry blossoms) and fulsome willows. The path being fortuitously people-free, I strolled peacefully for some time, pleased for the exercise. Having these moments to myself, for the first time in what seemed like years, allowed some unresolved matters to gurgle to the surface — time had not been my friend recently and much had been steamrollered over, instead of being dealt with. Reminders of several instances at home where I hadn't been treated with the respect I deserved highlighted the fact I needed to value myself and not feel the need to 'sell out' or 'perform' in order to be appreciated, loved or respected.

*

The Japanese are so obsessed by food that the TV which was on in the background while I ate my breakfast of shimeji, enoki and *kaiware* (daikon sprouts) omelette with a caramel shoyu reduction was broadcasting a program devoted entirely to cake. A panel of 20 individuals attempted to guess the signature dish baked by their fellow sweet-tooths. They cooed and gushed, before all was revealed in food-porn-ish close-ups, leaving me feeling mildly less food-obsessed for the experience.

On a competing channel, a roving reporter interviewed local patisserie and bakery owners in an effort to find the 'ultimate' Christmas cake. I am not talking dried fruit and nuts here, but serious over-the-top frou-frou constructions: mousses, custards, creams and foams, glazes, meringues and other intriguing elements — all appropriately white, red or green, in flavours of green tea or pistachio, white chocolate or berry. Marzipan Santas, snowmen, mushrooms and snowflakes battled it out to see who would reign supreme.

Another cooking program followed, showcasing crab, a winter specialty, as the key ingredient for the day. They whipped up *kani furai* (crumbed fried crab legs); *okayu* (a congee-like dish cooked in a *donabe*; see rice gruel with snapper on page 218), topped with creamy, soft scrambled egg; juicy chunks of crabmeat and chives, drizzled with ponzu (soy and citrus sauce); and also *chirashi zushi* (scattered sushi) involving crab, bamboo and cucumber. I was seriously hungry again by the end of the show.

I arrived at Arashiyama's Hanatouro ('Flower Lantern Festival') a little early for the walking tour I'd booked, so was able to investigate the local food stalls. I bypassed the oversized *okonomiyaki* ('as you like it' pancake/omelette) made with local leeks after noticing a *nikuman* stand. The fluffy, Chinese-inspired steamed buns contained the most divine, slow-simmered pork belly (*butaniko no kakuni* — see page 141) and I gobbled down two of them, lubricated with a cup of seasonal *amazake*, a sweet, gruel-like sake that is so low in alcohol it is served to children. Served hot, the sake warmed me to the bone.

While waiting for the guide, I also did a spot of shopping and purchased a small package of woody-scented incense with hints of cinnamon and nutmeg. I often find incense from other countries cloying and irritating to my nostrils, but Japanese incense is rather sublime.

Effervescent Emi-san led us through the forest's surrounding temples and shrines and over bridges illuminated by hundreds of lanterns — paper, bamboo and ceramic. It was a lovely stroll, but we were joined by thousands of Japanese seeking their Saturday evening's culture fill. Being 'packed like sushi' (as described by our guide) certainly added to the authenticity of the experience, but it didn't take long for me to hear the call of my spacious, comfy bed.

Shortly after, I was tucked up at home, my cosy apartment filled with an aroma that settled somewhere between campfire and freshly baked cookies.

*

I felt an instant rapport with Myong Hee over a leisurely breakfast. We ventured to her 'Winter Light' exhibition in a gallery situated in an old *machiya* (townhouse) oozing history in a winding backstreet of the Gion district. It was reasonably quiet, so we sat upstairs on tiny wooden stools drinking green tea and eating sweet *mikan* (mandarins) and sharing more personal details with each other than either of us had anticipated. The conversation was mostly philosophical and we connected like trusted friends. She admired my positivity, but I assured her that in recent times this had not necessarily been my outlook.

Myong Hee's current installation contained 108 pieces, each consisting of a rectangle of rice paper, onto which she had abstractly painted primary colours, before hand-stitching each piece 108 times in unique patterns. The number 108 is significant because it represents the 108 earthly desires, which, according to Buddhist belief, must be quelled.

When pressed, she revealed her initial influence had been a chronically depressed fellow she'd met many years prior, who at the time believed suicide was his only option. A monk suggested to the man that rather than end his life he repeat a specific physical prayer 30,000 times and that way — because taking the life of any living thing is unacceptable to Buddhists — if he died, he would do so in a more acceptable manner. The man prayed at the temple all day and night for a week, squat jumping to lie, face down, against the floor, then reverse jumping to a standing position. Although he was bruised black and blue, he felt no mental change. The monk then suggested increasing the count to 40,000. He continued the prayers and, almost spent, arrived, surrounded by bowing monks, at the magic number. Still alive and immeasurably frustrated, he reluctantly dragged himself onto the bus to go home. During the ride, he reported that his fellow passengers' faces morphed into animal features and, believing it to be divine intervention by way of enlightenment, his fate was redirected.

Myong Hee, going through a far less traumatic but nonetheless challenging period of her own, decided for reasons of health and discipline to perform 108 of the same physical prayers daily, and to this day continues to do so at around 5 am each morning. She is the picture of health and her creativity is constantly flowing. I interpreted her installation to be a testament to her perseverance and dedication to both her chosen form of 'meditation' and her art.

My own creativity stirred, I later strolled along the northern part of Teramachi, originally a temple town, now part of a shopping arcade filled with quaint shops and businesses. I flicked through antique Japanese art and calligraphy books, sifted through wads of beautiful handmade paper, admired modern artworks and dropped into small temples along the way. One temple housed giant pumpkins that would later be simmered in a sweet liquid for consuming during Tooji (the winter solstice held around 22 December). It is said that eating vitamin-rich pumpkins and taking baths with whole yuzu (citrus) during Tooji is good for preventing colds! Traditional confectionery purveyors peddled the wares of their ancestors, centuries-old fabric remnants were bundled and tied on cheap wire stands, and a nearby organic farmers' market was selling off the last of its pink and purple daikons and *kabura* (a winter daikon the size of a child's head) so the stallholders could return home for the day. Fresh leafy greens of edible chrysanthemums, dandelions, spinach and tight heads of cabbage and broccoli varieties sat beside expensive organic rice and homemade pickles. Needless to say, purchases were made ...

Nightfall came all too soon. It was dark, but I felt safe. I was in Kyoto, after all, and as people were still milling about, I decided to walk home. However, it was a fair distance and the foot traffic soon noticeably thinned. I was not used to walking on my own at night and allowed paranoia to get the better of me. Hearing footsteps behind me, I remembered a warning from Myong Hee not to walk alone too late. I quickened my pace as I mentally relived a harrowing situation from my old life in Tokyo when, on a train packed firmly enough for me to lift both feet from the ground without falling, I was groped by a *chikan* (pervert). With his back pressed firmly against me, he managed to wedge one cupped hand onto my crotch. My pulse started racing in mild panic as I recalled the vacant look on his face when I eventually freed myself, shoving him off me.

Suddenly, I was transported back to the present when, as if by magic, five chanting monks appeared in my line of vision and stepped onto the opposite end of a pedestrian crossing in sync with my own footsteps. They crossed in single file towards me in a scene that resembled the cover image on The Beatles' *Abbey Road* album. With my confidence restored, I ducked up a side alley, taking a shortcut to my apartment. Just a few steps away from my door I was greeted with a smile and a neighbourly '*kombanwa*' (good evening) from one of the handsome local rickshaw drivers. All was well.

Hungry from the long walk and flustered from my brush with imagined near death, I impatiently gulped down one of my most guilty Japanese pleasures — a creamy, molten corn *korokke* (croquette; see page 62) while I cooked the rest of my dinner, which consisted of my favourite burdock root salad (page 66), *kyuuri* (the best cucumbers in the world), mizuna for greens and a seared wagyu steakette with mushrooms (page 65). The meat's flavoursome fat melted through the wagyu, yielding a product similar to pan-fried foie gras. It surpassed all the quality beef consumed in my lifetime! The combination would have been entirely indulgent had it not been for the fact it comprised just a few mouthfuls of each.

Meals in Japan are all about enjoying a range of textures, flavours and colours in small quantities, which for me is the perfect way to eat.

*

shiwasu / juunigatsu – december / the 12th month

There is something rather wonderful about the light in Kyoto. It seems curiously unlike that in other parts of Japan, and indeed most other countries I've visited. It is almost physical — it envelops you, making you feel safe and open. The unexpected shadow castings and illuminations are all part of Kyoto's alluring and sometimes hidden personality.

shiwasu / juunigatsu – december / the 12th month

kuriimu korokke

cream croquettes
MAKES 12

It seems unlikely, but croquettes are so popular all over Japan that there are small stores devoted solely to them. Sold everywhere from high-end food halls to convenience stores, the most popular versions are either 'cream' style like this corn version (*koon kuriimu korokke* — my guilty favourite), or more simple with potato and minced (ground) beef, as in the recipe opposite, known as *minchi* (mince) *korokke*.

60 g (2¼ oz) butter
½ brown onion, very finely chopped
300 g (10½ oz/1½ cups) fresh corn kernels (about 2 large corn cobs)
1 tablespoon mirin
2 tablespoons saikyo miso (sweet white miso)
a large pinch of caster (superfine) sugar
a few drops of usukuchi shoyu (light Japanese soy)
50 g (1¾ oz/⅓ cup) plain (all-purpose) flour, plus extra for coating
500 ml (17 fl oz/2 cups) milk
2 eggs, lightly beaten
panko (Japanese breadcrumbs) or large stale white breadcrumbs, for coating
vegetable oil, for deep-frying

Melt one-third of the butter in a saucepan over medium–high heat. Add the onion and corn and cook, stirring regularly, for 3–4 minutes, or until the corn is just starting to soften. Reduce the heat to medium and mix in the mirin, miso, sugar and shoyu. Cook for a further 5 minutes, or until the corn is tender. Remove from the heat and set aside.

Melt the remaining butter in a second saucepan over medium–high heat. Add the flour and stir to combine. Gradually whisk in the milk until it has all been added and the mixture is smooth. Allow to come to the boil, then reduce the heat to medium and cook, stirring regularly, for about 35 minutes. At this stage the mixture will have thickened a little more and any floury taste will be cooked out. Remove from the heat.

Stir in the corn mixture. Pour into a wide plastic container and spread out evenly. Freeze for 1½–2 hours, or until the mixture is very cold and starting to freeze around the edges.

Meanwhile, put the egg, breadcrumbs and extra flour in three separate wide bowls in preparation for crumbing.

Take two rounded tablespoons of the chilled corn mixture at a time and quickly mould into oblong shapes, 8 cm (3¼ inches) long and 3 cm (1¼ inches) in diameter. Roll them in the flour, dip them in the egg, allowing any excess to drip off, then coat in the breadcrumbs. Place on a tray and freeze for at least 2 hours. The filling for these croquettes is very moist, so you must ensure the croquettes are at least semi-frozen before you cook them so they don't get too hot and explode.

One-third fill a large deep-fryer or saucepan with oil and heat to 170°C (325°F), or until a cube of bread dropped into the oil browns in 20 seconds. Cook the croquettes a few at a time for 3–4 minutes, or until dark golden and cooked all the way through. Drain well on kitchen paper and serve hot, sprinkled with a little salt.

Variation: You can also add some sesame seeds to the panko.

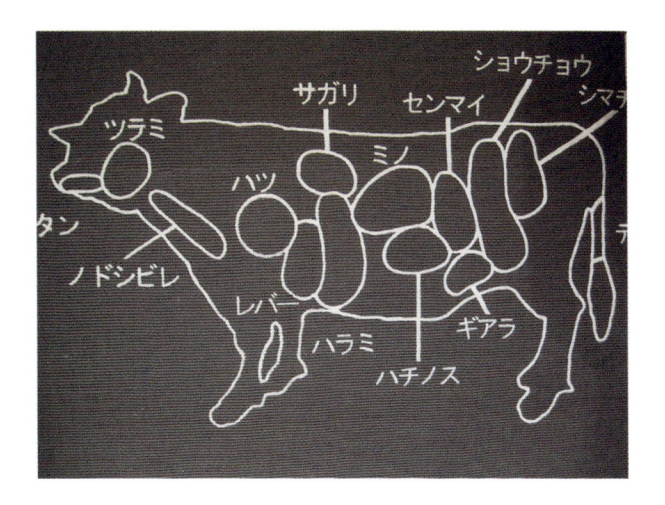

minchi korokke

sweet potato and beef mince croquettes

MAKES 12

250 g (9 oz) sweet potato
2 x 200 g (7 oz) floury potatoes
1 teaspoon sesame oil
10 g (¼ oz) butter
½ small brown onion, very finely chopped
200 g (7 oz) minced (ground) beef or pork
1½ teaspoons fine sea salt, or to taste
½ teaspoon caster (superfine) sugar, or to taste (optional)
¼–½ teaspoon Japanese curry powder (optional; see Note)
75 g (2½ oz/½ cup) plain (all-purpose) flour
2 eggs, lightly beaten
2 cups panko (Japanese breadcrumbs) or large stale white breadcrumbs
vegetable oil, for deep-frying

Put the sweet potato and potatoes, still in their jackets, in a large pot and cover well with water. Bring to the boil over high heat and cook for about 35 minutes, or until tender. Drain well and set aside until cool enough to handle. Peel, mash well and allow to cool completely.

Meanwhile, heat the sesame oil and butter in a frying pan over high heat and sauté the onion for 2–3 minutes, or until lightly golden. Add the meat and sauté, breaking up any lumps with the back of a fork, for 3–4 minutes, or until cooked through. Tip the meat into a colander and rest for 10 minutes to drain off any excess fat and liquid.

Mix the meat through the mashed potatoes. Season with the salt, a little sugar if needed, and the curry powder, if using. Cover and refrigerate for at least 1 hour, or until the mixture is cold enough to mould easily.

Take 2 tablespoons of the mixture at a time and shape into flat, oval-shaped patties about 7 cm (2¾ inches) long, 5 cm (2 inches) wide and 1.5 cm (⅝ inch) thick.

Put the flour, egg and breadcrumbs in three separate, wide bowls in preparation for crumbing. Lightly coat the patties in the flour, then dip them into the egg, allowing any excess to drip off, then coat them in the crumbs, pressing them on lightly to help them adhere. Refrigerate for at least 1 hour to chill well.

One-third fill a deep-fryer with vegetable oil and heat to 180°C (350°F), or until a cube of bread dropped into the oil browns in 15 seconds. Cook the croquettes in batches for about 3 minutes, or until crisp and golden. Drain on kitchen paper and serve hot, sprinkled with fine sea salt.

Note: Japanese curry powder is quite mild, full-flavoured and a little sweet. You can substitute any generic curry powder blend, but the Japanese mix will best achieve a distinctly Japanese flavour.

zenbu zen 64

yaki wagyu to enringi

wagyu with king brown mushrooms
SERVES 2–4 AS PART OF A MULTI-DISH MEAL

Wagyu is expensive, but I much prefer to savour a few small pieces of perfectly cooked, high-grade beef than tackle a huge steak of inferior quality.

2 teaspoons sesame oil
2 *enringi* (king brown mushrooms), cut lengthways into slices 3 mm (1/8 inch) thick
2 x 100 g (3½ oz) highly marbled wagyu sirloin steaks, cut into 1 cm (½ inch) slices
1 spring onion (scallion), green part only, very thinly sliced

DAIKON DRESSING
1 tablespoon niban dashi (page 29)
1 tablespoon usukuchi shoyu (light Japanese soy)
1 tablespoon mirin
2 teaspoons fresh or bottled yuzu juice or lemon juice
¼ teaspoon finely grated fresh ginger (optional)
2 tablespoons finely grated daikon (see Note), squeezed to remove excess moisture

Heat the sesame oil in a large, heavy-based frying pan over medium–high heat. Add the mushroom slices to the pan, spacing them well, and cook on each side for 2 minutes, or until lightly golden. Set aside and cover to keep warm. Increase the heat to high.

Meanwhile, combine all the dressing ingredients except the daikon in a small bowl and set aside. Do not make the dressing earlier than this — it needs to be freshly mixed for optimum flavour.

Slice a little fat from the beef, add it to the pan and heat until it melts. Season the steaks with a little salt. When the pan is nice and hot, add the steaks and cook on each side for 1 minute, or until well browned, but still rare inside. Remove from the heat and cover to keep warm.

Arrange the mushrooms decoratively on individual plates, or on one long rectangular plate. Cut the beef into 3 cm (1¼ inch) squares or strips (chopstick-friendly pieces) and, working quickly, place them neatly over or beside the mushrooms. Garnish with the spring onion.

Quickly stir the daikon into the dressing for spooning over the beef. Serve immediately.

Note: Don't use a regular grater for daikon. Inexpensive ceramic or plastic daikon graters, with raised points instead of blades, are available at Asian supermarkets; ginger graters will work too. The resulting texture is very different.

gobo sarada

burdock root salad

MAKES 1½ CUPS, OR SERVES 4–6 AS PART OF A MULTI-DISH MEAL

This earthy salad is addictive but also a little rich, so is only eaten in small amounts. It doubles easily for larger groups.

½ small carrot, finely julienned
1 *kyuuri* (Japanese cucumber), or ½ Lebanese (short) cucumber, finely julienned
100 g (3½ oz/1 cup) finely julienned or shredded burdock root (see Note)
1 small spring onion (scallion), white part only, very finely minced
black sesame seeds, to garnish

DRESSING

1 tablespoon toasted sesame seeds
2 teaspoons mirin
½ teaspoon shoyu
1 teaspoon caster (superfine) sugar
a few drops of Japanese sesame chilli oil or sesame oil
4 tablespoons Japanese mayonnaise (in the soft-squeeze bottle)

Sprinkle the carrot and cucumber liberally with salt and sit in a colander for 20 minutes to soften. Rinse well and squeeze tightly to remove any excess liquid. Set aside.

Meanwhile, bring a small saucepan of water to the boil. Add the burdock. When the water returns to the boil, cook for 3 minutes. Drain well and cool.

To make the dressing, finely grind the sesame seeds using a *suribachi* (ribbed Japanese mortar and wooden pestle). Mix in the mirin, shoyu, sugar and oil and stir until smooth. Scrape the mixture into a bowl, add the mayonnaise and mix well.

Add the burdock, carrot, cucumber and spring onion to the dressing and mix well. Place in a small dish, sprinkle with the sesame seeds and serve.

If you are not serving the salad straight away, you can cover and refrigerate it for up to 3 days, but mix it well again before serving.

Note: Burdock root is seasonal, but it is available frozen (julienned) from Asian food stores. It is ready to cook with — just thaw it before cooking for this particular recipe. If using fresh burdock root, first scrape the skin off it. Whittle the burdock into fine shreds (like you are sharpening a pencil with a knife, the old-fashioned way), into a bowl of cold water mixed with 1 tablespoon rice vinegar. Sit for 10 minutes to remove any bitterness and stop any browning. If using frozen burdock, this step is not necessary.

67 shiwasu / juunigatsu – december / the 12th month

Kyoto's famous flea markets are a great place to rub shoulders with locals. Literally. Although the markets are crowded from dawn until dusk in spring and autumn, rugging up for a winter morning's visit guarantees treasure for your efforts. Surely the perfect souvenir of both a trip to Japan, and the country's history, is something that resonates with you when fossicking through mounds of antique kimonos, ceramics, lacquerware and curios.

Pushed, shoved, pummelled and prodded — I was caught in a riptide in a sea of bargain hunters. It was the Toji Temple's final and therefore largest flea market of the year. I had been warned about the crowds, but had gone anyway. The tantalising pop of ginko nuts (or *ginnan* — the nut-like inner seed of the ginko tree) roasting on an open fire conjured images of a cosy Christmas, but I couldn't even get close enough to smell them, let alone buy any. I was paralysed by a thousand sets of elbows, hips and shoulders. I had to get out of there, but there was no visible escape route. Conveyor-belted to an area directly adjacent to the market, I witnessed people jostle against each other in an attempt to pray for the New Year. They enthusiastically rubbed a bronze tortoise for luck and wafted billowing incense smoke over any ailing parts of their bodies. From dodgy knees and wrists to balding heads — all were introduced to the vapours that were massaged in for good measure. I grabbed an armful of the vapours as I scooted along with the tide and waved it in my general direction, hoping it would find wherever it needed to be. The whole experience lasted around an hour, but only because I was physically unable to find my way out. I literally had no choice of direction. In a traffic jam of feet, I had to move wherever I was led until I was eventually spat out of a random exit.

While I was at the also-scarily-busy-but-nevertheless-wondrous Isetan food hall next to the marvel of modern architecture known as Kyoto Station, I was deviously offered some *kara-age* (fried chicken; page 71). It was so delicious it was impossible for me to leave the store without a take-home package — for research purposes, of course. This was no ordinary chook. Fine shavings of burdock root were dispersed through the crisp batter before frying, and the hot, golden nuggets were drizzled with a sweet and tangy glaze.

Rack me up for Guilty Pleasure No. 387, then downgrade the naughty rating with super-healthy burdock root and sesame; a nice trade-off.

I always eat more fried food in Japan than I would ever dream of eating at home. But Japanese deep-fried food is light and crisp, never greasy.

✻

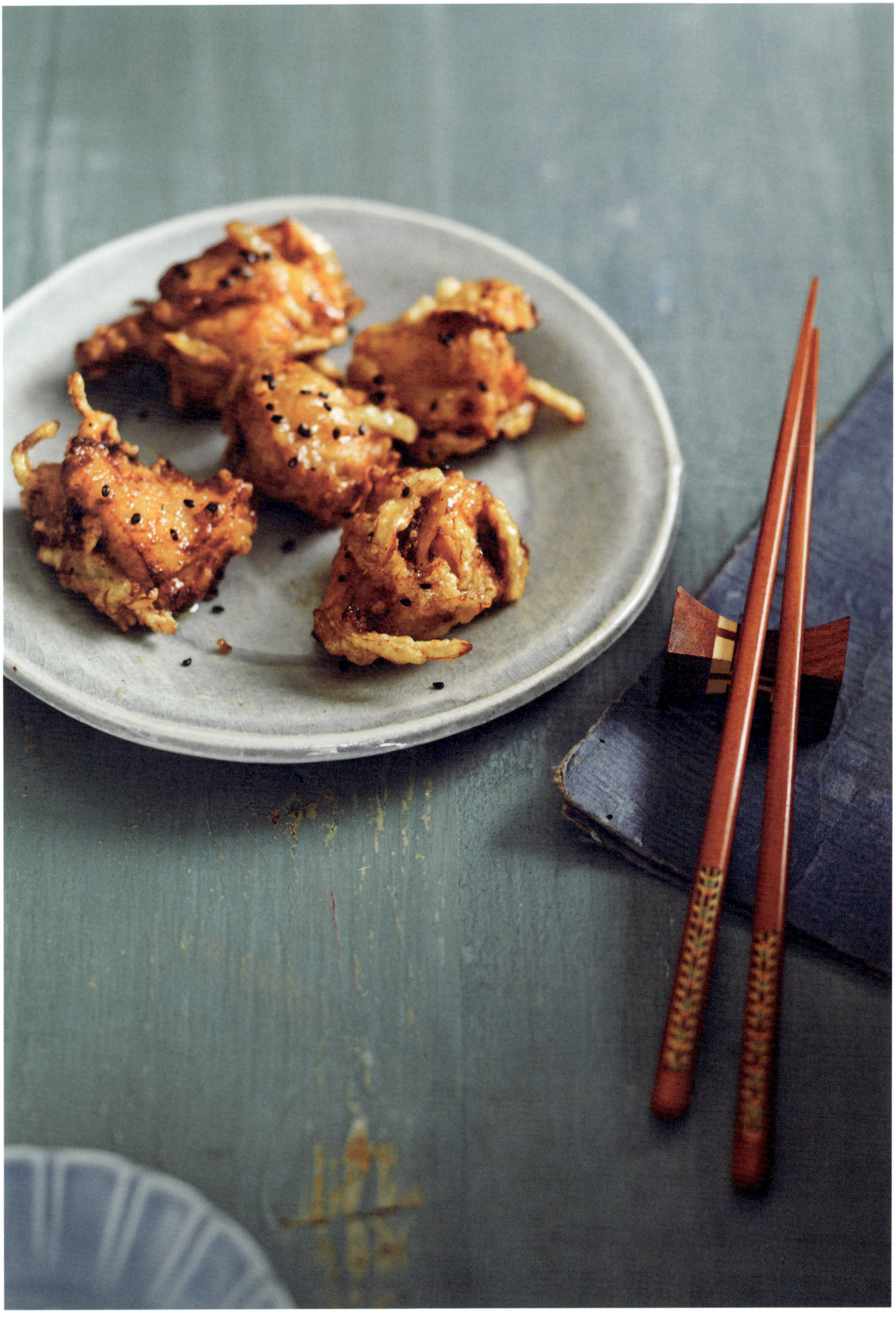

tori to gobo no kara-age

fried chicken

SERVES 6–8 AS PART OF A MULTI-DISH MEAL

Kara-age is the common name for Japanese-style fried chicken — and it's a knockout. *Age-mono* is the general term for fried food, and *-age* is the fried bit, which comes in handy when deciphering Japanese menus. Like gyoza (dumplings) and ramen (noodles), *kara-age* is an example of *wafu-chuka*, or Chinese-influenced Japanese food. This unusual version includes burdock root in the coating, and an addictive sweet and tangy sauce; however, feel free to omit both for a simpler version, which should be served with lemon wedges and a little sea salt on the side.

1 kg (2 lb 4 oz) chicken thigh fillets, skin on
2 tablespoons shoyu
2 tablespoons mirin
1 tablespoon sake
2 garlic cloves, crushed
1 teaspoon finely grated fresh ginger
vegetable oil, for deep-frying
120 g (4¼ oz/⅔ cup) *katakuriko* or potato starch, plus extra if needed
50 g (1¾ oz/½ cup) coarsely grated burdock root

SAUCE
80 ml (2½ fl oz/⅓ cup) rice vinegar
80 ml (2½ fl oz/⅓ cup) niban dashi (see page 29)
2 teaspoons usukuchi shoyu (light Japanese soy)
2 tablespoons caster (superfine) sugar
2 teaspoons fresh or bottled yuzu juice or lemon juice
a few drops of sesame chilli oil or sesame oil
1 slice of fresh ginger
1½ teaspoons honey
black or toasted sesame seeds (optional)

Cut the chicken into 4 cm (1½ inch) squarish pieces. Combine the shoyu, mirin, sake and garlic in a non-metallic bowl. Working over the bowl, squeeze the grated ginger in your hand, or in a small piece of muslin (cheesecloth), to extract the juice into the other ingredients — discard the fibrous remains. Add the chicken pieces and toss to coat. Cover and refrigerate for 30 minutes — no longer as the flavour will become too strong.

Combine all the sauce ingredients except the sesame seeds in a saucepan with 1 tablespoon water. Stir over high heat until the sugar has dissolved, then bring to the boil and cook for about 5 minutes, or until slightly syrupy. Remove from the heat, discard the ginger and set aside.

When ready to serve, one-third fill a deep-fryer or large heavy-based saucepan with oil and heat to 180°C (350°F), or until a cube of bread dropped into the oil browns in 15 seconds.

Tip the chicken pieces into a colander to drain off the marinade, then place them in a large bowl. Add the starch and burdock and mix well. The mixture should be a little sticky, but not too wet — if it is, add a little extra starch.

Cook the chicken in batches for 6–7 minutes, or until the coating is golden and crisp and the chicken is cooked through. Drain well on kitchen paper and keep warm in a low oven while you cook the rest of the chicken.

While the last batch of chicken is deep-frying, bring the sauce just to the boil again, then remove from the heat.

Place all the chicken in a large clean bowl and drizzle in half the sauce while tossing the chicken. Repeat with the remaining sauce, tossing well to ensure a light, even coating. Sprinkle with sesame seeds, if using, toss again, then serve immediately.

I was suddenly extremely tired and drained; the adrenaline from the newness of my situation was wearing off and warning me to slow down. I was meant to be stopping to smell the cherry blossoms, yet I had been running at quite a pace without realising it. But you can't go from 1000 to zero overnight, right? It was essential to slow down at a comfortable rate.

I was, however, both surprised and delighted to note that I had stopped keeping track of time. I threw on a few loads of washing and considered spending the day just lazing around, but the call of the Heian Jingu shrine, just minutes away, was too strong and I was still in the warped zone of worrying about not getting enough done each day. Through the imposing red, white and green entrance (which symbolises happiness and celebration, purity and life) I crunched my way over the expansive, white-gravelled front courtyard towards the main hall. Hearing the haunting strains, hollow knocks and echoes of traditional wood instruments, the voyeur in me quickly moved forward in search of its source. I stopped short upon sighting the austere beauty of a Shinto wedding ceremony.

The bride was covered from her hooded headpiece to her slipper-like footwear in a virginal white cloak of silk. Her face, only barely visible, was painted with very pale foundation, her lips brushed with only a subtle hint of colour. The groom in short black kimono and grey *hakama* (culotte-like pants) sat beside her in front of their 10 wedding guests. Both sets of parents wore black, although the fine embroidery at the base and on the *obi* (sash) of the women's kimonos was flourished with autumnal hues of gold, bronze and persimmon, or wintry hints of silver, ice blue and lilac.

The ceremony was still and hushed. The Shinto priest, also dressed in white, recited a solemn blessing inviting the spirits of the dead to enter the space. Afterwards, the *miko* (female shrine assistants), dressed in red and white, danced in honour of the deities that protect the shrine.

From the sitting position, the bride and groom bowed in unison towards the priest and the family posed for a smile-free portrait in respect of the seriousness of the occasion. It was a different atmosphere altogether once they walked into the main courtyard, and I deduced from the groom's goofy grin that this was not an arranged marriage. I left them to celebrate while I explored the peaceful garden.

In a seemingly insignificant side street I found an intriguing traditional restaurant frontage painted black. It was a little intimidating as I couldn't see inside, so — anticipating stares, uncomfortable pauses and whispers — I braced myself, slid open the door and stepped inside. The chef, hearing me close the heavy doors behind me, wandered out from the kitchen. A look of surprise ran across his face. I asked if it was okay for me to come in for lunch and he immediately ushered me through to the dining area, where two nervous kimono-clad young waitresses met me. The whole place was empty, so I assumed I was early. I selected a table in front of the tranquil inner courtyard garden and sat quietly. My lunch took a little longer than usual to arrive, so I checked the time. I was no longer wearing my watch, so I looked at my phone: it was 1.45 pm. Oh crap! In traditional Kyoto establishments, lunch service tends to end at 2 pm sharp. I apologised profusely to the waitress, who assured me it was okay. They had, in fact, already cleaned up after lunch and were preparing for dinner service — yet they still fired up the burners and cooked everything fresh for me. It was the kind of customer service one dreams about!

Where had the time gone? I had spent four oblivious hours in the Heian Jingu shrine and its stark winter garden. For the first time in a long time, I had been completely in the moment.

At home, I put the kettle on the stove and found the ritual of waiting for the water to boil curiously enjoyable.

*

Myong Hee's foodie friends from Takahama were in town and I joined them for dinner. They had gone to some trouble to select a venue where I could experience a wide range of local dishes. Through a narrow, nondescript doorway, we climbed an incredibly steep, rickety staircase, before being ushered into a private tatami room. I had hoped I would get used to this sitting-on-the-floor business, but my dodgy spine suffered almost the instant my backside hit the floor. Fortunately, having started sipping wine at 5 pm, it took only a glass or two more to anaesthetise the pain. I'd explained to my new friends that 5 pm was officially 'wine-o-clock' and they had embraced the concept with gusto!

Our hosts ordered a set course, adding a few extra favourites to the mix. They excitedly explained each dish and ingredient to me and were surprised when I recalled some of the names in Japanese before they did. I might not be able to converse in Japan on an intellectual level, but I can certainly contribute when it comes to cuisine — which we talked about for most of the evening. The 'international language of luuuurve' has nothing on the international language of food. Myong Hee later made the wise observation that love comes and goes, but food is a constant. For a moment I considered how often food may have replaced love in my life or comforted me from its loss.

I quickly brushed the thought aside when, for the second time in a week, I experienced a luscious *gomadofu* (page 252), this time topped with seaspray-fresh, creamy *uni* (sea urchin), freshly grated wasabi and a sweet chunk of lightly grilled scallop — a sensual awakening.

Kamo-negi nabe (page 76), a small ceramic hotpot dish containing sliced duck breast and leeks, was simple, but both savoury and richly warming. My companions explained the subtleties between Kyoto-style *kujo negi* (leek), with its greater white portion, versus the predominantly green *kanto negi* from the Tokyo area. In Japan, it's not only the chefs who know where their produce originates.

Tender strips of *ika* (squid) tempura were seasoned with lemon and spicy *shichimi togarashi* (seven-flavour spice mix) and drizzled with mayonnaise. It seemed more Spanish than Japanese, but as tempura was introduced to Japan by the Portuguese, it's not an impossible leap.

An *obanzai* platter arrived, including four small 'home-style' dishes: triangles of *aka konnyaku* (an opaque red jelly-like paste, coloured with a mild red chilli), which had a distinct paprika-like flavour but little heat; *tai namban* (fried snapper covered in a vinegar dressing with carrots, onion and daikon), which demonstrated more of the cuisine's Portuguese influence; small pan-fried rolls of *yuba*-wrapped *okara* (*okara*, the solids left after grinding soy beans to make soy milk, were wrapped in *yuba*, sheets of soy milk 'skin'; see page 84), and refreshing *shungiku no ohitashi* (edible chrysanthemum leaf salad in a light shoyu dressing, see page 79).

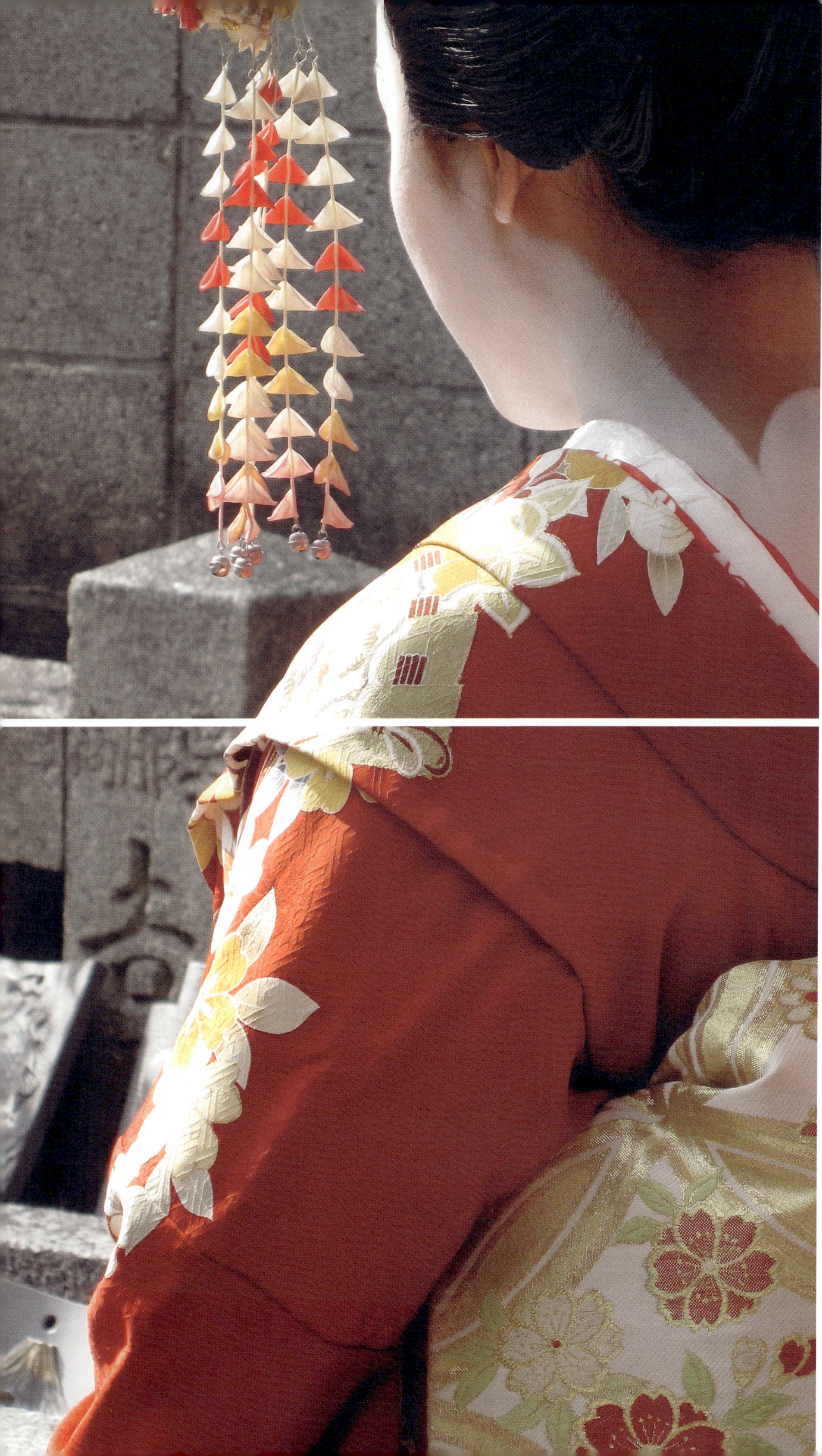
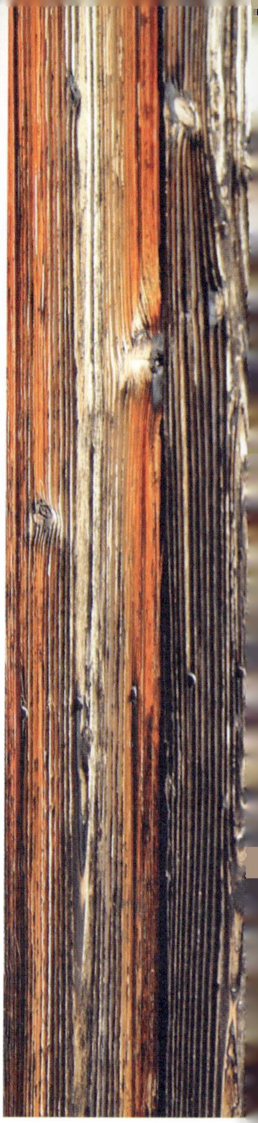
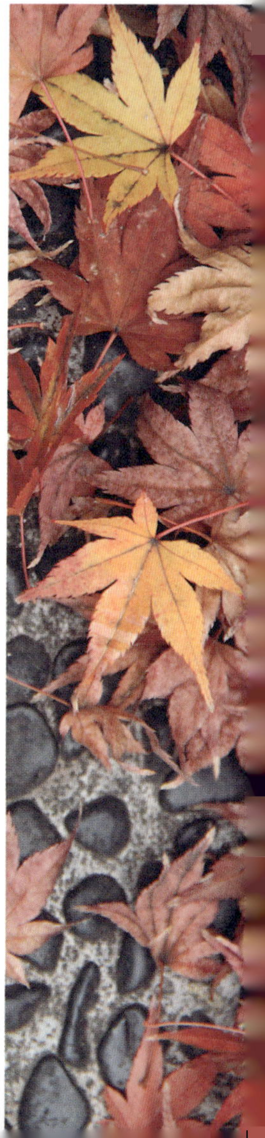

I was starting to feel a return of self.
One by one, tiny deflated pockets of my body
and soul were regenerating. I finally began
taking heed when my body called for rest.
I felt safe and happy, cocooned by the loveliness
and, to quote a wise friend,
'gentleness' of Kyoto.

kamo-negi nabe

duck and leek hotpot
SERVES 4–6 AS PART OF A MULTI-DISH MEAL

2 x 200 g (7 oz) duck breast fillets (see Notes)
ground sansho, for sprinkling (optional)
½ teaspoon sesame oil
3 pencil-thin leeks, cut into 4 cm (1½ inch) lengths (see Notes) — you'll need about 12 pieces
250 ml (9 fl oz/1 cup) tori dashi (page 208) or niban dashi (page 29)
1½ tablespoons sake
5 teaspoons mirin
2½ teaspoons shoyu

Pat the duck breasts dry with kitchen paper. Sprinkle the ground sansho, if using, lightly but evenly over the skin and rub it in using your fingers.

Heat the oil in a small *donabe* or small heavy-based, deep-sided frying pan over medium–high heat. Sear the duck, skin side down, for 2–3 minutes, or until the skin is evenly golden. Remove the duck from the pan and blot with kitchen paper to remove the excess oil.

Place the breasts skin side down on a chopping board and, using a sharp knife, cut them into slices 3 mm (⅛ inch) thick. Set aside.

Drain the duck fat from the pan and discard — there should just be a thin film on the bottom of the pan. Place the pan back over medium–high heat and brown the leeks for 30 seconds, then remove them from the pan and set aside.

Add the dashi, sake, mirin and shoyu to the pan and bring to the boil. Return the leeks to the pan and cook for 1 minute.

Quickly lay the duck slices in a single layer over the leeks and cook for 30 seconds, using chopsticks to gently push any duck that is still pink after that time briefly into the liquid. (If using a frying pan you can swirl the pan a little to assist even cooking.) Be careful not to overcook the duck — it should still be slightly pink in the centre and tender.

Serve in the *donabe*, or in small individual dishes.

Notes: Farmed duck is better for this dish — wild duck is a little tough and chewy for this style of cookery. If possible, choose leeks that are about 25 cm (10 inches) long and 2 cm (¾ inch) in diameter. They are available in greengrocers in winter.

77 shiwasu / juunigatsu – december / the 12th month

zenbu zen 78

shungiku no ohitashi

'drenched' chrysanthemum leaf salad
SERVES 4–6 AS PART OF A MULTI-DISH MEAL

This popular side dish can feature a variety of green vegetables (see Notes at the end of the recipe). It should be made very close to serving time, as once the chrysanthemum leaves are cooked and dressed they don't hold well.

- 1 small bunch (about 125 g/4½ oz) *shungiku* (edible garland chrysanthemum leaf — see Notes)
- 2 tablespoons ichiban dashi (page 29)
- 1 tablespoon usukuchi shoyu (light Japanese soy)
- 1½–2 teaspoons rice vinegar, or fresh or bottled yuzu juice, to taste
- 1 tablespoon mirin
- fine *katsuobushi* (shaved dried, smoked bonito) flakes or toasted sesame seeds, to serve (optional)

Trim the thick ends from the chrysanthemum stalks, then place the stems in a bowl of cold water for 30 minutes to help remove any grit and pesticides. Drain.

Bring a pot of water to the boil. Holding the tops of the leaves, dangle the stems in the water for 30 seconds, before dropping the whole bunch in for a further 30 seconds.

Drain and rinse the chrysanthemums under cold running water. When just cool enough to handle, gently squeeze any excess liquid out of the leaves with your hands. Cut into 5 cm (2 inch) lengths and place in a bowl.

Combine the dashi, shoyu, vinegar and mirin. Pour over the leaves and use your hands to gently turn them in the mixture. Transfer in neat bundles to small individual serving dishes, or place neatly onto one serving dish for guests to help themselves. Garnish with *katsuobushi* or sesame seeds if desired.

Notes: The slightly bitter garland chrysanthemum leaves, resembling those of the garden-variety chrysanthemum, are actually grown specifically for eating — do not confuse the two. Known in Japan as *shungiku*, they are generally only available in winter and are popular in *nabe* or hotpots, and sometimes tempura. As they are quite fragile, use them as soon as you buy them, or keep them sealed in a plastic bag in the fridge for use within 3 days of purchase.

English spinach, mizuna, daikon greens, wasabi greens, *nanohana* (canola/rape greens), broccolini and *komatsuna* (Japanese mustard spinach) can be used instead of *shungiku*. Cut the spinach and mizuna into 6 cm (2½ inch) lengths, place in a colander and pour boiling water over; rinse under cold water, squeeze out any excess water and dress as above.

All the other greens should be prepared as per the directions for the *shungiku*.

All of these greens can also be dressed with the *shira-ae* ('white' tofu dressing) on page 164.

Free-flowing wine had lubricated the linguistic skills of the only English-speaking member of the Takahama group, Ikeda-san. He encouraged me, although there was clearly no need, to try everything. It turned out he was a food farmer — growing rice, and a variety of Chinese anise used in Buddhist festivals — and was therefore very busy preparing to fulfil New Year orders. Over the past 15 years, he'd dedicated his spare time to becoming a 'novice' of Noh, the Japanese performance art known to drive Westerners insane with its shrill wailing music, with each 'song' lasting more than an hour. He'd been so hospitable I found it difficult to decline his invitation to attend a mesmerising performance the following month.

A small plate of knobbly brown discs interrupted us. Puréed *renkon* (lotus root), resembling parsnip mash, was coated in soba (buckwheat) groats and deep-fried. Full of nutty, earthy flavours, a little yuzu salt was the only seasoning required.

A handsome selection of sashimi was placed before us. *Anago* (conger/sea eel), lightly brushed with flame, married perfectly with tart *bainiku* (umeboshi paste; see the *butabara kushiyaki* recipe on page 173). Alongside it was *maguro* (tuna), *aji* (skipjack/horse mackerel) and *shima-aji* (striped skipjack). My dining companions were amused (read: mildly horrified) by the negligently small amount of wasabi I added to my shoyu. When I told them I 'preferred it mild' they jumped on me, insisting that wasabi is essential for killing any bacteria on the raw fish. I immediately upped my intake and have done so ever since, consequently developing quite an appreciation for the breath-catching green rescue remedy.

Kinome-yaki (fish lightly marinated in Japanese shoyu, then grilled and scattered with shredded *kinome* leaves) was tender yet robust. Still-sizzling wagyu, its rich meat slightly smoky from the fire, was enhanced by a tiny squeeze of lemon. We were onto our eighth dish but, to be polite, I managed to 'force' down a couple of slices.

I have become so accustomed to the near-global law against smoking in restaurants that I was a little stunned when a cigarette was lit by one of our group. I have always thought it seemed rather sacrilegious to smoke while eating ... but this was Japan! And although the number of smokers is decreasing, the act is still prolific and I reminded myself to be tolerant.

Fortuitously, a small dish containing layers of flattish squares resembling the slightly wrinkled skin of cooling custard soon distracted me. It was my introduction to the Kyoto delicacy *nama yuba* (fresh soy milk skin; see page 84). It looked less than appealing, but once it passed my lips I swore I could hear angels singing. Much like a very soft burrata cheese, it was creamy, moist, just holding together, but with a texture like none other and without the fatty residue of dairy. With a dot of freshly grated wasabi and a few drops of good-quality shoyu, it was simple and divine. A wholesome treat that feels somewhat unholy by nature of its sensuality.

We did not require any more food, but my hosts, noting my euphoric appreciation of *nama yuba*, ordered some *yuba* chips — deep-fried in sesame oil. Wafer-thin, with a deep malty nuttiness, sprinkled with sea salt and dosed with very finely sliced spring onion, they were lip-smackingly moreish.

My stomach had stretched, but I didn't care. I was on overdrive — and didn't baulk too much when the tempura arrived. Thankfully it consisted of a paltry three items: small *kisu* (whiting), fanned baby *nasu* (eggplant/aubergine) and whole *piman* (pimiento) — all delicious!

Closely following was another first for me — *nama fu* (fresh wheat gluten). *Fu* is the dried version that, when reconstituted in hotpots or soups, swells to spongy shapes; it has never done much for me. This was completely different: more like a slightly chewy handmade gnocchi! It was served *dengaku*-style (using the same sauce as the tofu recipe on page 53, but without the added *kinome*) — skewered, topped with miso and grilled. Delicious!

The final installation arrived. Although it would have been deemed impolite, I was prepared to forgo the rice course. However, it was studded with my new-found love, *nama yuba*, and topped with *ankake* (a slightly sweet, thickened amber sauce of shoyu and dashi), fresh shiso and grated wasabi. After a few bites, I was in lust with the sensation and its simplicity; it was one of the most deeply comforting foods I had eaten in some time.

I was so drunk with gastronomic ecstasy that I was almost hallucinating. Semi-crippled by back pain and dead legs caused by too many hours sitting on the tatami, I was more than ready to leave.

But then there was dessert — and, as I was taught more than 20 years ago, *betsu onaka* (the Japanese concept of two separate stomachs, one reserved for sweets) would allow me to partake.

I hobbled out, stuffed to the gills, in awe of the generosity of strangers (not least because my meal was paid for) and inspired by new introductions.

*

In Japan, soy milk is rarely consumed as is; rather it is part of the tofu- or *yuba*-making process. However, the recipe on page 84 explains the method for making soy milk, so feel free to use it as you would regular purchased soy milk. Just note that it won't be as sweet, as there is no added sugar.

83   shiwasu / juunigatsu – december / the 12th month

nama yuba

fresh soy milk skin

MAKES 4 NAMA YUBA SERVINGS, OR 1 LITRE
(35 FL OZ/4 CUPS) SOY MILK

Unlike the skin that forms on regular milk when it boils, which turns my stomach, this curious foodstuff made by boiling soy milk is quite a delicacy. It may not sound all that inviting and it takes some patience to make a batch, but it is worth making — if only once, to experience this unusual treat. The most crucial elements are good-quality (preferably Japanese) soy beans and pure water, otherwise the *yuba* will be inferior and bitter.

Nama yuba is highly regarded both for its healthful properties (high protein and fibre) and its deliciously creamy texture and flavour, with slightly nutty, malty undertones. It is great served warm from the pot with a little good-quality shoyu or ponzu (a soy and citrus sauce) and freshly grated wasabi or ginger. It can also be served cold the same way.

Nama yuba, when allowed to dry out just a little, can also be deep-fried and seasoned with salt or *shichimi togarashi* (seven-flavour spice mix) for a crisp snack of *yuba* chips — served with lots of finely sliced spring onion on top.

Dried *yuba* is more readily available than fresh *yuba*, and once lightly rehydrated is used to wrap foods for simmering or deep-frying. It can also be shredded and used in stir-fries, soups or rice dishes. *Yuba* is popular in Chinese cookery, and there is some debate whether it was introduced to Japan alongside Buddhism, or whether the recipe was in fact taken back to China from Japan.

235 g (8½ oz/1¼ cups) whole dried soy beans
good-quality usukuchi shoyu (light Japanese soy), to serve
freshly grated wasabi or ginger, to serve

First, make soy milk (*tonyu*). Put the soy beans in a large container and fill with water. Cover with plastic wrap and soak at room temperature for about 15 hours, or until the beans have doubled in size. (If the weather is particularly warm, soak them in the fridge.) Drain, discarding the water, and rinse the beans.

Pour 2 litres (70 fl oz/8 cups) fresh water into a large pot. Bring to the boil over high heat, then reduce to a simmer. Line a large colander with a large square of doubled-over muslin (cheesecloth) and place it over a larger bowl. Set aside.

Put half the beans in a blender or food processor with 250 ml (9 fl oz/1 cup) of the simmering water, then process until as smooth as possible. Scrape into a bowl and repeat with the remaining beans and another 250 ml (9 fl oz/1 cup) simmering water. Then pour all the bean purée back into the remaining simmering water and stir to combine. Remove from the heat and pour the mixture into the lined colander.

You need to work quickly, but the mixture is hot, so wear clean rubber gloves for the next step and take good care.

Bring the edges of the cloth together, then twist and twist to form a firm bag. Hold tight to the twist so the beans cannot escape; press and squeeze the bag with your other hand, over the colander, to extract the liquid.

If the mixture is still too hot to handle, you can use a wide wooden spoon or the base of a jar to help press out the liquid. If the bowl underneath becomes too full, tip the milk off into another bowl. When you are certain that you cannot get any more milk out of the beans you can stop pressing. You should have about 1 litre (35 fl oz/ 4 cups) of soy milk.

The cloth bag will be filled with a grainy, nutritious substance called *okara* — don't throw this away as it can be used in the stir-fried tofu lees recipe on page 140.

Bring all the soy milk to the boil in a large pot over medium–high heat, then reduce to a simmer and cook for 5 minutes. Remove from the heat and leave to cool — the milk will thicken slightly on cooling, making it look more creamy. The soy milk is now ready to chill and use as you would dairy milk, or you can proceed with making the *nama yuba* below, or the tofu on page 116. The soy milk will last 3 days in the refrigerator.

To make *nama yuba*, place the soy milk in a *donabe* or a ceramic-lined saucepan and bring to a very gentle simmer — do not let the milk boil, otherwise the skin won't form. It will take about 1½ minutes for a fine skin to cover the top of the liquid. Use a chopstick to slide under one edge and lift off the skin to a waiting dish.

Keep repeating this step until the milk is used up — however please note that you will need to reduce the heat as the level of milk in the pan decreases. Also, towards the end, the soy milk can start to caramelise and then burn on the bottom, and can make the *yuba* bitter, so it is best to stop at that point.

The very best way to eat *yuba*, in my opinion, is to have it straight from the pot, dipped into a little shoyu and some freshly grated wasabi or ginger.

If you have access to four small *donabe* and individual burners, this is a fun dish to have family or guests make themselves at the table.

If making it ahead of time, wrap the *yuba* in plastic wrap and store in an airtight container in the fridge for up to 4 days. *Yuba* also freezes well for up to a month.

Note: Store-bought soy milk can be used to make *yuba* and tofu — but only if the sole ingredients are soy beans and water. Most commercial varieties produced outside Japan contain sugar or preservatives and they will not work. Look for pure soy milk in Asian food stores (it is sometimes sold in tetra paks).

Once you have soy milk at hand, it is simple to turn it into fresh tofu — see the recipe on page 116.

zenbu zen 86

I began slowing down. Finally, the coil started to release. I sat on the plastic stool in my ice-blue bathroom sighing while the hot water showered over my back. The desire was strong to stay in and laze around with a book — something I hadn't done in a long time. I smiled at the memory of youthful summer holidays spent lounging around the pool, reading and intermittently napping without guilt, and wondered if I would ever experience that kind of satisfying inertia again.

But with my nagging guilt on autopilot, I didn't allow myself the indulgence and so dressed and threw myself into it. I did, however, spend less time out and about than I normally might have, and made a further small concession by purchasing items for dinner that would give me a break from cooking the evening meal. They were small, but crucial, steps towards a wind-down.

I chose healthy *furofuki daikon* (page 91) and a spring onion salad with a mustard miso dressing (see right), plus some deliciously indulgent eggplant and pork *hasami-age* (page 88).

While in the store I sampled *shogacha* (ginger tea; see page 204) and became instantly hooked. I purchased a jar, knowing it would serve me well through winter with its warming properties. It is now my 'go-to' drink if I have the sniffles or am feeling a little off.

*

negi no karashi sumiso-ae

pencil-thin leeks with mustard miso dressing

SERVES 4 AS PART OF A MULTI-DISH MEAL

6–8 pencil-thin leeks, or very crisp, thick spring onions (scallions) or shallots

MUSTARD MISO DRESSING
3 tablespoons saikyo miso (sweet white miso)
1 tablespoon sake
1 tablespoon vinegar or fresh yuzu juice (or use half–half)
2 teaspoons caster (superfine) sugar
¼–½ teaspoon *karashi* (Japanese mustard) or hot English mustard, to taste

Trim the leeks or spring onions, then separate the whites from the greens. Cut each into 5 cm (2 inch) lengths. Bring a pot of water to the boil, then reduce to a simmer. Add the whites and cook for 1 minute, then add the greens and cook for a few seconds. Drain in a colander and plunge into a bowl of iced water until all the heat has dissipated. Drain well.

Combine all the dressing ingredients well, then toss with the leeks or spring onions and serve.

This dish also lasts well for a couple of days, kept covered in the fridge.

hasami-age

fried 'sandwiches'

MAKES 12 PIECES, TO SERVE 4–6 AS PART OF A MULTI-DISH MEAL

If made with eggplant, these stunning little 'sandwiches' are called *nasu no hasami-age*; with lotus root they are known as *renkon no hasami-age*. The *ankake* sauce is best kept for more robust versions, such as eggplant with pork. Lotus with prawn (shrimp) is more delicate and just requires a little shoyu and yuzu.

12 eggplant (aubergine) slices, each 1 cm (½ inch) thick, cut from an evenly shaped eggplant that's about 7–8 cm (2¾–3¼ inches) in diameter; or use 12 lotus slices, each 7 mm (3/8 inch) thick (see Note)
katakuriko or potato starch, for dusting
vegetable oil, for deep-frying

FILLING
250 g (9 oz) minced (ground) pork, chicken or prawn
1 spring onion (scallion), very finely minced
1 garlic clove, crushed
1 egg white
2 teaspoons sake
3 teaspoons usukuchi shoyu (light Japanese soy)
½ teaspoon finely grated fresh ginger
2 shiso leaves, very finely shredded (optional)
½ teaspoon fine sea salt
½ cup panko (Japanese breadcrumbs)

ANKAKE SAUCE (OPTIONAL)
250 ml (9 fl oz/1 cup) niban dashi (page 29)
60 ml (2 fl oz/¼ cup) mirin
2 tablespoons usukuchi shoyu (light Japanese soy)
3 teaspoons *kuzu* or arrowroot
1½ tablespoons caster (superfine) sugar

Mix all the filling ingredients in a non-metallic bowl using clean hands. Cover and refrigerate for 30 minutes.

Lay the eggplant or lotus slices out flat and sprinkle the surface with starch. Place 2 tablespoons of the filling mixture on half the slices — you may need a little less if the lotus is small; you can therefore make a few extra 'sandwiches'! Smooth the filling over to an even thickness. Sandwich together with the remaining six slices, placing them 'dusted' side down. Press lightly to adhere. Use a pastry brush to dust the sandwiches all over with some more starch.

One-third fill a deep-fryer with oil and heat to 170°C (325°F), or until a cube of bread dropped into the oil browns in 20 seconds.

While the oil is heating, make the *ankake* sauce, if using. Combine all the ingredients in a saucepan and stir until smooth. Stir over medium–high heat until the mixture boils, then reduce to a simmer. Cook for 45 seconds, or until glazy, then turn off the heat.

Deep-fry the 'sandwiches' a few at a time for 5–6 minutes or until golden and cooked through. Drain on kitchen paper. Cut into halves, forming 12 semi-circles.

Place on a platter or individual plates and spoon over the *ankake* sauce, if using.

Note: If you are using fresh lotus, place it in water with a little rice vinegar as soon as you peel it. This will remove any bitterness and prevent it discolouring.

Tip: If you don't wish to deep-fry the 'sandwiches', you can pan-fry them until golden, then finish them in a preheated 180°C (350°F/Gas 4) oven for a few minutes.

89   shiwasu / juunigatsu – december / the 12th month

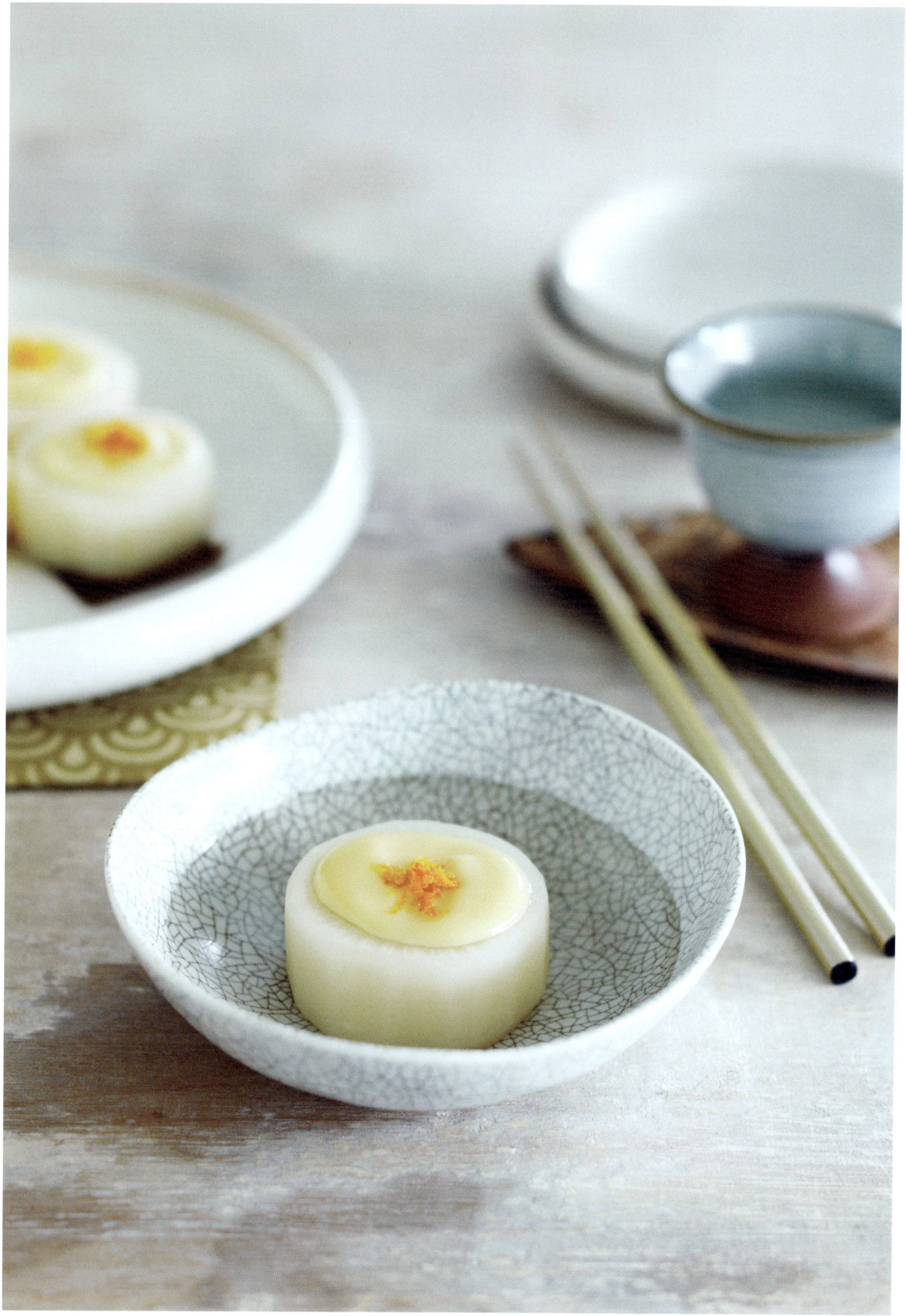

furofuki daikon

simmered daikon with yuzu miso sauce

SERVES 6 AS PART OF A MULTI-DISH MEAL

Daikon is sweetest at the stem end, and grows gradually more sharp and pungent towards the pointy tip. The sweet end is usually eaten raw in salads, the middle part is cooked in simmered dishes, and the pointy end is grated for use in fresh-flavoured dressings, such as the one with the *yaki wagyu to enringi* recipe on page 65. This dish uses the middle section of the daikon.

This yuzu miso topping is very popular in Kyoto, but other types of miso can be used for variety — aka and hatcho are the most popular after saikyo miso, and can be taken to a new level with the addition of toasted sesame seeds or chopped walnuts, or a touch of honey. All of these toppings are also good on fried eggplant (aubergine) slices and tofu.

15 cm (6 inch) length of daikon, cut from the centre of a medium-sized daikon, about 300 g (10½ oz)
6 cm (2½ inch) piece of kombu (dried kelp)

YUZU MISO SAUCE
3 tablespoons saikyo miso (sweet white miso)
2¼ teaspoons fresh or bottled yuzu juice or lemon juice
3 teaspoons mirin
60 ml (2 fl oz/¼ cup) ichiban dashi (see page 26)
½ teaspoon very finely grated yuzu zest or lemon zest

Cut the daikon into six slices, each 2.5 cm (1 inch) thick. Use a sharp knife to peel the slices then bevel (trim off) the sharp edges which will help the pieces to stay whole during the cooking process. Cut a deep cross in one face of each disc, which will ensure even cooking.

Place the kombu on the base of a large saucepan and add the daikon, cross side down. Fill with cold water and place a Japanese drop-lid or cartouche (a round of baking paper) over the top. Bring almost to the boil over a medium–high heat. Immediately reduce to a simmer and cook for 1½ hours or until very tender.

Towards the end of cooking time make the topping. Combine all the ingredients except the zest in a saucepan. Cook, stirring over medium heat for a few minutes or until hot.

Drain the daikon, place cross side down and top with a little of the yuzu miso sauce. Sprinkle over the zest and serve one piece on small, individual serving dishes. It should be soft enough to cut with chopsticks or a spoon.

Note: Saikyo miso is a mild white miso stocked in the refrigerated section of Japanese grocery stores. It is sweeter, smoother and less salty than most other types of miso and is used frequently in Kyoto cuisine.

For the first time in more than 40 years I was in a country where Christmas Day is not a holiday. It was business as usual and with my mind set on the task of finding a gift for a fellow *gaijin* friend who was hosting lunch, I found myself in yet another beautiful, buzzing food hall. Everything seemed so very right, even if no one was stopping to wish me a 'merry' day. Any recognition of the Western event is purely related to commercialism. If the Japanese celebrate, it is only ever on Christmas Eve, which is considered a special night for romance.

My friend's kids, who are now 18 and 22, collected me from the train station; I've known them since they were babies and I suddenly felt old. Glasses were clinked and gifts were exchanged before we shared a juicy roast chicken — somewhat of a luxury in Kyoto, as they are extremely difficult to purchase whole. They are, however, notably easier to gain possession of than a turkey, which, if you did manage to find one, you'd be hard-pressed to serve up any way but raw, because Japanese cuisine does not support the use of an oven. Plus, most Japanese households don't enjoy the luxury of space. That's not to say chicken isn't popular in Japan, but it is almost always either threaded onto skewers or cut into small pieces for easy navigation by chopsticks.

Inside my Christmas cracker was a quote from American industrialist and philanthropist John D. Rockefeller: 'If you want to succeed, you should strike out on new paths, rather than travel the worn paths of accepted success.' It struck a major chord with me.

In true Aussie style, we spent the afternoon draped over comfy lounges drinking cups of tea. A car drove slowly past the house playing the kind of sweet tune you might associate with an old-fashioned ice-cream truck.

When I quizzed teenager Emilee she replied, matter-of-factly, 'Oh, that's just the tofu people', who apparently make tofu fresh each day and sell it from their cars, a practice also carried out by the *yamaiimo* (roasted sweet potato) man and the ramen noodle family.

Possibly outstaying my welcome, but enjoying the company, I managed to linger long enough for dinner. While we waited for the main course Emilee, keen to introduce me to more Japanese delicacies, peeled back the seal from a pot of *natto*, the much-maligned fermented soy bean product. I had sampled a tiny, forgettable portion many years ago, but had never seen it prepared. I initially noticed its sweaty-sock smell and its appearance, which was quite tacky and slimy. Emilee added a little shoyu and hot mustard and, using chopsticks, enthusiastically scratched the surface of the beans to release the flavour and to help the saucy goop adhere. She lifted a little out of the bowl to check the consistency, which had become more foamy and creamy, and I gagged at what looked like a spiderweb of spittle. Few things turn my stomach, but I persevered and was surprised to find it tasting yeasty and not entirely unpleasant. I am pleased to report that I have since enjoyed *natto* in various guises and am almost convinced of its merits.

Dinner was a consoling *takenoko gohan* (bamboo shoot rice; see opposite), chock-full of earthy sweet young bamboo shoots from the surrounding forest — slightly crunchy, but teamed well with nutty fried tofu. On the side was a dainty *kyuuri* (cucumber) and ham salad with sesame dressing — the perfect end to my cross-cultural 'Kuristomasu' Day in Kyoto.

*

takenoko gohan

bamboo shoot rice

SERVES 6 AS PART OF A MULTI-DISH MEAL

In Japan this dish is commonly cooked in a rice cooker, but it's also sometimes cooked in a *donabe* or clay pot, which is great for presenting at the table, and is also more traditional. For this recipe I used a heavy-based, flameproof casserole dish.

- 25 g (1 oz) piece of *age-tofu* (fried tofu sheet), measuring about 16 x 8 cm (6¼ x 3¼ inches)
- 450 g (1 lb/2 cups) medium-grain white rice
- 200 g (7 oz) bamboo shoots, cut into pieces about 5 mm (¼ inch) thick, 1 cm (½ inch) wide and 2 cm (¾ inch) long; outside Japan I buy frozen shoots in large pieces, but you can also use the tinned variety
- 750 ml (26 fl oz/3 cups) ichiban dashi (page 26)
- 1½ tablespoons usukuchi shoyu (light Japanese soy)
- 2 tablespoons sake
- 2 tablespoons mirin
- ½ teaspoon salt
- shredded nori, to garnish (optional)

Place the tofu sheet in a colander and pour boiling water over the top to remove any excess oil. Drain and cut into small rectangular pieces measuring about 1 x 2 cm (½ x ¾ inch).

Place the rice in a large *donabe* or heavy-based, flameproof casserole dish. Add the bamboo shoots and tofu. Combine the liquid ingredients and salt, pour the mixture over the top, then bring to the boil. Cover with a lid and immediately reduce the heat to low. Cook for 40–45 minutes, or until the rice is tender.

This dish is best served immediately as part of a multi-dish meal and makes a nice change from plain rice. Fluff the rice with rice paddles to mix all the ingredients through before serving; you can garnish it with shredded nori if desired.

Note: Some people stir a knob of butter through the rice at the end of cooking. It is certainly not traditional, but tastes great.

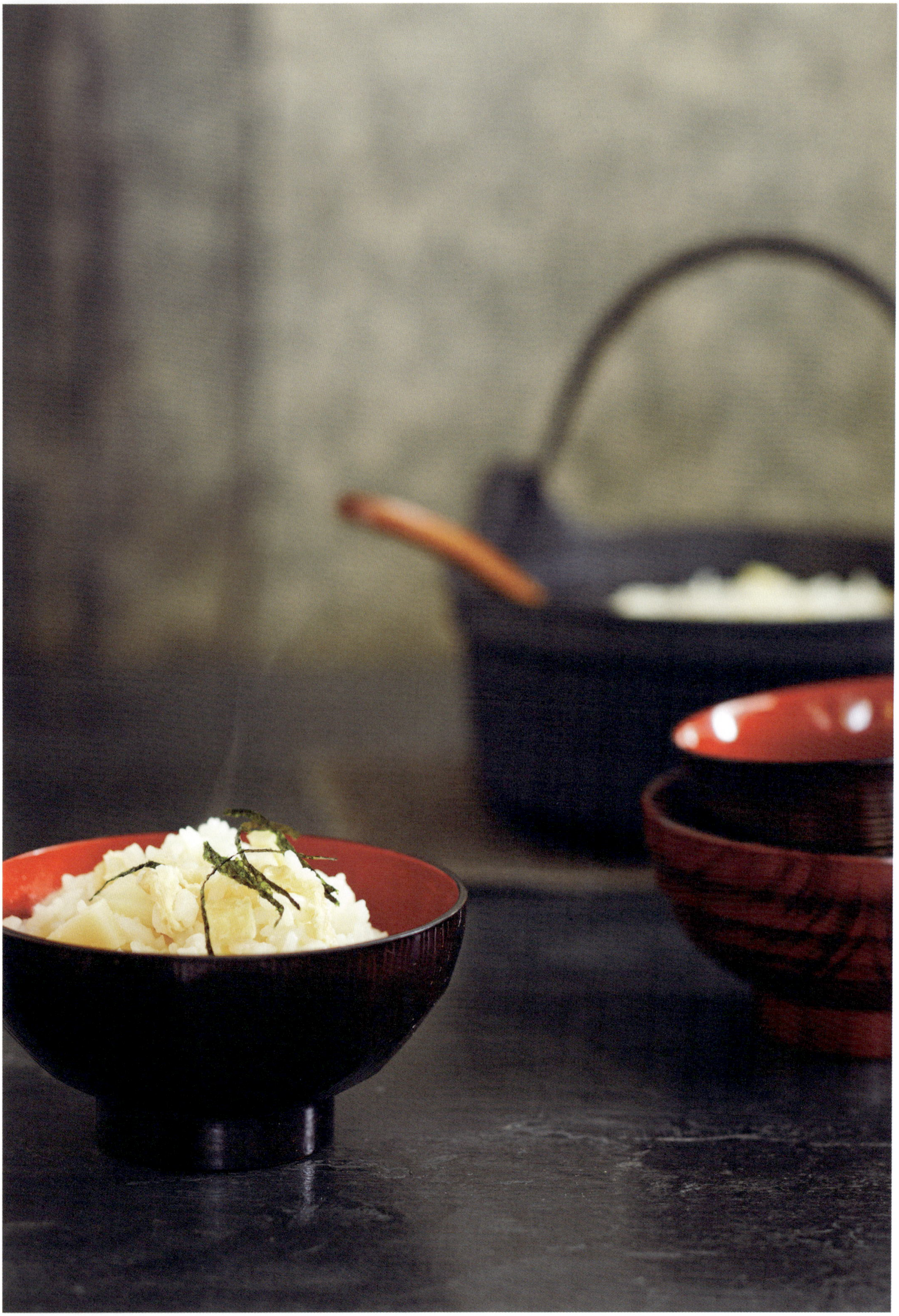

Although most Japanese blush redder than the rising sun after just one or two drinks, sake plays an important role in the culture. Sake barrels are often found as offerings at temples and shrines, are given as gifts on important occasions, and the rice-based libation is itself consumed at temples during certain ceremonies such as New Year's Eve. One particular beer brand is even named after one of Japan's seven lucky gods.

At a charming party for Myong Hee, an older gentleman lawyer, with the means to eat very well in this town, explained there are restaurants here that you cannot access unless you are a regular, or are accompanying a regular. These are usually establishments with a very long history, which have developed their craft over an extended period and only desire patrons who will appreciate the technique, presentation and effort behind their beautiful food, which generally means 'no *gaijins* allowed'. Connoisseur diners will attend and sit very quietly, never under the misguided notion they are 'there for a good time'. It is about serious consideration of the atmosphere, cuisine, ceramics and other antique serving ware — and the sake, which is sipped slowly and appreciated. If, for example, sushi is ordered, it is by the single piece, out of respect for the sushi master who has trained for years to be able to present this morsel of the most incredibly fresh seafood, cut with precision and deftly adhered to perfectly cooked and seasoned rice. The diner in such an establishment is required to appreciate the subtleties of the cuisine, as one might regard another art form.

I have since dined in such a place and found it takes some gumption to see out a meal while the scrutinising stares of the chef and faithful regulars are piercing holes through your skull, finding it impossible to conceive that a Westerner might actually understand or appreciate this 'superior' cuisine.

Another woman at our table, an artist, was trained in *kaiseki*, a multi-coursed, high-end cuisine that artistically represents the seasons. She was keen to share her secrets on preparing fish and vegetables and, with no understanding of English, sketched cute diagrams of specific fish presentation onto a napkin for me. I was warmed by her eagerness to share and impressed by her pride in the country's haute cuisine.

Everyone's glass was filled and waiting, but not a sip passed a single pair of lips before we introduced ourselves around the table, explaining our connection to our host. Given there were 20 of us, it was thirsty work.

Gazing at the organic restaurant's central stairwell, carved from a huge tree trunk, fond memories of Enid Blyton's *The Magic Faraway Tree* sprang to mind, and the food that followed was as riveting as that from the book. A mother-and-son team deftly handled a range of *kyo-yasai* (nationally renowned, superior-quality vegetables grown in the Kyoto area) and the first dish on the table was a bowl of the most remarkable potatoes: *kyo-ebiimo* or Kyoto 'prawn potato' (a potato/yam cross), named because of their slightly curved shape and distinguishing striped skin. They had been simmered in dashi with wakame seaweed and the texture was so smooth that, although whole, it was as though they had already been mashed with butter and cream and moulded back together, the centres textured like mascarpone. Incredible!

Rare and wispy baby *gobo* (burdock root) had been cooked tempura-style, as were some crisp lotus rounds. An excellent *oden* (winter hotpot), consisting only of daikon and tofu, was cooked in an intense but perfectly balanced dashi. A refreshing raw daikon salad with sweet persimmons was accented with a shredding of aromatic shiso. More burdock root, the broader *horikawa* variety, was tossed with a delicious sesame dressing; über-fresh sashimi salad was drizzled with a shoyu vinaigrette; and giant oysters, although kissed with a subtle hint of smoke after being cooked over an open flame, managed to retain their perfect sea flavour. The customary rice offering included dried baby scallops and fragrant ginger. Every bite of every dish was clean, nurturing and enchanting.

After dinner we sang 'Happy Birthday' around a small, plain cake flavoured with organic matcha (green tea powder) and stood in a circle for the 'present exchange', which played out like 'pass the parcel'. I conveniently scored a wine opener before Myong Hee presented us each with a segment of her 108 stitch-art installation. As a ring-in, I felt completely undeserving, but overwhelmingly touched.

As we were leaving, the older gentleman caught my eye and, with a most serious face, informed me he would 'wait for my book with anticipation', as he believed it was my 'duty to educate the world about Japanese cuisine'. No pressure! I meekly responded I would 'do my best'. As it turns out, Kyoto natives tend to welcome foreigners who express an interest in the local culture — and several of them went out of their way to make a point of telling me this. He added that Kyoto is the best place in Japan to learn about the core of the country's cuisine, as it was still the most deeply cultural of all Japanese cities. I knew he was on the money.

At that juncture, I realised there was no point fooling myself that I was going to gain more than a loose overview of the intricacies of Kyoto cuisine — let alone the full gamut of Japanese cuisine — within a few months! It would take a lifetime of being based in Japan researching the many aspects of the cuisine to gain even a well-rounded understanding, and I felt completely out of my depth thinking about the enormous task ahead. Everything I uncovered led to a whole new layer of information, from which hung pockets of detail that on closer inspection would sprout wings and beckon me to continue the expedition towards understanding. I would certainly never learn it all. I discovered that Kyoto is a city of hidden life — what you see on the surface is merely that — and her people will only let you in so far, at which point you must somehow prove your worthiness and only then might the doors start to unlock. It is basically a combination of right place, right time, right people and a particularly respectful, willing and open frame of mind that enables one even the slightest chance of commencing the journey.

Mine, after more than 20 years of travelling in Japan, was only just beginning.

*

When not overly crowded, the Nishi Otani mausoleum can be one of the most spiritual and calming spots in Kyoto: it is an enormous hillside complex completely covered with an intricate street plan of pale, silvery-grey Shinto pillars containing the ashes of those who have passed on.

On the final few days of each year, families make a pilgrimage to spruce up their loved ones' resting places in preparation for the New Year. Armed with buckets and brushes, they stop en route to buy flowers and incense and fill vases with spring water. It is traditional that all homes (including those of the deceased), businesses, shrines and temples are scrubbed and polished from top to toe, until glistening, by New Year's Eve. This act helps to expel any residual bad energy from the past year in order to attract the good spirits of the New Year. Decorations of kadomatsu (pine and bamboo) and *shimenawa* (sacred straw festoons) are set in place in *genkan* (entrances) and *tokonoma* (spiritual altars) for good luck, and the streets take on a proud but humble glow.

I glanced around a small sub-shrine and realised I had been there before: with my father, when I was 15 — the only time we travelled overseas together. My mood was tinged with sadness, but I sensed him join me, in the quietness, enjoying the view across thousands of blue Kyoto rooftops. A plump ginger cat kept one curious eye on us as she stretched in the sun.

*

Although literally freezing, it was an absolutely glorious start to the last day of 2009. Determined to make the most of the morning light, I rugged up like an Eskimo in preparation for climbing around the local Kurodani Temple complex.

I was welcomed by blissed-out Buddhas sharing palm-to-palm signs of peace with their elegant, tapered fingers, and felt instantly rewarded for my effort. However — as if being alone in a secluded graveyard wasn't enough to give me goosebumps — a mischievous airflow soon whipped around the aged buildings, with the resulting reverberations echoing like ghoulish howls. Despite the supernatural cries, I knew that I was safe. The experience was a rare and surreal treat, and it was what I craved that day. Before long, the family groups arrived for the ritual plot cleaning and began to spread out over the densely inhabited terraced hillside. When the air was thick with essence of bleach and the brisk sound of contaminant removal, I took my leave.

I arrived home with a selection of typical *osechi ryori* (New Year's cuisine): *kuromame* (black soy beans) and *kurikinton* (vibrant yellow chestnuts and sweet potatoes in syrup), and the makings of *kohaku namasu* (daikon and red carrot pickle, page 104), *toshikoshi soba* (year-crossing soba noodles, page 100) and *ozoni* (New Year's soup, page 105).

Although not naturally blessed with the cleaning gene, I swept, vacuumed and polished my place until it sparkled. I refreshed the bedding, distributed candles, lit incense and arranged New Year's greenery in the *tokonoma*, then commenced kitchen preparations just as small snowflakes began to drift by my window, providing a divine cleansing of the building externals.

*

shiwasu / juunigatsu – december / the 12th month

toshikoshi soba

year-crossing soba noodles
MAKES ENOUGH FOR 4 LARGE SERVES OR 8 SMALL PORTIONS

Soba noodles represent health and long life. Their long strands are eaten before midnight on New Year's Eve, symbolically linking one year to the next.

Feel free to use your own choice of toppings in this dish, keeping it as simple as you like. Finely sliced shiitake or strands of enoki mushrooms, green leafy vegetables or finely shaved daikon or shredded bamboo shoots are great additions — anything that doesn't require too much cooking.

You can replace the prawns or *kamaboko* with slivers of other cooked meats, such as chicken, pork, duck or even beef.

SOBA (BUCKWHEAT NOODLES)
325 g (11½ oz/2½ cups) organic, stone-ground buckwheat flour, plus extra for sprinkling
150 g (5½ oz/1 cup) plain (all-purpose) flour
250 ml (9 fl oz/1 cup) cold water, plus an extra 1–2 tablespoons

SOUP
1.5 litres (52 fl oz/6 cups) niban dashi (page 29)
170 ml (5½ fl oz/⅔ cup) usukuchi shoyu (light Japanese soy)
125 ml (4 fl oz/½ cup) mirin
125 ml (4 fl oz/½ cup) sake
25 g (1 oz) piece of *age-tofu* (fried tofu sheet)
8 cooked prawns (shrimp), or 12 slices *kamaboko* (cooked fish paste cake)
2 spring onions (scallions), very thinly sliced
shichimi togarashi (seven-flavour spice mix), optional

This is a tactile recipe — hands are best used to determine the correct consistency, so roll up your sleeves.

Put the buckwheat flour and plain flour in a large bowl and mix to combine well. Gradually mix in the 250 ml (9 fl oz/1 cup) cold water while you agitate your fingers left and right until the mixture starts to clump together. Lift out handfuls of larger clumps and crumble them back into the bowl to evenly distribute the moisture. Gradually add a little more cold water, mixing in the same way until you can squeeze the clumps together and they hold their shape easily — but they shouldn't feel too wet.

Gather the dough into a ball and knead it on a lightly floured bench for 10 minutes to work the gluten, which will stop the noodles breaking too easily. The dough should be soft, pliable and just a little sticky.

Break the dough in half and roll each between your hands into a smooth ball. Dust your bench with a little extra buckwheat flour, then use your hands to press a dough ball out to a thick oblong disc, about 7 cm (2¾ inches) wide and 14 cm (5½ inches) long — with the shorter ends left and right.

Use a rolling pin to neatly and thinly roll the dough out to a thickness of about 1.5 mm (1/16 inch), and about 45 cm (17¾ inches) long and 24 cm (9½ inches) wide. If the dough gets sticky, sprinkle it with a little extra buckwheat flour; make sure you sprinkle the top and lightly smooth it over with your hands to evenly distribute it before the next step.

Working left to right, fold one short end over to meet the other short end. Sprinkle the surface again with extra buckwheat flour and smooth it over with your hands.

Using a very sharp, long, thin-bladed knife with a cutting edge as straight as possible — a very fine cleaver would be excellent, or a specially crafted soba knife if you can find one! — trim the edges so they are neat.

Starting at the right-hand edge, carefully cut the dough into thin strips about 1.5 mm (1/16 inch) wide, using the edge of a ruler as a guide if you need it. (The reason you double the dough over is to reduce the cutting time; however, you do need to carefully separate the layers into single noodles before you cook them. You can avoid the separation process by simply cutting the noodles from the original rolled layer, but this may take a little longer.)

Carefully arrange the noodles into two mounds on a wide shallow bamboo basket or tray.

Repeat the rolling and cutting with the second dough ball. You will end up with four noodle mounds in total — being one quantity per person.

Bring a large pot of water to the boil. Add one mound of noodles to the pot, then stir with the wide end of a chopstick or the handle of a wooden spoon to keep the noodles separated. Don't be tempted to add more than one serve of noodles at a time, as the pan will be too crowded, resulting in uneven cooking. You will need to repeat the cooking process for each mound of noodles.

When the water returns to the boil, add about 250 ml (9 fl oz/1 cup) cold water, which should halt the boiling momentarily. Return to the boil again, add another cup of cold water and bring back to the boil. Add one final cup of water and bring to the boil, then immediately scoop out the noodles with a wide wire-mesh strainer.

Rinse briefly with cold running water, gently rubbing with your hands to remove excess starch if necessary. You are now ready to either place each portion in one large or two small deep bowls for topping up with soup.

To make the broth, pour the dashi, shoyu, mirin and sake into a large saucepan and bring to the boil over medium–high heat. Meanwhile, put the tofu sheet in a colander and pour boiling water over it to remove the excess oil. Pat dry with kitchen paper and thinly slice.

Neatly place a little pile of tofu on top of each bowl of noodles. Next to that, slightly overlapping, place two prawns or three slices of *kamaboko*, and a pile of spring onion next to that.

When the broth is hot, carefully ladle some into each bowl so that it just covers the noodles. Serve with the *shichimi togarashi* on the side for sprinkling over, if desired.

Note: The cooking liquid from the noodles is reportedly full of nutrients, and is used as either a base for the broth the noodles are served in, or as a base for other soups.

Soba noodles are great in winter with piping-hot broth, but can also be served chilled in summer on a flat bamboo basket with a sauce to dip them into. This dish is called *zaru soba*, named for the basket.

New Year's Eve in Japan is a very different experience to what many in the West are used to. It is a far more deeply reflective time. The year that has been is farewelled in peaceful ceremony. All is cleansed, both physically and spiritually, in preparation to move forward gracefully into the oncoming year. It is a time of thanks and positivity and a reminder of the Zen philosophy of impermanence.

shiwasu / juunigatsu – december / the 12th month

kohaku namasu

daikon and red carrot pickle
SERVES 6–8 AS PART OF A MULTI-DISH MEAL

Kohaku means 'red and white', and signifies happiness and celebration in Japanese culture. This simple light pickle is served during Oshogatsu, the New Year's holiday celebration, when it is ideally made with Kyoto's famous red carrots, and at other times is served as a side vegetable or salad. This dish will last up to 1 week in the fridge — in fact some people won't even touch it until it has matured for a few days.

20 cm (8 inch) piece of daikon, peeled and cut into two 10 cm (4 inch) lengths
1 small carrot, trimmed to a 10 cm (4 inch) length
1 teaspoon sea salt
5 cm (2 inch) square of kombu (dried kelp)
80 ml (2½ fl oz/⅓ cup) rice vinegar
5 teaspoons caster (superfine) sugar
1 tablespoon mirin
¼ teaspoon usukuchi shoyu (light Japanese soy)

Use a mandoline or very sharp knife to very thinly slice both the daikon and carrot lengthways — the slices should only be about 1 mm (1/32 inch) thick. Stack up a few slices at a time and carefully cut them, lengthways again, into strips 2 mm (1/16 inch) wide. Place in a colander, sprinkle with the salt and mix to combine.

Sit the colander over a bowl and mix the daikon and carrot occasionally for 20 minutes, gently kneading with your hands so they become softened and pliable. Rinse well and gently squeeze out any excess water, which will help ensure the dressing is not diluted and that the vegetables stay crunchy.

Put the kombu in a non-metallic container with a lid and place the carrot and daikon on top.

Put the vinegar, sugar and mirin in a small saucepan and stir over medium heat until the sugar has dissolved. Remove from the heat, stir in the shoyu, then pour over the carrot and daikon. Refrigerate for at least 4 hours, mixing occasionally.

The pickles are now ready to serve; you can drain off the vinegar if desired.

Variation: Lotus root can be used instead of daikon. As soon as you peel it, place it in water with a little rice vinegar to remove any bitterness and to stop it discolouring. Cut the lotus into two pieces, then trim lightly around the outer surfaces, tracing the holes so the cross-section surface resembles a chrysanthemum (the Japanese imperial crest). Cook in boiling water for about 10 minutes, or until lightly tender. Drain well and slice thinly before placing in the vinegar solution.

It is said that serving lotus at New Year is auspicious, as you can look through the holes to enlightenment.

It isn't traditional, but sometimes people will put some red chilli in this dish, to add to the festive colour and for extra bite.

ozoni

New Year's soup
SERVES 4

This hearty New Year's soup varies from household to household and is often made with a clear broth. However, in Kyoto it is popular to add the local saikyo miso for enhanced sweetness and texture. Ideally, *ozoni* is made on New Year's Eve, leaving New Year's Day free to spend time with family; however, the *mochi* (glutinous rice cakes) are best cooked just prior to serving.

1 litre (35 fl oz/4 cups) niban dashi (page 29)
200 g (7 oz) skinless chicken thigh fillets, cut into small bite-sized pieces
1 thin Japanese leek, sliced 1.5 cm (5/8 inch) thick on an angle
4 fresh shiitake mushrooms, the centres cut into a cross, with just a thin sliver removed from each cut, for decoration
8 carrot slices, each about 1 cm (½ inch) thick, either kept as plain discs, or with flower shapes stamped out
2 baby or 'finger' daikons, cut into rounds 1 cm (½ inch) thick, or 2 daikon slices, each about 1 cm (½ inch) thick, cut into quarters
1½ tablespoons shoyu
1 tablespoon sake
2–3 tablespoons saikyo miso (sweet white miso)
8 *kamaboko* (cooked fish paste cake), sliced about 7 mm (3/8 inch) thick
8 round *mochi* (glutinous rice cakes)
40 g (1½ oz/1½ cups) *komatsuna* (Japanese mustard spinach), *shungiku* (edible chrysanthemum leaf) or English spinach leaves, very lightly blanched and refreshed
finely julienned yuzu or lemon zest

Place the dashi, chicken, leek, mushrooms, carrot and daikon in a large saucepan and slowly bring to the boil over medium–high heat. Reduce the heat to a simmer, skimming any foamy residue from the surface. Cook for 20 minutes, or until the carrot is just starting to soften.

Mix together the shoyu, sake and miso. Add a little of the hot cooking liquid to dissolve the miso, then pour into the pan and stir to combine. Add the *kamaboko* and cook for a few minutes more.

Meanwhile, heat the grill (broiler) to high. Place the *mochi* on a foil-lined tray and grill (broil) them on one side for about 60–90 seconds, or until puffed and golden. Turn them over and cook for a further minute, or until puffed and golden — you need to watch the *mochi* carefully, as they can turn from golden to burnt (even alight!) very quickly. I cook my *mochi* under an open flame gas grill, but if you are using an electric grill it may take a little longer.

Season the soup with sea salt to taste. Divide the *mochi* among four deep bowls. Arrange the greens to one side of the *mochi* and ladle the broth into the bowls (the heat will cook the greens). Sprinkle with the yuzu zest and serve immediately.

zenbu zen 106

I joined millions of Japanese nationals watching TV's Kohaku (the New Year's Red and White Song Contest), while proudly scoffing my noodles. Not yet feeling part of the local community, I chose to stay in my toasty apartment rather than brave the chill and queue for my chance to swing a huge log-on-a-rope into an enormous brass bell at the local temple. Exactly 108 deep gongs — known as Joya-no-Kane — would ring out through the town, in promise of quelling each unsavoury human desire.

In the spirit of things, I submitted my own form of reflective prayer — a list of 108 things I was grateful for, which was my own cathartic way of saying 'goodbye' to the strains of the past year. I needed to start the New Year afresh with positivity, appreciation and thankfulness for the life I live.

Just before midnight, the first of the bells solemnly chimed. The sombre ritual, in tribute to the importance of year's end, is performed at Buddhist temples only, as is the case with funerals. Shinto shrines are generally reserved for celebrating new beginnings, such as marriage and childbirth, and the New Year is ushered in shortly after the final tolling of the midnight gongs.

Joyful cheering resonated from the Heian Jingu shrine, where Hatsumode (first shrine visit of the year) had begun. Every year, several million people walk from their quiet *sayonara* temple session to the nearest shrine for hot *amazake* (a sweet, gruel-like sake) and other traditional festivities.

Even though I was on my own, the night was magical and I remained energised until 2 am — full of anticipation and already embracing 2010.

*

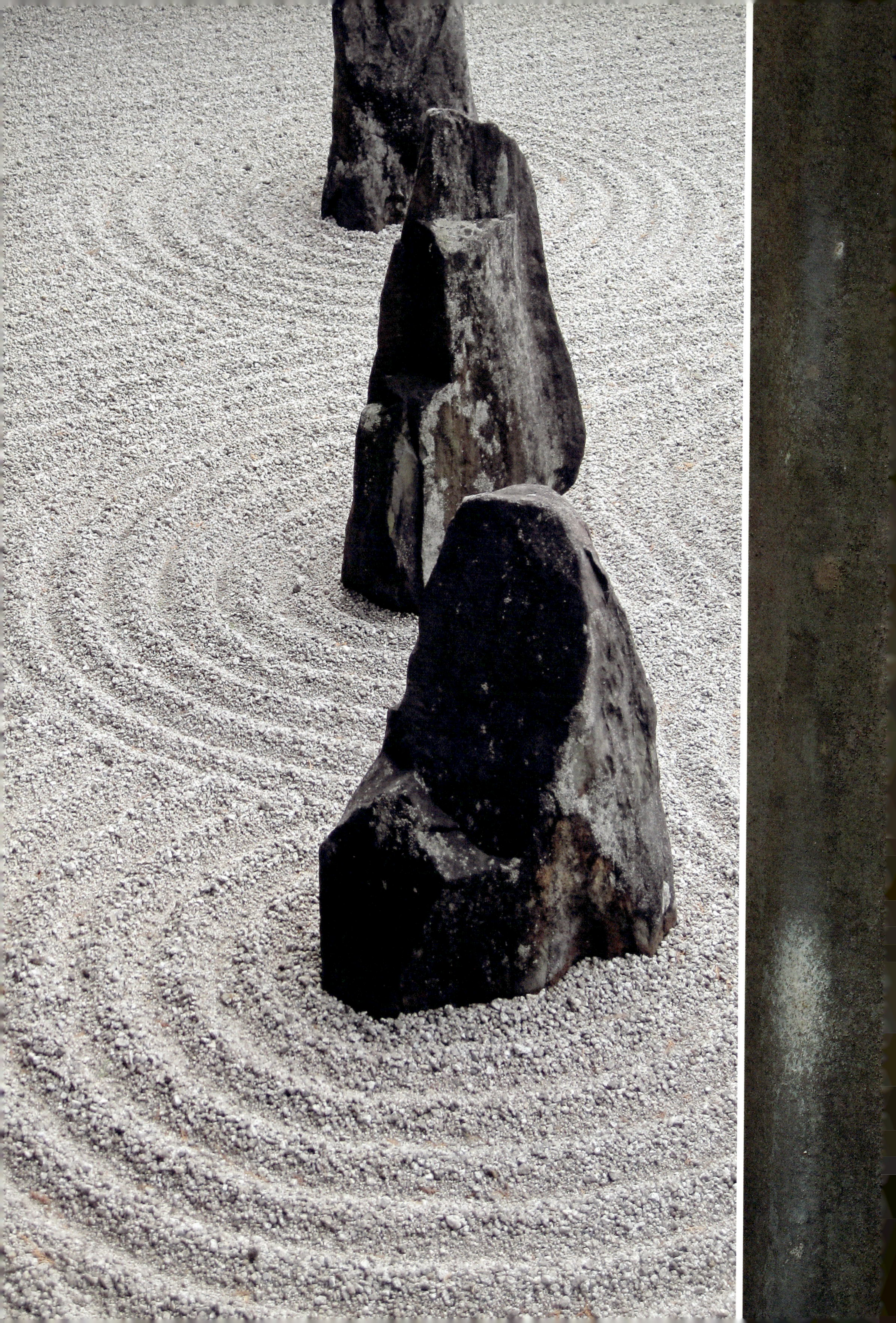

mutsuki/ichigatsu

JANUARY | THE 1ST MONTH

CHAPTER 3

THE 1ST MONTH

According to the old calendar, Mutsuki is the month when friends and relatives visit and cordial relationships are formed – a month of harmony.

january

mutsuki / ichigatsu

A new day, a new decade, a new life. I opened my front door and peeked at the fresh snow on the mountaintops — it finally felt like winter and I was chuffed to be engaging in my first Hatsumode (my first shrine visit of the year).

A 'real-feel' temperature of −11°C (12°F) did not deter the thousands of Japanese who filed through the imposing shrine gates. They were steered in an orderly fashion across the courtyard into the main hall, where a special New Year's blessing was taking place. I watched carefully for a while before joining in with the locals. I tossed a coin into the receptacle, took a few steps back and clapped twice to attract the gods' attention. I'm not religious but, like many Japanese, I am happy to take the best symbolic bits of Buddhism and Shintoism; I bowed my head and prayed for the predictable.

Desperate to know their destiny in the year ahead, many pilgrims take part in the wild shaking of *omukuji* (fortune) canisters. If bad omens are determined, one must tie the fateful paper to the wire fence provided in order for the gods to 'take care of it' for you. If the reading is positive, it is taken home to refer to throughout the following 12 months.

While others were buying lucky *hamaya* (sacred arrows) or *kumade* (rakes), I forked out for some dinky food-inspired amulets: a cheery *sakura* (cherry blossom) for happiness; yuzu for longevity; and an ineffectual-looking *momo* (peach) with which to ward off evil.

Hungry with food reference, I headed home to enjoy my hearty *ozoni* (page 105). Knowing that TV newscasters seem to delight in reporting 'death by *mochi*' statistics every New Year, I was a little wary, but as it's usually the infirm, elderly or small children who are at risk of choking on this wondrous rice cake, I threw caution to the wind and tucked in.

Traditionally, two large, concrete-like *mochi* rounds are placed in the *tokonoma* (spiritual altars) as a New Year offering, after which they should be sledge-hammered into smaller pieces for adding to the New Year's *ozoni*. I managed to perfectly grill and puff my *mochi* until a thin crust formed around the gooey innards. How a solid rock of dried mashed rice ends up molten when grilled is beyond me! Cheating death, I met the challenge of a second, smaller bowl.

*

zenbu zen 110

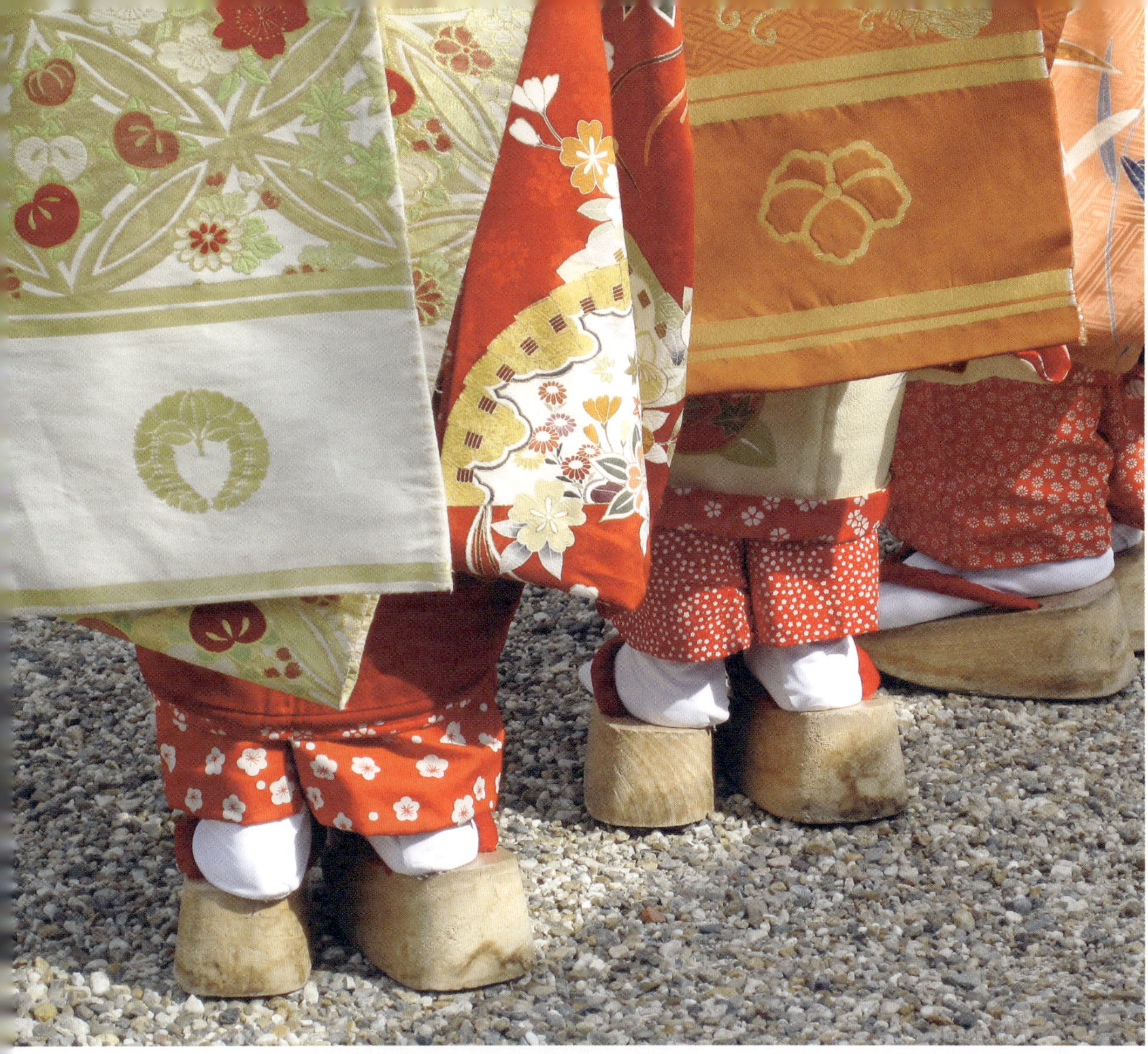
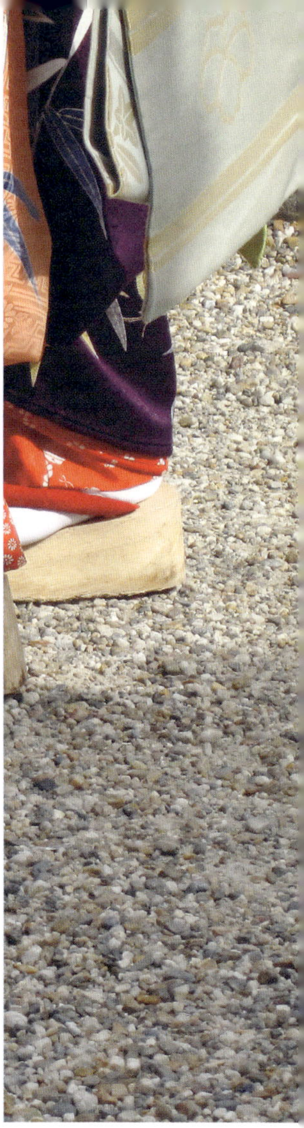
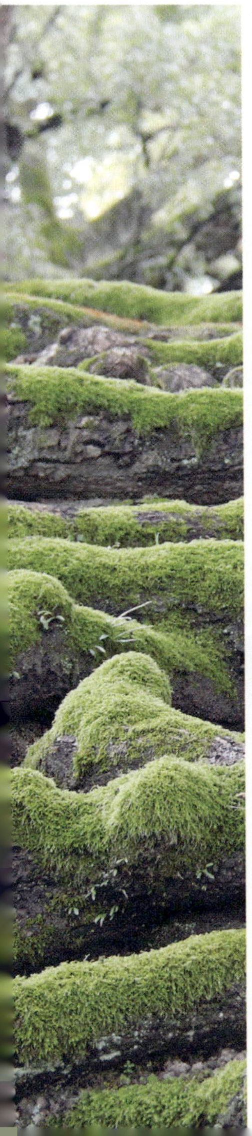
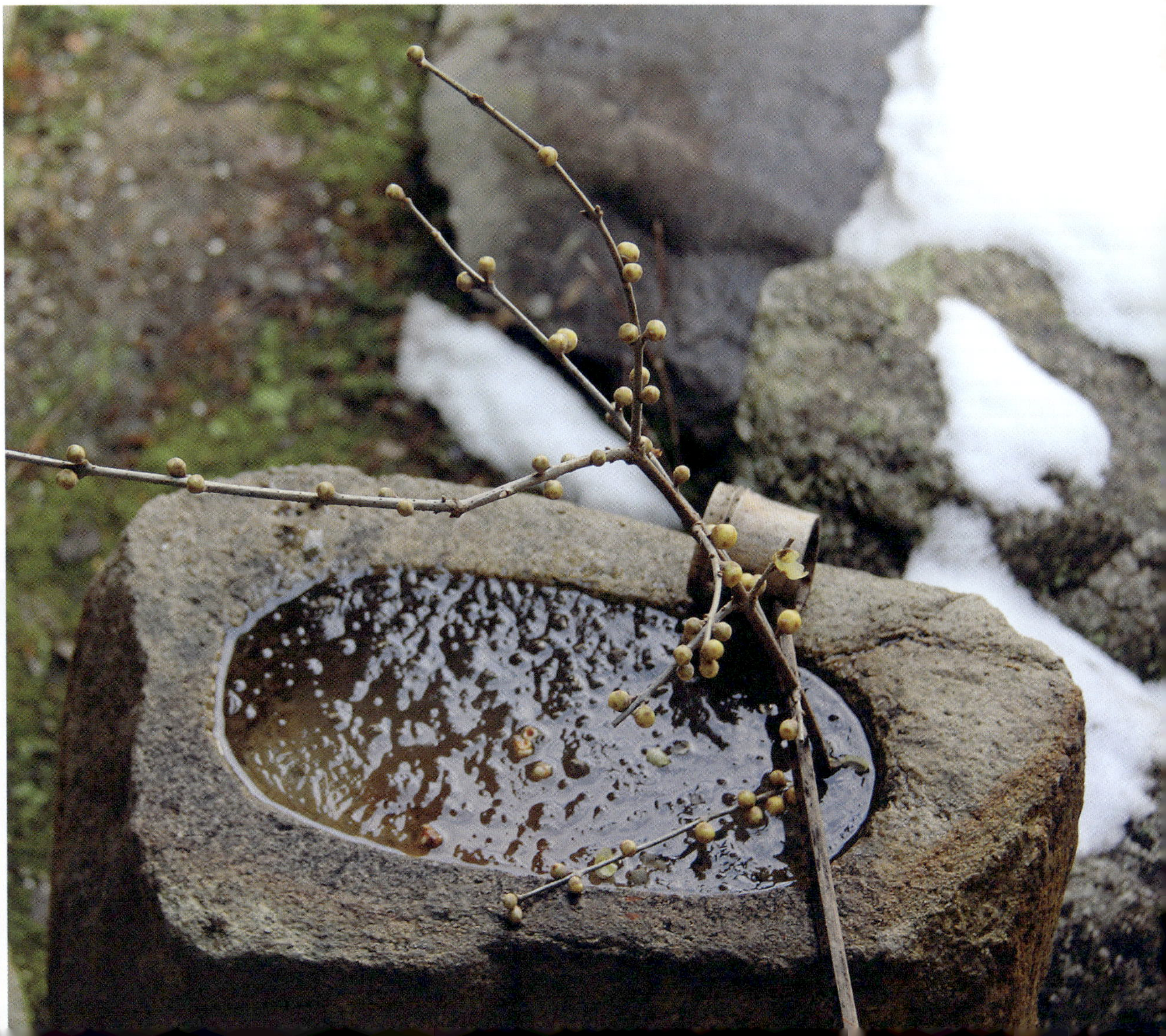

My hair was brittle from weeks of warm air-conditioning and months of medication, and my lips were so chapped it felt like gremlins had snuck in while I was sleeping and glued on tiny squares of cellophane. I also had to settle for a sponge bath each morning, as the bathroom was literally freezing. A slightly unsettling scenario!

In the kitchen, it felt like I was learning to cook all over again. Some *ebiimo* (a yam-like potato) simmered in homemade dashi tasted damn fine, despite turning a shade of purplish-grey, and a red-skinned, creamy-fleshed sweet potato became almost fluorescent yellow once it soaked up some boiling water. I scored, seared and glazed *konnyaku* — a bland grey jelly made from the starchy root of a plant known as *konjak*, or devil's tongue — to see if it really could replace beef or chicken when glazed with teriyaki sauce, and then tried both lightly and heavily cooking several *yurine* (lily bulbs) to gain an understanding of their textural properties. I garnered that just a few moments too long could mean the difference between al dente and complete disintegration.

*

Myong Hee and our now mutual friend, Mayumi, arrived with a gift of lacquered chopsticks wrapped in their own portable fabric pouch. Environmentally conscious Mayumi dispenses these handmade gifts like educational leaflets, hoping people will use them in preference to the disposable versions offered in many Japanese restaurants.

The soy bean is king in this town, and for lunch the ladies chose a famous tofu restaurant. The hero of this set-course meal is *oboro dofu* (page 116), the panna cotta of tofu. It is served, junket-like, in a bowl with a duvet of thickened dashi containing saffron-fine threads of carrot, shiitake and *mitsuba* (Japanese trefoil) — a fresh Japanese 'parsley' that grows wild, but is also cultivated. The simple dish felt gentle on my stomach.

A bowl of rice is traditionally placed on your left in this kind of set meal so that you pick it up and hold it at chest level, while using chopsticks in your right hand. The miso soup should be placed on the right, but is cupped in both hands to drink from.

Kazunoko (sacs of herring roe) preserved in salt, then soaked overnight before use, are firm and slightly crunchy to the bite. Their fishy flavour was not to my taste and I struggled to swallow it all, but the *nama yuba* (page 84) was my saviour, cleansing my palate for the next dish.

Beside some baby bamboo shoot, taro and *fu* (wheat gluten) sat an unusual green stem resembling thin celery: it was *fuki*. Mayumi relayed the legend that if you crush up its large, slightly bitter leaves and mix it with raw egg, then drink it — just once in your life — you will never have a stroke. Eating Japanese cuisine her whole life, she was hardly likely to be high risk ... and then a small basket of tempura arrived to test the theory.

There was also a small dish of deeply flavoured *kombu no tsukudani* (page 115), which was originally designed to recycle leftover kombu from dashi. Apparently 'good' housewives still do this, but these days, it is common for people to use powdered dashi. I vow to 'recycle' kombu whenever I can to avoid wastage.

Nori tsukudani (see page 113) is also a great way to use up leftover nori sheets. I spread it on toast, and use it to flavour soups and stews.

tsukudani

Tsukudani fall under the category of side dishes (*okazu*) that are made 2–10 days before serving. They are regularly consumed, in small amounts, at traditional breakfasts, alongside plain rice (or a rice gruel called *okayu*; page 218), miso soup (page 46), *tsukemono* (pickles; see pages 154–155 and 158–159), sometimes a soft-boiled egg, *natto* (fermented soy beans) or grilled (broiled) fish and other fresh vegetable dishes.

Tsukudani are specifically made to store well and are thus handy for New Year celebrations too.

Often salty or with an intense flavour from preserving or being cooked in shoyu or vinegar, these dishes are consumed in very small amounts — see the serving suggestions opposite and on page 115.

nori no tsukudani

nori preserves
MAKES ABOUT ¾ CUP

Apart from its more standard uses explained to the left, this dish, being paste-like, is great for seasoning soups or stews. I am also a fan of spreading it on toast or rice crackers as a snack.

4 nori sheets, about 12 g (¼ oz) in total
125 ml (4 fl oz/½ cup) sake
1½ tablespoons koikuchi shoyu (dark Japanese soy)
1 tablespoon usukuchi shoyu (light Japanese soy)
2 tablespoons *kurosato* (Japanese black sugar) or dark brown sugar

Toast the nori lightly over a gas flame or under a grill (broiler) for a few seconds, until it starts to bubble slightly and soften. Remove from the heat quickly as it can burn easily. As it cools it will crisp up.

Tear the nori into small pieces and place in a saucepan with the sake and 250 ml (9 fl oz/1 cup) water. Bring to the boil, reduce the heat and cook at a rapid simmer for 15 minutes — watch it carefully so the liquid doesn't boil over.

Add the dark and light shoyu and sugar and stir until the sugar has dissolved. Reduce the heat to very low so the mixture is just simmering. Cover with a cartouche (a round of baking paper, with an air vent cut in the centre) and continue to simmer, stirring occasionally, for 40–45 minutes, or until the mixture becomes thick and sludgy.

Spoon the mixture into a sterilised jar, seal and allow to cool — it will thicken a little more on cooling. The preserves can be refrigerated for up to 3 months.

zenbu zen 114

kombu no tsukudani

kombu preserves
MAKES ABOUT ½ CUP

60 g (2¼ oz) rehydrated kombu (dried kelp), leftover from making ichiban dashi (see page 26)
2 tablespoons rice vinegar
1 tablespoon mirin
1 tablespoon sake
3 teaspoons *kurosato* (Japanese black sugar) or dark brown sugar, plus 1 tablespoon extra
1 tablespoon koikuchi shoyu (dark Japanese soy)
1 tablespoon usukuchi shoyu (light Japanese soy)

Cut the kombu into 2 cm (¾ inch) squares and place in a bowl with the rice vinegar and 500 ml (17 fl oz/2 cups) water. Set aside for 1 hour to tenderise the kombu — it should become slightly slimy.

Place the kombu and its soaking liquid in a saucepan with the mirin, sake and the 3 teaspoons sugar. Bring to the boil, reduce the heat to low and simmer for 1 hour.

Add the dark and light shoyu and extra sugar and simmer for another 25 minutes, or until the liquid has almost been absorbed and the kombu is very soft and looks a little glazed. You may need to shake the pan occasionally to stop the kombu sticking. Remove from the heat and allow to cool. As the mixture cools, the remaining liquid will be absorbed and the kombu will firm up a little.

Enjoy as a cold snack with a cold beer in summer, or as a small side dish with a meal, as you might enjoy *tsukemono* (pickles). Its saltiness works very well against a foil of plain white rice; it can also be chopped or shredded and used as a filling for rice balls or sushi. It will last in the fridge for up to 3 months.

Variation: Rehydrated shiitake mushrooms from making shiitake dashi (page 29) are also very popular prepared in this way — minus the soaking-in-vinegar step. Thin slices are often used as one of the fillings in a combination *futomaki zushi* (sushi roll).

tofu

set soy milk
SERVES 4–6

Tofu is simple enough to make once you have pure soy milk at hand. I can't resist it straight from the pot in soft curds (*oboro dofu*) — drizzled with shoyu and maybe a squeeze of yuzu juice and some shallots. *Shichimi togarashi* (seven-flavour spice mix) or grated fresh wasabi or ginger are also great condiments.

Store-bought soy milk from an Asian grocery store can be used to make tofu if the only ingredients it contains are soy beans and water, but most varieties available outside Japan contain sugar or preservatives and they will not work.

1 litre (35 fl oz/4 cups) pure soy milk (homemade, from the *nama yuba* recipe on page 84, or store-bought)
2 tablespoons liquid nigari (see Note)

Place the soy milk in a large saucepan and bring to the boil over high heat. Immediately reduce the heat to medium, and when the temperature reaches 80–85°C (175–185°F), adjust the heat slightly until this temperature holds steady.

Pour in the nigari and stir gently until the mixture just starts to thicken and separate. Turn off the heat and cover for 10 minutes.

You can use a slotted spoon or small wire-mesh ladle to scoop the warm curds straight into your dish for eating with a spoon. Alternatively, you can pour the whole amount into a colander lined with dampened muslin (cheesecloth), then wrap the muslin back over the top of the mixture and weigh it down slightly with a plate for about 15 minutes; this will yield a soft tofu — like commercially available 'silken' tofu.

For a firmer tofu, place an extra weight — such as a bowl filled with cold water — on top of the plate. The heavier the weight and the longer the tofu is weighed down, the firmer the texture will become.

You can store tofu in an airtight container, covered with clean water, in the fridge for a few days.

Note: Nigari is a coagulant consisting mainly of magnesium chloride. It can vary in strength, so use my measure as a guide and then add a little more or less as required.

You will also need a cooking thermometer to check the milk is at the right temperature before adding the nigari.

mutsuki / ichigatsu – january / the 1st month

Down-to-earth yet elegant Mayumi, originally from Awajishima — a small island between Honshu (the main island) and Shikoku — is a font of knowledge on traditional cuisine. Living in an extended family household, she cooks almost every day. Her mother insisted on sharing traditional cooking methods with her when she was growing up in the 1970s. At the time, there was a huge boom in international foods and pre-made dishes and many Japanese women cast off their aprons for the thrill of the new. As a consequence, in conjunction with the recent breakdown of the extended family matrix, many households are now unfamiliar with more authentic Japanese dishes and ingredients.

Mayumi's home town is famous for its oranges, milk, beef, flowers, lettuce and onions. She's an advocate for quality, fresh produce, and revealed that savvy housewives all around Japan only shop in the morning, in order to make the most of the premium market selection. She reminisced about old-fashioned after-school treats of rice balls topped with *kinako* (roasted soy bean powder) and sugar, and grilled *mochi* (glutinous rice cakes), brushed with shoyu and wrapped with nori. A little different from chocolate biscuits or banana bread! I found that the less complex the range of flavours I consumed, the more I began to appreciate and enjoy the subtleties of basic foods and the Japanese flavour profile.

After a long walk, towards Kiyomizu Temple, which involved weaving through the crowds that gathered to pay respects to both the 800-year-old camphor tree outside Shoren-in Temple and the famous weeping *sakura* (cherry blossom) in Maruyama park — the latter of which was reportedly dying and had sent shockwaves through the town — we escaped the throng by ducking down a quaint side alley into a snugly bohemian *ryokan* (traditional inn) for coffee and a sweet. The kitchen was bare as it hadn't officially reopened for New Year, but the chef improvised, whipping up a traditional sweet from roasted, powdered *hadaka mugi* (naked barley) mixed with warm water and seasoned with a bit of salt and *kurosato* (Japanese black sugar). The thick paste, eaten with a spoon, came crowned with a single organic pecan, a dried cherry and a cranberry, and was surprisingly tasty when served with coffee brewed on the potbelly stove. The air was crisp and clear and we chatted for almost two hours before venturing to dinner.

When we eventually arrived at the restaurant, hidden away in the Gion maze, we were met with welcoming shouts of '*irrashaimase*'. After struggling with my boots for the sixth time that day, we entered a private room where the ladies' close friends, Kikuko and Yukari, were waiting for us.

Given that I had dispensed with politeness by ordering some sake for myself, instead of the wine the ladies preferred to drink, they felt it appropriate payback to order me a serving of *heshiko* (mackerel fermented in *nuka* — rice bran). They assured me it was 'sooo good with sake' and urged me to taste it.

The deep-brown withered fish chunks looked very unappealing, so I quickly popped a 2 cm (¾ inch) square piece into my mouth and chewed on the slightly sweet, jerky-like mass. I chewed ... and chewed ... finally gulping down the masticated remnants with a large flush of sake. Poker-faced, the girls innocently enquired whether I liked it? Honestly, it wasn't horrendous — just kick-in-the-teeth intense! My dining companions then quietly picked up their chopsticks, breaking off a tiny flake of fish at a time. This was a lesson they might well have provided before I nearly asphyxiated myself.

Also newly introduced to me were three considerably more comforting slow-cooked dishes: *gyuusuji to konnyaku no miso-ni* (beef tendons with *konnyaku*, slow-simmered in a rich miso-based sauce; see page 124); *tako no yawarakani* (meltingly tender sections of fat octopus tentacles, softened in bancha tea; page 122) and *buri to daikon no nimono* (a popular Kyoto winter dish of daikon and yellowtail fish, still on the bone, simmered in a shoyu-based broth; see page 125). All excellently hearty yet healthy winter fare.

*

Where there is an ending, there is a beginning. The close of one year allows the next to open. In Japan there are two opportunities for this – by observing New Year's celebrations for both the Gregorian calendar (the end of December to early January), and the Chinese-based seasonal division. The first *Setsubun* (parting of the seasons) of each year is held, with great gusto, around 3 February.

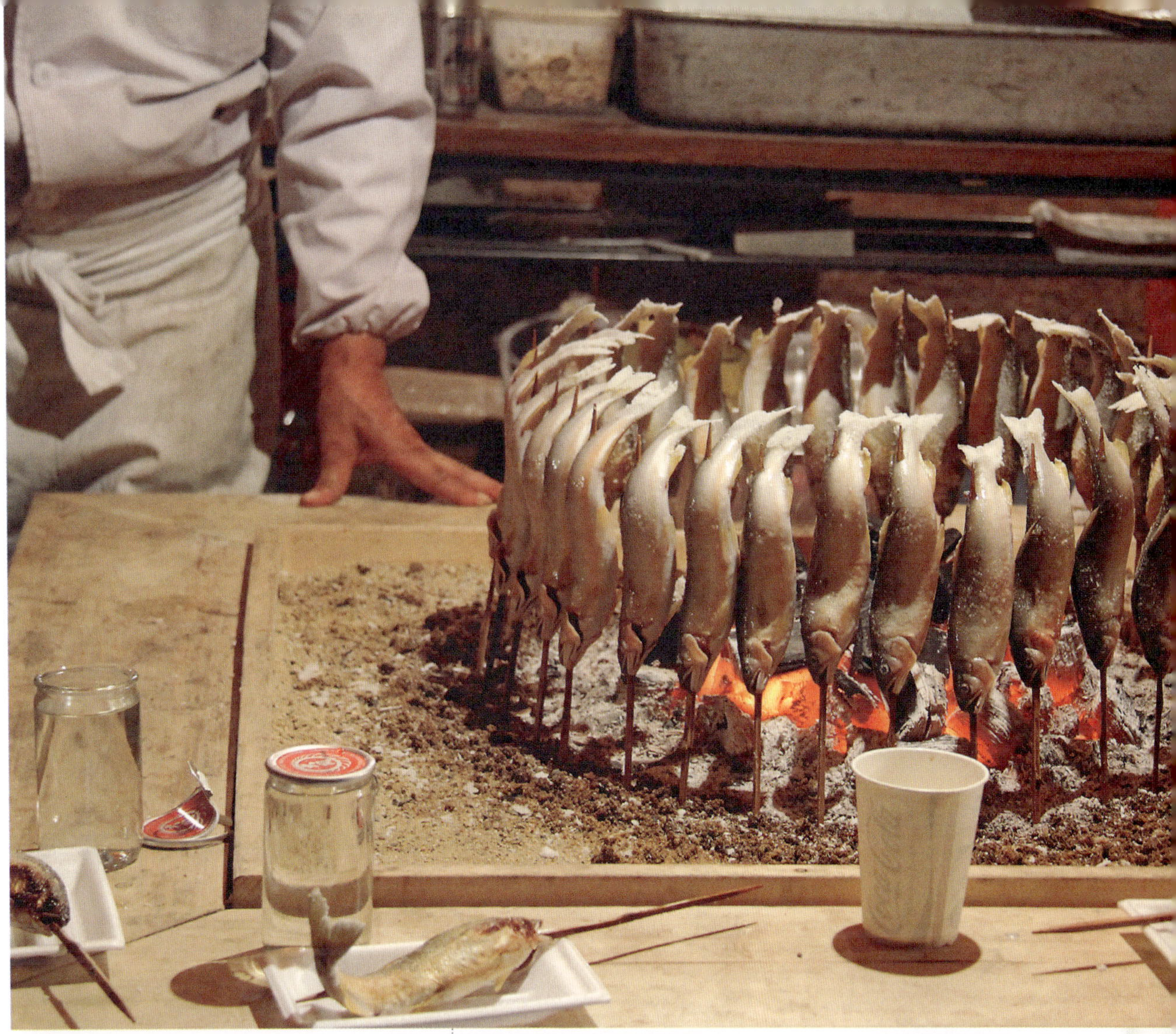

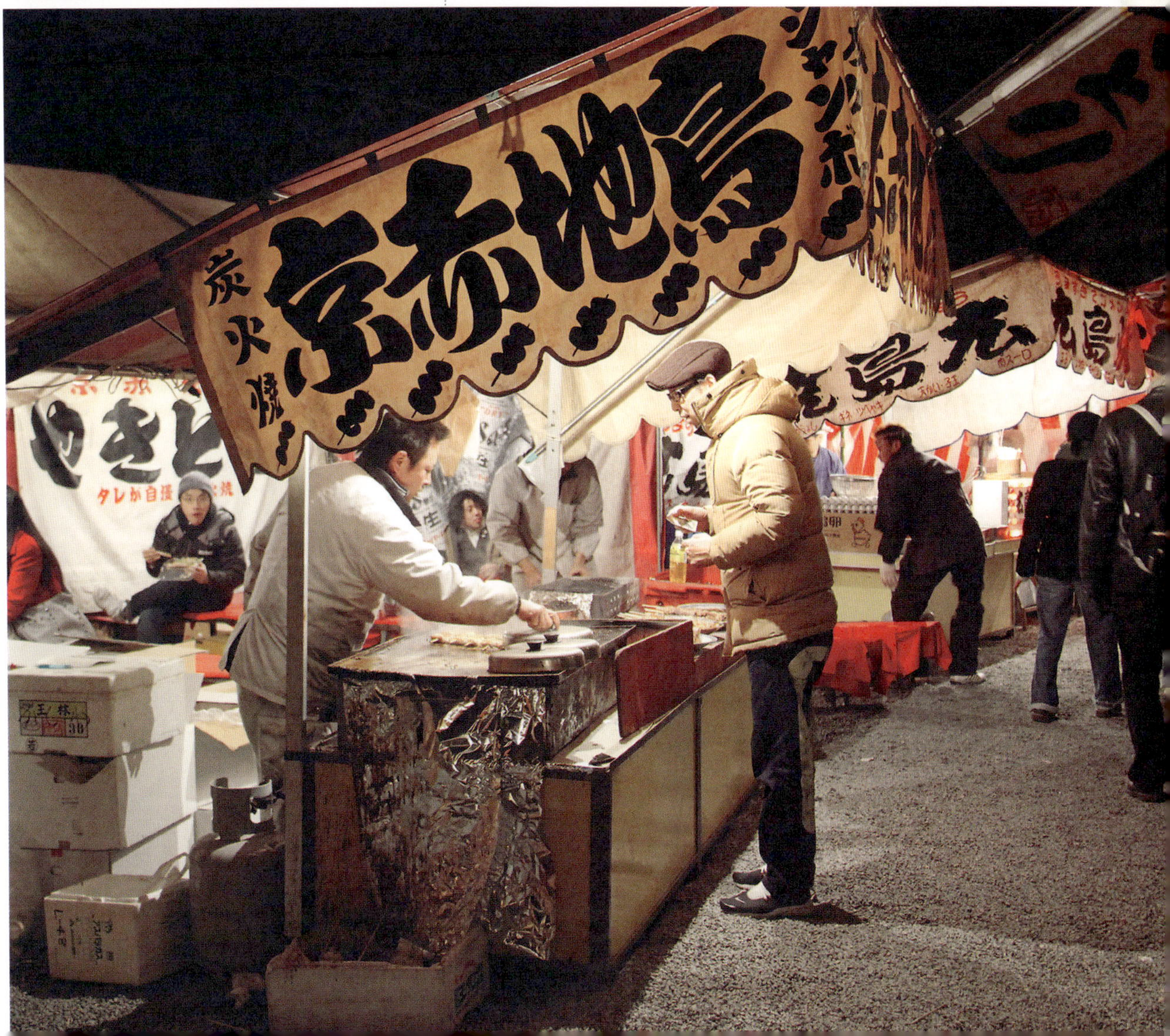
炭火焼
京赤地鳥
ジャンボ

tako no yawarakani

tender simmered octopus
SERVES 4–6 AS PART OF A MULTI-DISH MEAL

1 octopus, about 600 g (1 lb 5 oz)
3 tablespoons bancha tea leaves (see Note)
375 ml (13 fl oz/1½ cups) kombu dashi (page 29)
2½ tablespoons koikuchi shoyu (dark Japanese soy)
125 ml (4 fl oz/½ cup) sake
80 ml (2½ fl oz/⅓ cup) mirin
finely shredded shiso, or a sprig of fresh *kinome* (sansho leaf), to garnish (optional)

Freeze the octopus for at least 24 hours, and up to 48 hours — freezing is believed to start tenderising the octopus as it helps break down the cellular structure.

Remove the octopus from the freezer and allow to thaw. Grasp the tentacles and pull them away from the head; pull out all the innards, then rinse the head well.

Remove the eyes from the octopus using a sharp knife, then cut the head in half lengthways. Cut off the tentacles to give four lots of two-tentacle pieces (the octopus will be chopped into smaller chunks later).

Place the tea leaves and 1 litre (35 fl oz/4 cups) water in a pot with the octopus over medium–high heat. When the water comes just to the boil, reduce the heat to a simmer. Place a vented cartouche (a round of baking paper with an air vent cut in the middle) on top. Simmer the octopus for 40 minutes, or until reasonably tender. Remove from the water and drain well.

When the octopus is cool enough to handle, pick off and discard any bits of tea, then cut the head into 4 cm (1½ inch) square pieces, and the tentacles into 5 cm (2 inch) lengths.

Place the dashi, shoyu, sake and mirin in a clean saucepan with the octopus pieces over medium–high heat. Bring to just below the boil, then reduce to a simmer and cook for 15–20 minutes, or until the octopus is very tender and has taken on a brownish hue.

Remove from the heat. Carefully transfer the octopus into attractive piles in small individual bowls, then pour over a little of the cooking liquid. Serve garnished with shiso or *kinome* if desired.

Note: Bancha is an unrolled, coarse type of green tea that includes the leaves and twigs. It is considered to be of lower quality than other teas, being from a subsequent harvest to the first crop or 'flush' of tea. However, the slight bitterness in its matured leaves is offset by the sweetness in the twigs, and it is considered an everyday green tea that is low in caffeine. Kyo-bancha or Kyoto-style bancha is roasted, and can be significantly smoky in flavour depending on the producer.

123 **mutsuki / ichigatsu** – january / the 1st month

gyuniku to konnyaku no miso-ni

simmered beef tendon, cheek and konnyaku

SERVES 6 AS PART OF A MULTI-DISH MEAL

As the beef tendons (*gyuusuji*) have little meat, I have added beef cheeks to this recipe, being one of the few beef cuts that cooks for the same length of time as the tendon. The *kampyo* (dried gourd) is readily available in Japanese grocery stores and does add flavour to the dish, but if you can't find it you can leave it out.

- 300 g (10½ oz) beef tendon (see Notes)
- 600 g (1 lb 5 oz) beef cheeks
- 1.5 litres (52 fl oz/6 cups) niban dashi (page 29)
- 2 pencil-thin leeks, cut into 4 cm (1½ inch) lengths on a slight angle
- 1 carrot, thickly sliced on an angle
- 18 cm (7 inch) strip of *kampyo* (dried gourd)
- 250 g (9 oz) block of *konnyaku*, cut into 2 cm (¾ inch) squares (see Notes)
- 2 tablespoons shoyu
- 60 ml (2 fl oz/¼ cup) mirin
- 250 ml (9 fl oz/1 cup) sake
- 2 teaspoons finely grated fresh ginger
- 2 garlic cloves from the *miso zuke* recipe (page 158), finely chopped (optional)
- 3 tablespoons hatcho miso (see Notes)
- 1 tablespoon *kurosato* (Japanese black sugar) or dark brown sugar

Trim the beef tendon and cheeks of excess fat and sinew. Put the tendon in a saucepan of cold water and bring to the boil over high heat. Cook for 5 minutes, then pour into a colander and rinse well. Meanwhile, cut the cheeks into 4 cm (1½ inch) squarish pieces. When the tendon is cool enough to handle, cut it into 4 cm (1½ inch) lengths.

Place the tendon and cheeks in a clean saucepan with the dashi and bring to the boil. Reduce the heat to a simmer and place a Japanese drop-lid or vented cartouche (a round of baking paper, with an air vent cut in the middle) on top. Simmer for 2¼ hours, occasionally lifting off the cartouche to skim off any scum that has risen to the surface.

Add the vegetables, *konnyaku*, shoyu, mirin, sake, ginger and garlic, if using. Increase the heat to high to return to the boil, then reduce to a simmer again. Replace the cartouche and simmer for another 2 hours.

Remove the cartouche. Pull out the now softened *kampyo* and chop it, then return it to the pan. Add the miso and sugar and stir to combine well. Cook for a further 30 minutes, or until the cheeks and tendon are very tender and the sauce has thickened.

Notes: If you can't get beef tendon, you can replace it with 300 g (10½ oz) beef cheeks.

Konnyaku is a high-fibre, bland, greyish jelly made from the starch of the *konjak*, or devil's tongue root. It has very few calories and is used to bulk out foods as it absorbs the flavour of whatever it is cooked with. It is believed to be good at 'cleansing' the system.

Hatcho miso is a dark, rich miso that tastes both sweet and salty.

buri to daikon no nimono

simmered japanese yellowtail and daikon

SERVES 4–6 AS PART OF A MULTI-DISH MEAL

This dish, known in short as *buri daikon*, is popular in winter when yellowtail is at its most flavoursome, the fish being oilier to insulate it from the cold waters. Other rich, oily fish can be substituted. If, like me, you prefer a milder flavour, try a sweet-fleshed fish like snapper (given as an option below), or instead of fish on the bone, opt for thick fillets — perhaps tuna.

You can serve this dish straight away, but in Japan it is most often enjoyed after a day's refrigeration. In fact it is often served at room temperature, where the sauce is at its most gelatinous and wobbly (from the gelatine in the fish bones) and considered a delicacy.

This may not be your cup of tea, but I do recommend refrigerating and gently reheating the dish for a more rounded flavour.

18 cm (7 inch) length of daikon
3 cm (1¼ inch) piece of fresh ginger, thickly sliced
80 ml (2½ fl oz/⅓ cup) shoyu
125 ml (4 fl oz/½ cup) sake
60 ml (2 fl oz/¼ cup) mirin
2 teaspoons *kurosato* (Japanese black sugar) or dark brown sugar
half a whole small yellowtail, head left on, or 1 whole small snapper, head left on — you'll need about 1 kg (2 lb 4 oz) fish in total, gutted and scaled (see Note)
very finely shredded yuzu zest or fresh ginger, to garnish
mitsuba (Japanese trefoil) leaves, to garnish (optional)

Peel the daikon and slice into discs 3 cm (1¼ inch) thick. Trim off the sharp edges to stop them breaking up during cooking. Place in a large saucepan with the ginger and 1.25 litres (44 fl oz/5 cups) cold water. Bring to the boil and cook for 40 minutes.

Add the shoyu, sake, mirin and sugar to the pan. Return to the boil and cook for a further 20 minutes.

Meanwhile, cut the fish into squarish pieces about 5 cm (2 inches) in diameter. It can be difficult cutting through the larger bones, so use a sharp, heavy knife or cleaver and take care. Place in a colander, sprinkle with salt and leave for 20 minutes. Pour boiling water over the fish to rinse away any impurities, then rinse well under cool running water to remove any remaining blood or grit. This step will ensure the fish's aroma and flavour is not too strong.

Add the fish to the pan and cook for 20–22 minutes, or until the fish and daikon are very tender and have a brown hue from absorbing the cooking liquid.

Serve in a wide deep bowl, garnished with yuzu or ginger and scattered with a few *mitsuba* leaves, if desired.

Note: Yellowtail can vary wildly in size; if possible, use a full half of a medium-sized yellowtail, which should be about 1 kg (2 lb 4 oz). The sauce and daikon in this dish work well to cut through the oiliness of the fish, and also work well with other rich, fatty meats such as pork belly or duck. If using a mild, white-fleshed fish, you may like to add some dashi to dilute the base sauce flavour slightly, so it is not overpowering.

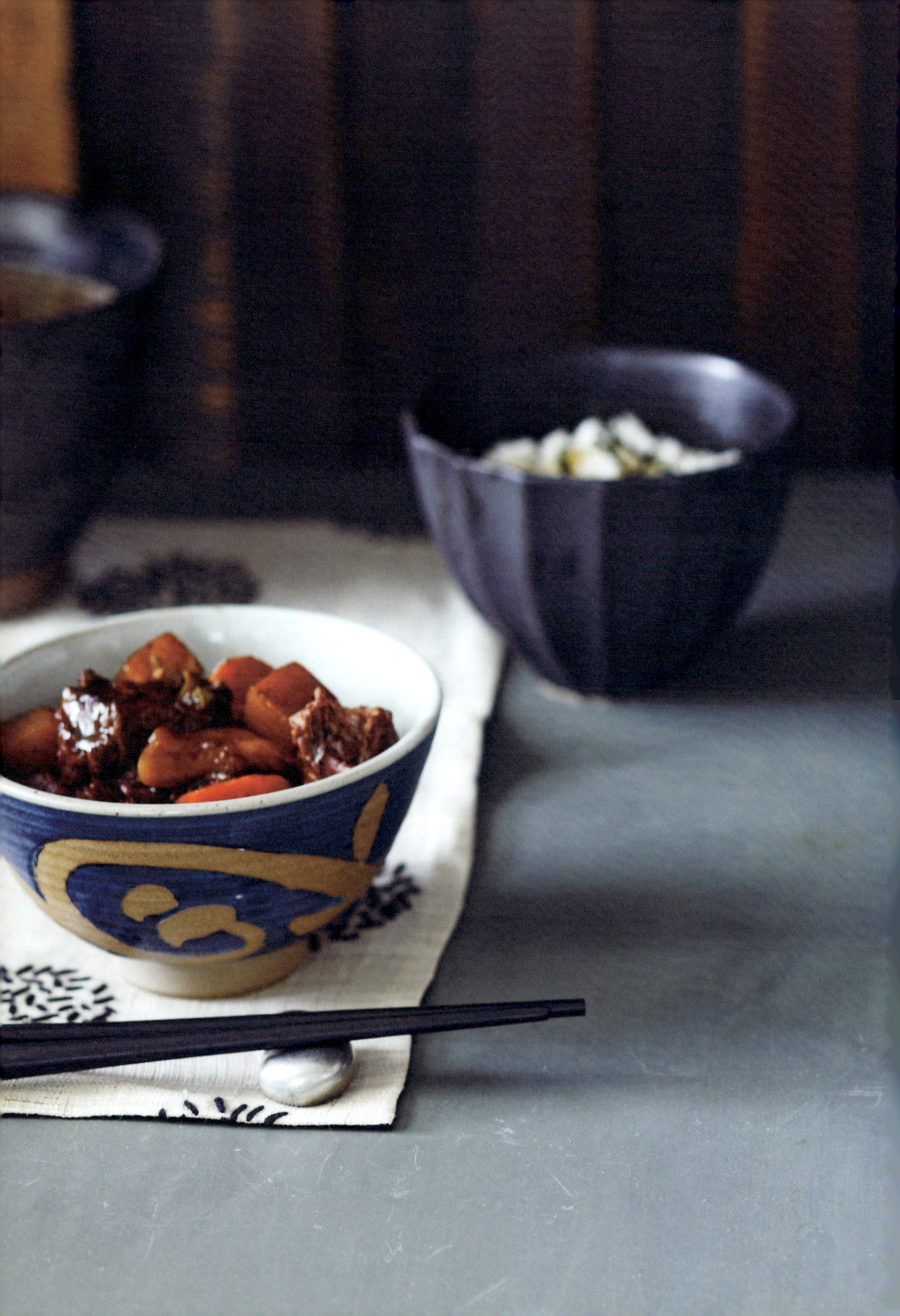

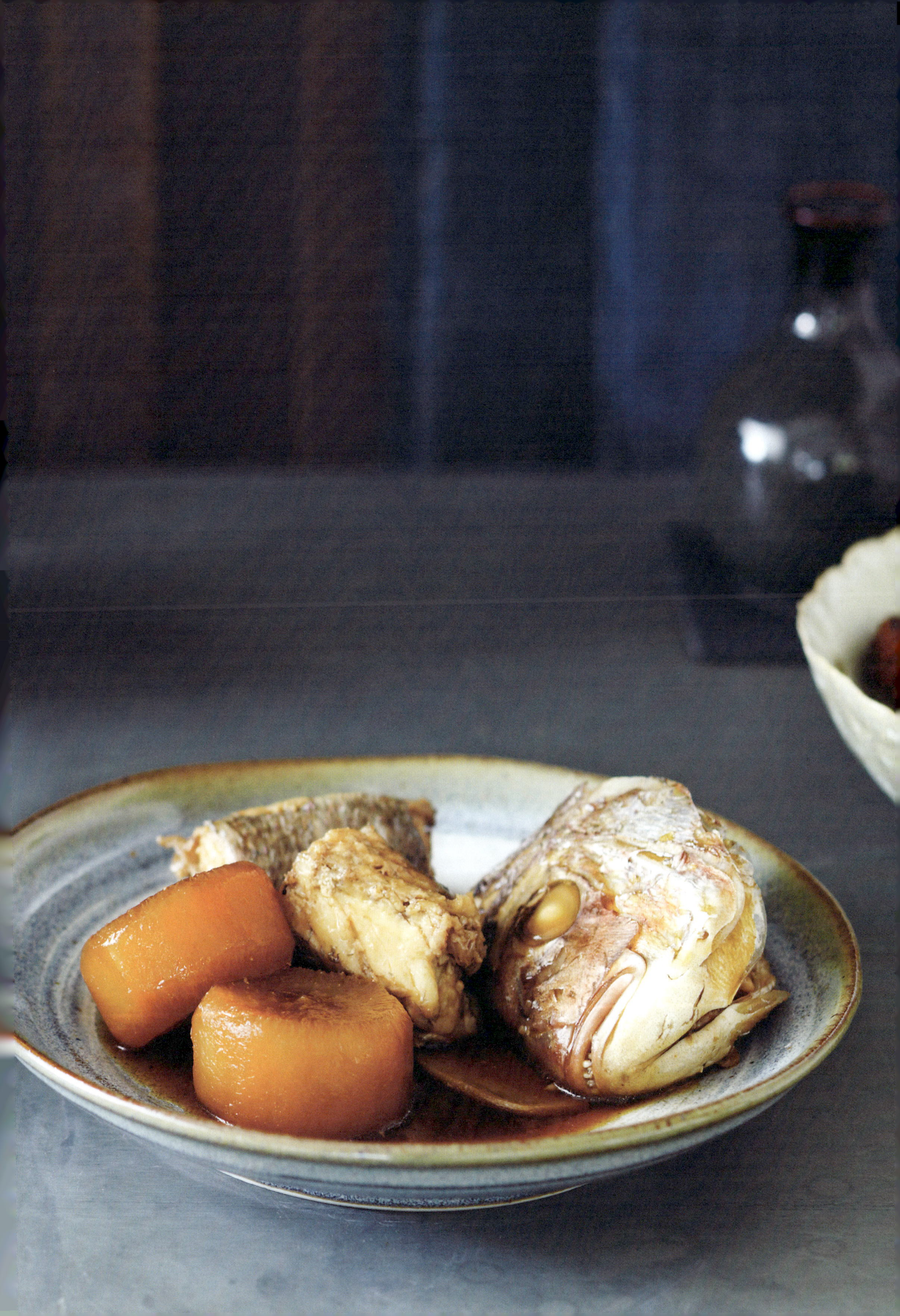

After a freezing morning under the meandering *torii* (gateway) of the Fushimi Inari Shrine, I was warmed to the core in a cruddy little mum-and-dad joint churning out really good fried stuff. A prickly *obaachan* (grandmother) elbowed me for a table that we stubbornly ended up sharing until I spilt miso soup over myself, which prompted her to toddle away, as fast as her legs could carry her, to distance herself from the uncouth foreigner.

I rewrapped myself in winter packaging and returned to the weather. Closer to my destination of Tofukuji Temple, the thunderous booming of taiko drum practice became an appropriately atmospheric soundtrack to my jungle-cat-like roaming around moss-muted temples and pruned vestibules of loveliness. A little off the tourist path, my alone time was interrupted when I realised I was being followed ... a sign to move on. One tends to become a little complacent about safety in Kyoto, but it still pays to have your wits about you in secluded areas.

I retreated, quickly scurrying homewards to simmer up a pot of reassuring *nanakusa gayu* (rice soup with seven herbs). The combination of *mitsuba* (Japanese trefoil or parsley), shepherd's purse, cudweed, chickweed, henbit, turnip and daikon greens would ensure good health for the year — and, with my recent track record, every little bit would help.

*

An early start meant pulling into the car park of a postage-stamp-sized bakery in the middle of nowhere for a quick breakfast. Although the exterior wasn't much, it was a vault of decadence inside. I was able to secure half the shop before my quickly multiplying competitors got a look-in. In Kikuko's car we ravaged individual loaves, still warm from the oven and filled with the most deliciously sweet *anko* (page 146) that had ever passed my lips. Who knew a red paste made from azuki beans could taste this good? I wanted to smother it on everything imaginable: buttered toast, ice cream, ear lobes ...

Believing the experience was likely the climax of my day, I could easily have returned home a happy woman, but we pressed on until we arrived at a spartan village on the outskirts of Nara. With a little time to spare before a ceremony set to honour the Jyoruri-ji Temple's head monk for his work within the greater Buddhist community, we made a short visit to the main hall for the annual unveiling of its national treasures — statues carved more than 900 years ago. It was a brief but spiritual experience connecting with these ancient offerings that represented a magnificent period of history. I sat in traditional pose, staring in awe.

The surrounding grounds were more open and natural than many of the more groomed Kyoto temple offerings. A small graveyard recycled broken stone lantern tops as markers, and a total of 17 cats patrolled the area. Within the confines of a roped-off area was a large circle constructed from thousands of thin branches, reminiscent of a sacred Druid stone formation. Noting my curiosity, Myong Hee divulged that it was, in fact, her most recent art installation; after spending a day in the forest meditatively collecting fallen timber, she had painstakingly trimmed all to 60 cm (2 foot) lengths before wrapping each in one of five coloured cloths, then placing them over the stones of what was likely the foundation of an ancient building. The branches all faced one vertical log in the centre where 'the energy from the garden angels' would be focused. Lost in the moment, we arrived late for the ceremony and scurried back to the hall, quickly kicking off our boots before sliding back the *shoji* screen and onto the tatami in front of the altar. Myong Hee's paper lanterns were lit and dotted around the room, and the space filled with an intoxicating mix of incense, *sencha* (green leaf tea) and warm bodies.

The monk and his disciples slowly shuffled into the room, deep in cantation. Throughout the chanting, powdered incense was intermittently sprinkled over a burner, producing a thin waft of smoke for conducting over prayer books with a wand-like stick. Although I am not Buddhist, I felt both welcomed and privileged to be at this sacred, mesmerising blessing. The rest of the room joined in with the low humming and I closed my eyes, absorbing the vibrations of their vocal musings and the deeper, engaging brass chimes of the prayer bowl.

Green tea and small bowls of piping-hot *zenzai* (*mochi* rice cakes in sweet azuki bean soup), a typical sweet for that time of the year, felt both comforting and nurturing. However, I almost lapsed, ungratefully, into a sugary coma during the 90-minute speech, of which I understood two words. I was relieved to note several heads also bowed — not in prayer, but in sleep. Through a small gap in the *shoji* screen I spied a shaven-headed nun preparing tea and was grateful that lunch would soon be served ...

Lemon-sized *onigiri* (rice balls), capped with toasted sesame seeds, arrived on a procession of trays from the kitchen. A low table was covered in small dishes containing nori sheets for wrapping the rice, plus a wide range of pickles and condiments, such as shiitake *tsukudani* (see Variation to recipe on page 115), dried tofu rehydrated by simmering in sweet dashi, luscious homemade umeboshi pickles, tasting more of plum than salt (unlike the commercial variety), daikon pickles with yuzu, *tamagoyaki* (egg and dashi omelette), and small taro — all excellent foils for the perfectly cooked white rice. Bowls of miso chock-full of *yama imo* (yam), daikon, *konnyaku* and carrot were also handed around the room. Humble offerings packed with pure, delicious flavours and characteristic of food cooked from the heart.

An elderly gentleman proudly tapped the small sake barrel brewed by his daughter in nearby Wakayama and siphoned its contents into flasks for pouring. Female sake brewers were non-existent until the recent rise in interest by the younger female population, and I was heartened to see this father so accepting of his female offspring's chosen field. Exaltations were expressed from around the room, declaring it '*sugoi oishii*' ('amazingly delicious!') — which it absolutely was. The day was so cold I managed to polish off a third *ochoku* (small ceramic sake cup) when it was offered.

We finished the humble meal with small pieces of a large, lacy, wholesome 'biscuit' and yet more tea, while chatting to the so-called 'second monk' — Sekigawa-san. As fortune would have it, he is a teacher of *shojin ryori* (Buddhist vegetarian cuisine), and enthusiastically invited us to his house for a lesson the following week. He also happened to know Mari Fujii — another expert on *shojin ryori*, whom I had been hoping to meet. Myong Hee smiled knowingly and advised I was experiencing '*go-en*'. Seeing the puzzled look on my face, she explained that it meant 'when natural connections are made, happening just as they should'. I also heard it described as 'honourably good luck in terms of relationships'. I returned her smile, two-fold. This was a definite nod to the essence of the whole trip — what I had hoped would happen in 'letting go'. *Go-en* had connected me to Myong Hee and then to all her wonderful friends and their connections. *Go-en* is a term that will resonate with me until death … or dementia.

For a long time, the need for things to occur organically had been grabbing at my intestines, keeping me conscious. I was reminded that when I made the decision to come to Japan to write this book it 'came to me' as a really strong urge, an almost physical pull that I was unable to be released from — so I went with it and as soon as I did, things fell into place: the extraordinarily cheap airfare, the perfect apartment to rent, a book deal and a good wodge of unexpected royalties turning up in my bank account … just like that!

I was warned by a friend to get myself organised with meeting people, as 'things don't happen easily in Japan'. I wondered if I had been kidding myself that this would all just flow naturally, but intrinsically I believed it would all be okay, so I respectfully disregarded her advice.

The people I consequently met and learnt so much from were generally those whom I casually met along the way. What this cemented for me was that this really was the way to live my life. Today, I find that I communicate and work most freely when I am connecting and disconnecting as naturally as the sun and moon move in and out of our day and trusting that I come into contact with all for a reason.

Our bellies full and souls enriched, we began the process of taking leave, which is always a drawn-out affair in Japan. After bowing and nodding and exchanging *meishi* (business cards) and details with our fellow guests, we crawled into a smaller room where the head monk and a few VIPs sat puffing away on cigarettes, keeping warm under the *kotatsu* (low heated table). We knelt, placing our hands on the tatami in front, fingertips angled towards each other, and bowed from the waist, noses almost tipping the floor, in a gesture of great respect while, for the entire duration, they exhaled putrid smoke from their lungs in our general direction. The irony and humour of the circumstance will remain forever etched in my memory.

*

In celebration and hope for good business for the coming year, the Ebisu Festival was in full swing. I turned my nose up at the deep-fried battered umeboshi (pickled 'plum') on a stick and instead perched in front of a small stage at the Ebisu-jinja Shrine where the *miko* (shrine maidens) whirled to live *shakahachi* tunes. A long queue formed to knock loudly on the temple wall in hope that the spirit of the partially deaf lucky god Ebisu, an unfortunate character born half boy/half leech, would hear their prayers. The longer I stayed, the more insanely busy it grew, to the point where I fled for fear of being trampled.

My feet, at this point, were in need of much attention, so I took myself to the gorgeously fitted out Hyatt Regency Hotel where I had booked a massage and facial at Riraku Spa. I had timed my morning well: as the last moments of sunlight faded behind looming rainclouds I was heading underground to be pampered. I changed into my robe and paper undies and removed my 'under-bra' as instructed, ready for my two-and-a-half-hour *ne-ne* package. Mami-san explained she'd

I mention the concept of *go-en* ('natural connections') several times in this book – as much to remind myself of its message, as to share it. Life is a little easier when you let go of expectation and instead allow natural momentum to bring things your way. However, letting go of fears, trusting with an open mind and heart, and only giving as much energy to any given situation as is healthy isn't easy. I will still be learning until the day I leave the earth, but the practice is so rewarding.

perform my 'bodywork' first, followed by an organic facial. She poured a small cup of sake into a wooden footbath and gestured for me to soak my feet — insisting the sake would warm my body. She tapped some spicy powdered incense onto my palms and mimed for me to rub them together in a circular motion before taking three deep breaths to relax myself. Popping silkworm cocoons onto the tips of her fingers, she proceeded to clean my embarrassingly ill-cared-for feet, rubbing in tiny rotations. I selected some oil from a beautiful tray containing *rirakusing* — detoxing and energising scents. I melted quickly and deeply and was reminded of the importance of physical touch. I was near sleep by the time my facial got under way. It started with an azuki bean powder scrub, followed by grapeseed and jojoba cleansing oil. A warm, gel-like seaweed mask scented with *sudachi* lime was then brushed over my face. Mami-san's fingertips fluttered all over my features before applying 'peach moon' herbal facial water. It was over all too soon.

I walked away from this nurture fest at 5 pm feeling completely re-energised. I was not yet ready to head homewards so I walked with no particular plan, for how long I'm not sure, just allowing my legs to take me wherever they felt inclined. Just being.

*

I was starting to feel a return of self. One by one, tiny deflated pockets of body and soul were regenerating. I finally began taking heed when my body called for rest. I felt safe and happy, cocooned by loveliness and, to quote a wise friend, the 'gentleness' of Kyoto.

From my bed, where I had indulgently overslept, I could hear drumming — sparking a reminder it was Seijin no Hi, or 'Coming of Age' Day, when those who have turned 20 in the past year (or by March in the current year) come together in yet another festive celebration. Girls were dressed in formal kimonos, and rather unflattering fluffy white shoulder drapes, while most of the lads sported spiffy Western suits, and exaggeratingly cruised about in small swarms, as though in a scene from Quentin Tarantino's *Reservoir Dogs*.

Collective clicking from parents' cameras sounded like a swarm of rampant cicadas, the disturbance compounded by the number of unofficial, slightly pervy 'paparazzi' who joined them. I shuddered to realise I was probably one of them! But it was only when one of the mothers proudly offered up her two charges for a photo opportunity with me that the tables were turned — within seconds there were at least eight male photographers crouching, leaning, towering and lurching as their phallic lenses hunted us like starlet 'game' stepping onto the red carpet. I felt naked. A bitter taste from a spoonful of my own medicine had me moving on rather quickly while primly smoothing down my ruffled feathers. I vowed to be more respectful when thrusting my own camera about!

I strolled for a long time, first exploring the pristine park surrounding the Imperial Palace, before languidly snaking my way from temple to temple as I headed north-west towards Kinkakuji ('The Golden Pavilion'). Before too long, I realised that an impromptu pit-stop to watch models parading kimono fashions in the old textile district of Nishijin had stuffed up any chance of reaching my destination before closing time. But I couldn't have given two hoots.

I kept moving, discovering unfamiliar parts of the city, liberated by not having to be anywhere or do anything.

When I reached Senbon Dori, a long shopping strip in an area that feels stuck in the 1970s, I realised it was probably my destination all along. The area is a bit daggy, but curiously attractive with its ramshackle stores selling aluminium saucepans, cheap slippers and exquisite silk scarves. It exuded an 'old school' essence that I had not experienced for some time: it wasn't an ancient village, but it felt like the life force of the town. Perhaps it is ironic, but I've since heard that at one time during Kyoto's 1200-year-history, under the cover of night, Senbon Dori was the designated thoroughfare for transporting Kyoto's corpses to a central burial ground.

The area was bustling with locals shopping for perishables of fresh leafy greens, fish, tofu or other household essentials and chatting like you might to a neighbour over the fence. They were dressed more casually than in other parts of Kyoto, in what might be considered the Japanese equivalent of 'trackie-dacks'. Gilded Kinkakuji had nothing on the atmosphere in that rustic little pocket.

Inspired, I went home with some sweet pork, *okara* (soy grits; see page 140), an armful of fresh vegetables and a sense of belonging.

*

Although tatami matting is yielding and slightly spongy to walk on, the sensation of padding across it barefooted or in socks is utterly grounding. The scent and texture of the rice straw flooring is unmistakably Japanese, and instantly reconnects me to the country whenever I return. Although first introduced as a luxury item during the Heian period, tatami are usually found in at least one room of every traditional or modern home.

mutsuki / ichigatsu – january / the 1st month

miso butaniku no nabe

miso pork hotpot
SERVES 4–6 AS PART OF A MULTI-DISH MEAL

The stew or hotpot dish known as *nabe* is named for the special lidded ceramic or cast-iron cooking vessel it is prepared in — namely the *donabe*, commonly shortened to *nabe*. A *nabe* can of course be cooked on the stovetop in a regular heavy-based pot or deep-sided saucepan, but is traditionally cooked at the table over a portable flame.

Nabe are great for communal dining, particularly in the cooler months. Often, as with other hotpots, the broth is first brought to a simmer in the *nabe*, then the ingredients are neatly and attractively placed in individual groups around the pot, with items taking the longest to cook usually added first. If the ingredients all have equal cooking time, they can be brought raw in the pot to the table before cooking.

The thinly sliced ingredients means a relatively quick cooking time; delicate greens are added just before serving.

500 ml (17 fl oz/2 cups) niban dashi (page 29)
125 ml (4 fl oz/½ cup) mirin
5 tablespoons saikyo miso (sweet white miso)
2 tablespoons shoyu
1 teaspoon finely grated fresh ginger
500 g (1 lb 2 oz) pork belly, cut into long slices about 3 mm (⅛ inch) thick (see Notes)
2 pencil-thin leeks, cut into 4 cm (1½ inch) lengths on a slight angle, or 1 regular leek, white part only, cut on a slight angle into slices 2 cm (¾ inch) thick
1 large carrot, cut on an angle into slices 7 mm (⅜ inch) thick
8 tiny *koimo* (Japanese taro), peeled (optional)
150 g (5½ oz) piece of fresh lotus root, peeled, sliced 5 mm (¼ inch) thick and placed in acidulated water (see Notes)
150 g (5½ oz) shimeji mushrooms, pulled apart into small clusters
80 g (2¾ oz/3 cups) *shungiku* (edible chrysanthemum leaves; see explanation on page 79) or *komatsuna* (Japanese mustard spinach)
steamed rice, to serve
shichimi togarashi (seven-flavour spice mix), to serve (optional)

Place the dashi, mirin, miso, shoyu and ginger in a large jug and mix to combine.

Start around the outside edge of a large *nabe* or heavy-based, deep-sided saucepan and attractively arrange the looped-over pork, leek, carrot, taro, lotus and mushrooms so they are leaning up against each other, but kept as areas of individual ingredients so it is easy to select pieces of each ingredient when the dish is served.

Carefully pour the liquid ingredients down one side of the *nabe* so as not to disturb the decorative ingredients. Place over high heat — either on the stovetop or a portable gas burner — and bring to the boil, skimming off any foam that rises to the surface during the process.

Reduce the heat to a simmer and put the lid on. Cook for 30 minutes, or until the lotus and taro are tender. Turn off the heat, then carefully tuck the chrysanthemum leaves into one corner so their tops are still above water. Pop the lid back on, leave to sit for a few seconds to help wilt the leaves, then serve, allowing each guest to help themselves to a little of each ingredient with long communal chopsticks and a small ladle for the broth.

The *nabe* should be eaten in individual bowls, with rice on the side in separate rice bowls. Diners may sprinkle the dish with *shichimi togarashi* as desired. Use chopsticks to eat the ingredients from your bowl and the rice — then, when finished, it is perfectly acceptable in Japan to pick up the bowl and drink the remaining broth. Chopsticks are often the only cutlery served for an entire meal, so it simply makes sense to drink the broth if you are not presented with a spoon.

Notes: If you can't buy pre-sliced pork from the fresh or frozen section of an Asian grocery store, nicely ask your butcher to freeze some boneless pork belly and then cut it 3 mm (⅛ inch) thick on a meat slicer. Alternatively, allow it to thaw slightly before cutting it yourself with a very sharp, large knife. Loop the pieces in half before placing them in the pot for a neat presentation.

If you can't find fresh lotus root (*renkon*), you can use thawed frozen lotus root slices, or 200 g (7 oz) bamboo shoot wedges.

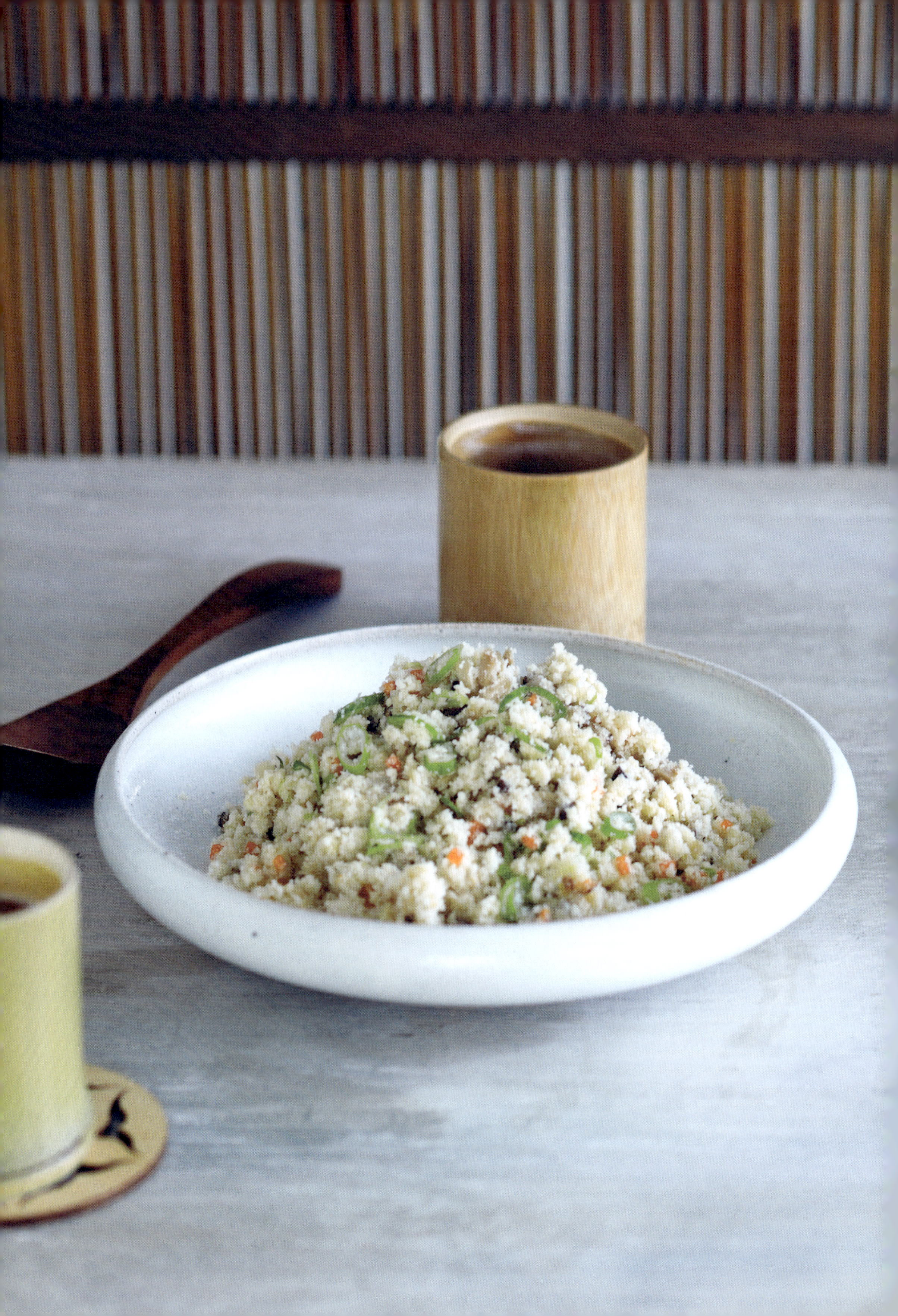

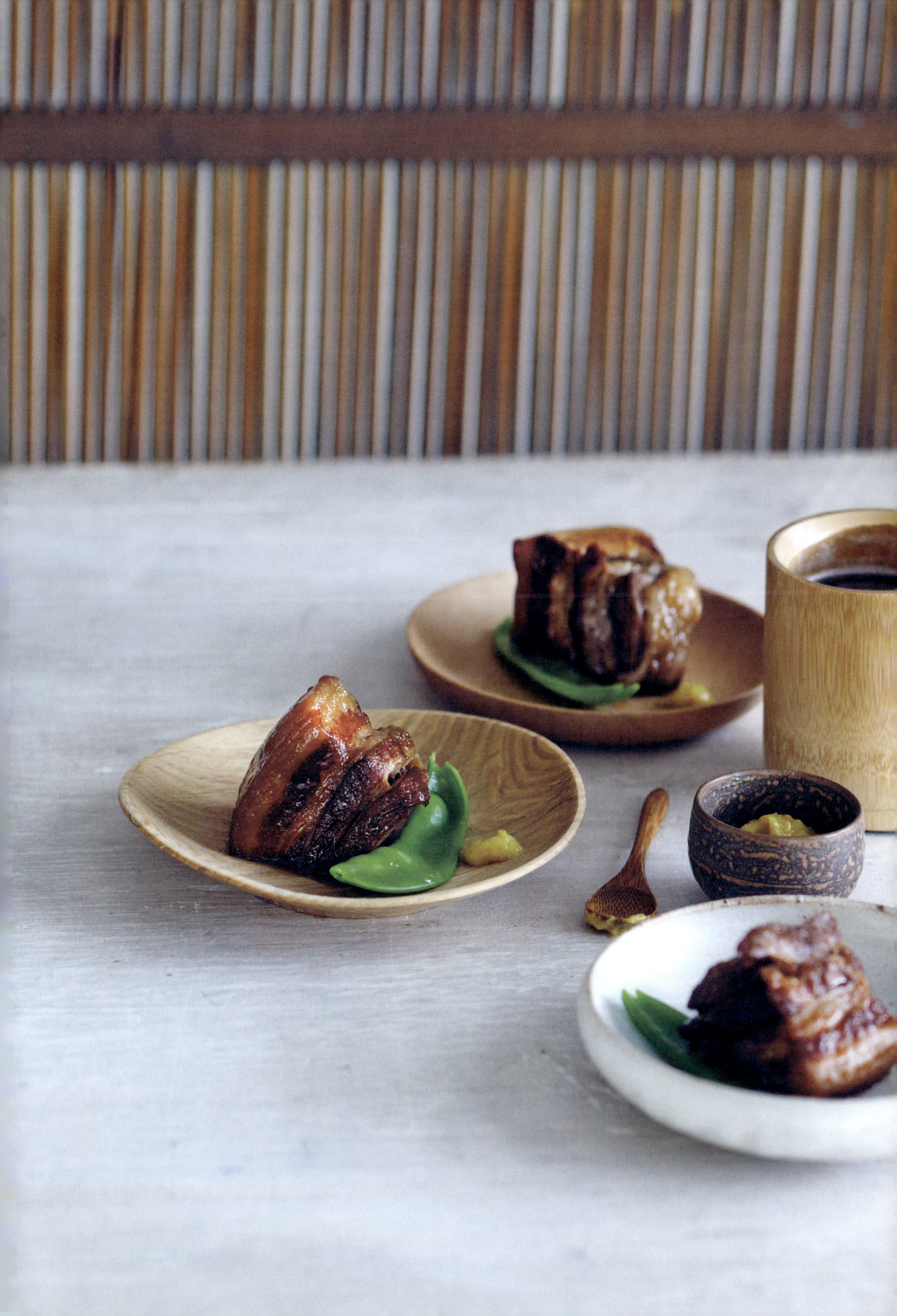

okara itame

stir-fried tofu lees and vegetables
SERVES 4–6 AS PART OF A MULTI-DISH MEAL

During soy milk production, a by-product of leftover 'milked' beans is formed — *okara*. Nutritious, filling and low fat, *okara* is often added to soups and side dishes in an effort not to be wasteful. In high-scale production it is used as feed for farm animals.

There are also many possibilities for using *okara* in Western cooking — mix it with vegies for meat-free rissoles, use it instead of bread or rice in stuffings, or add it to soups or stews for bulk. When dried out and toasted in the oven it can be used as a cereal or a crunchy topping for bakes. It will also freeze well for a couple of months. If you made it your mission, I'm sure you could find many other ways to use *okara* instead of throwing it away. Here is a simple, flavoursome recipe from my kitchen.

1 teaspoon sesame oil
2 teaspoons vegetable oil
2 spring onions (scallions), thily sliced, keeping the greens and whites separate
½ carrot, very finely diced
1 garlic clove, finely chopped
½ teaspoon finely grated fresh ginger
300 g (10½ oz/2 cups) *okara* (leftover from making the soy milk on page 84)
2 rehydrated shiitake mushrooms, very finely diced
50 g (1¾ oz/⅓ cup) bamboo shoots, very finely diced
250 ml (9 fl oz/1 cup) dashi (see Note)
2 teaspoons usukuchi shoyu (light Japanese soy)
1 tablespoon mirin

Heat the sesame and vegetable oils in a frying pan over medium–high heat. Add the white part of the spring onion with the carrot and stir-fry for 3 minutes, or until the spring onion is lightly golden.

Add the garlic and ginger and stir-fry for 30 seconds, before adding the remaining ingredients, except the spring onion greens. Stir to combine, bring to the boil, then reduce the heat and simmer for 15 minutes, or until the liquid has evaporated.

Stir in the spring onion greens and season to taste with sea salt. Serve either hot or at room temperature.

Note: You can use your choice of dashi here — kombu dashi (page 29) or shiitake dashi (page 29) for vegetarians, or niban dashi (page 29) otherwise. You can of course use tori dashi (page 208) if serving this dish as a side for a chicken main.

butaniku no kakuni

slow simmered pork belly in shoyu and black sugar

SERVES 6–8 PEOPLE AS PART OF A MULTI-DISH MEAL

Introduced to Japan from China, this dish, also called *rafute*, is tender as butter and has a lovely sweet shoyu flavour. Although there is quite a lot of fat in pork belly, it also contains a substantial amount of collagen. Much sought-after in Japan, pork belly is always eaten in small amounts as part of a multi-dish meal; it is also sliced and served over ramen noodles, and in fluffy steamed buns called *nikuman*.

This dish is great over rice, in a noodle soup or as part of a multi-dish meal that includes rice and an assortment of vegetable dishes.

1 tablespoon vegetable oil
800 g (1 lb 12 oz) piece of boneless pork belly, cut into 6 x 4 cm (2½ x 1½ inch) rectangular pieces
50 g (1¾ oz) fresh ginger, cut into thick slices
2 pencil-thin leeks, or 1 small leek, split down the centre, but kept hinged together
1 litre (35 fl oz/4 cups) niban dashi (page 29) or water
310 ml (10¾ fl oz/1¼ cups) sake
1½ tablespoons usukuchi shoyu (light Japanese soy)
1½ tablespoons koikuchi shoyu (dark Japanese soy)
60 g (2¼ oz/⅓ cup) *kurosato* (Japanese black sugar) or dark brown sugar
1½ tablespoons Japanese black vinegar (optional)
4 eggs, boiled for 4 minutes, then cooled and shelled (optional)
6 blanched, trimmed snow peas (mangetout), to garnish
karashi (Japanese mustard) or hot English mustard, to serve

Heat the oil in a large frying pan over medium–high heat. Add the pork and cook, turning now and then, for about 5 minutes, until golden on all sides. Remove from the pan, place in a colander and pour boiling water over to rinse off the excess oil.

Place the pork in a large saucepan with the ginger, leek, dashi and sake and bring to the boil, skimming off any scum that rises to the top.

Add a Japanese drop-lid or a vented cartouche (a round of baking paper, with an air vent cut in the middle). Reduce the heat and simmer for 2¼ hours, or until the pork is quite tender.

Stir in the light and dark shoyu, sugar and vinegar and cook for a further 1 hour, or until the pork is very tender — as knives and forks are not served at Japanese meals, the pork should be tender enough to break with chopsticks.

Turn off the heat, then remove and discard the leek and ginger. Add the eggs, if using, submerging them in the liquid.

Allow the pork to sit and soak up more of the sauce for 45 minutes. Alternatively, you can allow the dish to cool slightly, then transfer to a bowl, cover and refrigerate overnight — if you do this, you'll be able to scrape off the excess fat that settles on the top of the dish.

When ready to serve, gently reheat the dish. Carefully cut the eggs in half. Serve garnished with snow peas, with the Japanese mustard on the side, to help cut through the richness.

If you prefer a thicker sauce, remove the pork and eggs from the pot and thicken the sauce slightly either by reducing it over the heat, or stirring in some *kuzu* starch or cornflour (cornstarch) that has first been mixed to a paste with a little water.

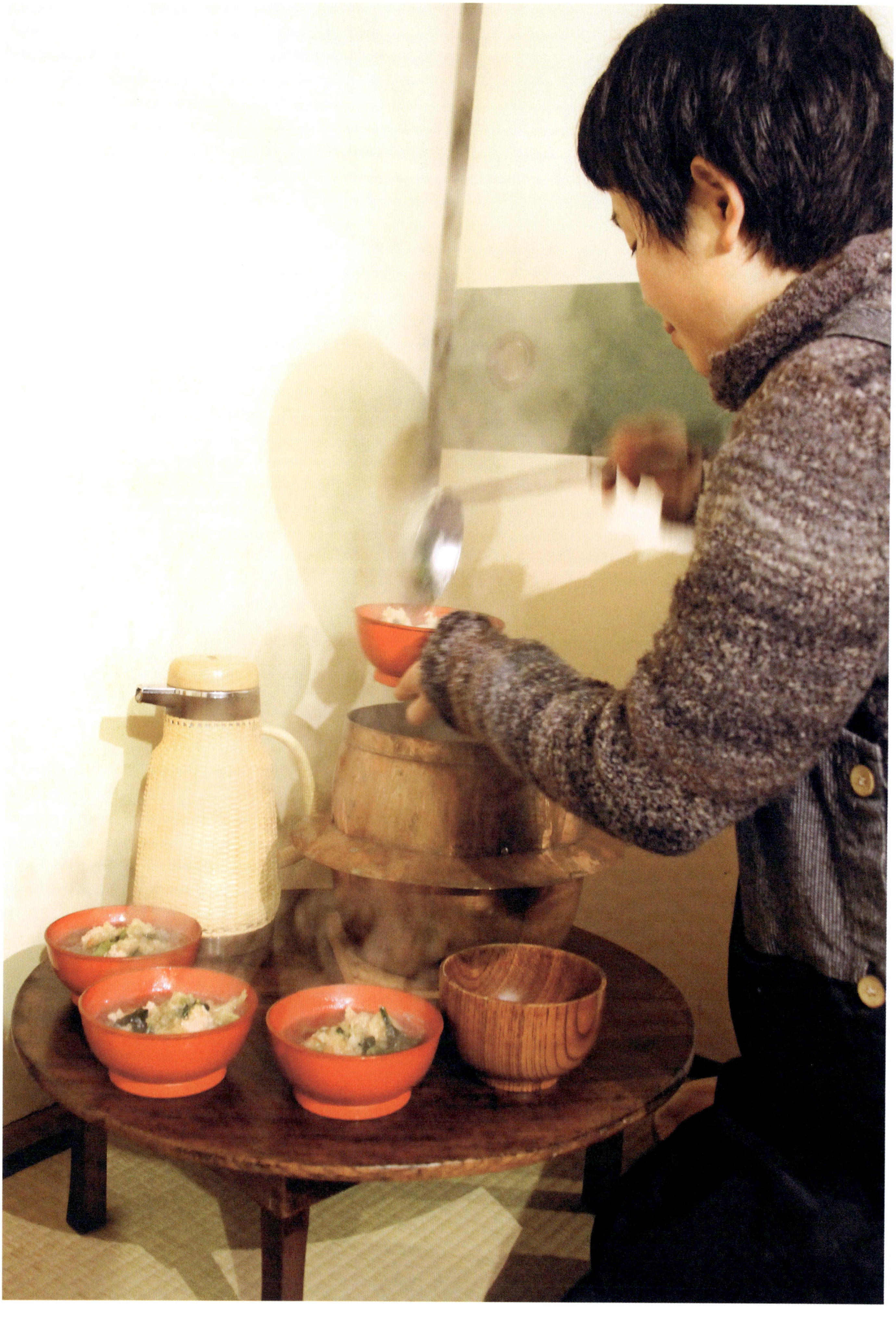

During a half-hour train trip to Kameoka, to learn more about traditional Japanese cookery, I was transported to a place that felt far more distant than it actually was. Minutes after leaving the city, we raced through a pitch-black tunnel in the mountainside and exited into a vista of mist-shrouded foliage and sunken gorges filled with rapidly flowing phosphorescent water. I could well have been travelling via time machine. I contentedly watched 'my' town slip further and further away.

A friend of a friend, Akemi, met me at the station en route to the city hall, where she introduced me to eight farmers' wives who have taught traditional Japanese cookery to local housewives for more than 20 years. Kameoka, though landlocked and lacking creatures of the marine variety, is agriculturally rich and provides many Kansai homes with some 100 varieties of seasonal vegetables including *edamame* (fresh soy beans), *komatsuna* (Japanese mustard spinach), *junsai* (a pond plant resembling frog spawn) and *sansai* (mountain vegetables). Its river fish are highly regarded, as are its *torigai* — a type of clam that is dried and preserved for use in summer sushi. Kameokans are famous for *yomogi mochi dango* (green mugwort dumplings filled with red beans and wrapped in a *yomogi* leaf for shape and texture), and *senmaizuke* (1000-piece pickles), made from wafer-thin slices of the famous round winter daikon, proportionate to a toddler's noggin.

The women were a little wary at first and early during my interview, without provocation and completely off-topic, boldly blurted out that none of them were 'professional' and quickly added that I 'shouldn't be concerned about that'. I respectfully responded that I was not in the least bit concerned and that, in my opinion, home cooks were often just as good if not better than professionals, and there was nothing more wonderful than food cooked with heart and soul. I also concurred that it was imperative the type of information they possessed was shared and passed down through the generations for fear it could be lost forever. I assured them I was honoured to be talking with them. And who wouldn't be? They had some 500 years of combined knowledge and experience between them! With that, they relaxed, nodding with approval. The barriers had been lowered an increment. I'd passed the first test.

Emphatic that the younger generation should understand their own food culture, their classes include: seasonal *ryori* (food) for the summer festival of Obon; autumn's Kameoka festival; spring specialties to celebrate the blossoming of Kyoto; and two winter classes covering *oshogatsu* (New Year's) *osechi ryori* and *tsukemono* (pickles). The ladies believe that most young Japanese, particularly those living alone, have no idea how to cook, preferring to buy pre-made foods or dine out. We chatted for almost an hour, Akemi patiently translating what I could not communicate: I learnt they made their own miso paste and tofu (page 116), and that some of them even grew the soy beans with which to make both. One woman even made her own *koji* (rice culture), crucial to making both miso and sake.

They enquired, as had many on this trip, about Australia's food culture. Cringing at the thought of comparing the two, I told them that as a 'new' country comprised of people from many different ethnic backgrounds, we had borrowed from established cuisines as varied as British, Italian, Greek, Chinese, Thai and Vietnamese. They were astounded to learn that many

Australian home cooks are quite daring in the kitchen, also dabbling in French, Spanish, Turkish, Lebanese, Malaysian, Indian and Japanese cuisines. While there is a diverse range of foods available in Japanese restaurants, most home cooks in Japan rarely stray from cooking their national cuisine, and only prepare Korean, Chinese or 'Western' cuisine on rare occasions. It was gratifying to be reminded that Australian cooks are open to celebrating a wide range of culinary cultures, and it is both curiosity and lack of inhibition that educates our palates.

While discussing the New Year's celebrations, I volunteered that I, too, made *toshikoshi soba* (year-crossing soba noodles; page 100) and *ozoni* (New Year's soup; page 105). Their eyes lit up with surprise, before narrowing with suspicion, and then quizzing me on whether my *mochi* (glutinous rice cakes) were round or square? Realising it was a test, I grimaced and squeaked out a response: 'Square?' Their tongues tut-tutted, indicating I had succumbed to the 'inferior' Kanto (Tokyo region) style. Kansai *mochi* is round. Fail.

Educating me further, they declared Japanese rice is the best in the world as it is grown in pure mountain water ... which apparently is also the best water in the world ... and therefore makes the most pure-tasting, finely textured ice and the best sake and tofu in the world. *Mochiron* ('of course'), ladies, *mochiron*.

When our time was up, I presented the women with a thank-you gift of gorgeously wrapped sweet biscuits. As is customary, they acted appropriately embarrassed and feigned refusal a few times before accepting. As they fervently began digging through their handbags I couldn't help but wonder what they might 'return' with — lint-encrusted escapee mints perhaps? It was then my turn to be genuinely embarrassed as they presented me with whole chestnuts cooked in syrup, *manju* (dumplings) with white azuki bean paste, and a New Year's offering containing *mikan* (mandarin), dried *kaki* (persimmon), *kuromame* (black beans cooked in syrup) and a twisted knot of kombu (dried kelp).

But the biggest prize by far was some homemade *yokan* (a jelly-like paste made from azuki beans, sugar and agar agar; see page 146), a treat I fondly remember enjoying with fragrant green tea while working at Japan Airlines in Sydney in my late teens. Every mouthful nodded to that time in my youth, which had cemented my relationship with Japan.

*

You don't have to look hard to find beauty in Kyoto. Many handcrafted knives, pots, bamboo whisks and the like are still created with the highest degree of refinement by local artisans. Most are expensive, as you would expect, but pre-loved objects like these wooden moulds (in various sizes, for shaping confectionery or rice for celebrations) can be picked up in antique shops or flea markets for a fraction of the price — at the very least making for an exquisite ornament!

yokan

red bean confectionery
MAKES ABOUT 36 PIECES

Yokan, a firm, slightly fudgy, jelly-like red bean paste, was developed as a dessert in the Edo period and is commonly served with green tea. Traditional versions are sometimes simply garnished with whole or chopped chestnuts or sweet potato, or flavoured with green tea or persimmon. However, contemporary versions are available in specialist stores in all manner of flavours, colours and patterns — some exquisitely designed for the seasons.

Before you can make the yokan you need to make anko — a red bean paste that is used in a number of Japanese desserts and confections. I could eat a bowl of anko with a spoon, and have done. It's fabulous on buttered toast with matcha (green tea powder) sprinkled over the top, or served with chocolate or vanilla ice cream and kinako (roasted soy bean powder) as a yoshoku (Western-style) sundae.

The recipe below makes about 4 cups of anko, so you'll have about 2 cups left over. The leftover anko can be stored in an airtight container in the fridge for about 1 month, and also freezes well for up to 3 months.

Besides using it to make more yokan, or sampling it as explained above, you can use it to fill a variety of Japanese sweets, such as dorayaki (page 264) or nama yatsuhashi (page 260; also known as otabe when filled with anko). Or make some green tea dacquoise or macarons, add anko and whipped cream and devour.

ANKO

330 g (11½ oz/1½ cups) dried azuki beans
440 g (15½ oz/2 cups) caster (superfine) sugar
1 teaspoon sea salt

1 stick kanten (agar agar), about 7.5 g (¼ oz) — readily available in Japanese grocery shops
100 g (3½ oz/½ cup) kurosato (Japanese black sugar) or dark brown sugar

First, make the anko. Soak the beans in a large bowl of water — in the fridge if the weather is particularly hot — for about 16 hours.

Drain the beans and place in a large saucepan with 1.25 litres (44 fl oz/5 cups) fresh water. Bring to the boil over high heat. Reduce to a simmer, skim off any foamy residue from the surface, then cook for about 35 minutes, or until the beans are tender and just starting to break up around the edges. There should be little water left at this stage.

Add the caster sugar and salt and stir until the sugar has dissolved. Cook over low heat, stirring regularly, for 1½ hours, or until the beans are very, very soft and semi-crushed, and the surrounding liquid is thick. I like my *anko* left a little chunky for a more textural mouthfeel, but if you prefer you can process the mixture with a hand-held stick blender for a smoother result. Remove from the heat.

To make the *yokan*, soak the *kanten* in a bowl of cold water for 1 hour. Squeeze to remove any excess water, then break into small pieces.

Put the *kanten* in a saucepan with 375 ml (13 fl oz/ 1½ cups) cold water and heat until it dissolves. Add the sugar and stir until dissolved.

Strain the mixture through a fine sieve into a clean saucepan. Add 2 cups of the *anko* (refrigerate or freeze the rest). Stir over medium–low heat for about 20 minutes, or until the mixture thickens slightly. Remove from the heat.

Rinse a 24 x 16 cm (9½ x 6¼ inch) mould (such as a rectangular cake tin) with cold water so it is a little damp. Pour the *yokan* mixture into the mould and allow to cool to room temperature. Cover and refrigerate until ready to serve.

To serve, cut into small rectangles and enjoy with green tea.

Variation: I have included below a *yoshoku* version of rum, raisin and walnut, but feel free to experiment with coffee, vanilla, dried apricots, *umeshu* (Japanese plum wine) and ginger. *Mizu yokan* (water *yokan*) is a less dense, more wobbly-textured *yokan* and is eaten chilled in summer.

To make a rum, raisin and walnut version, soak 1 tablespoon raisins in 2 tablespoons rum for 2 hours. Chop the raisins finely and add, along with the rum and 1½ tablespoons chopped toasted walnuts, to the *yokan* mixture just before pouring into the mould.

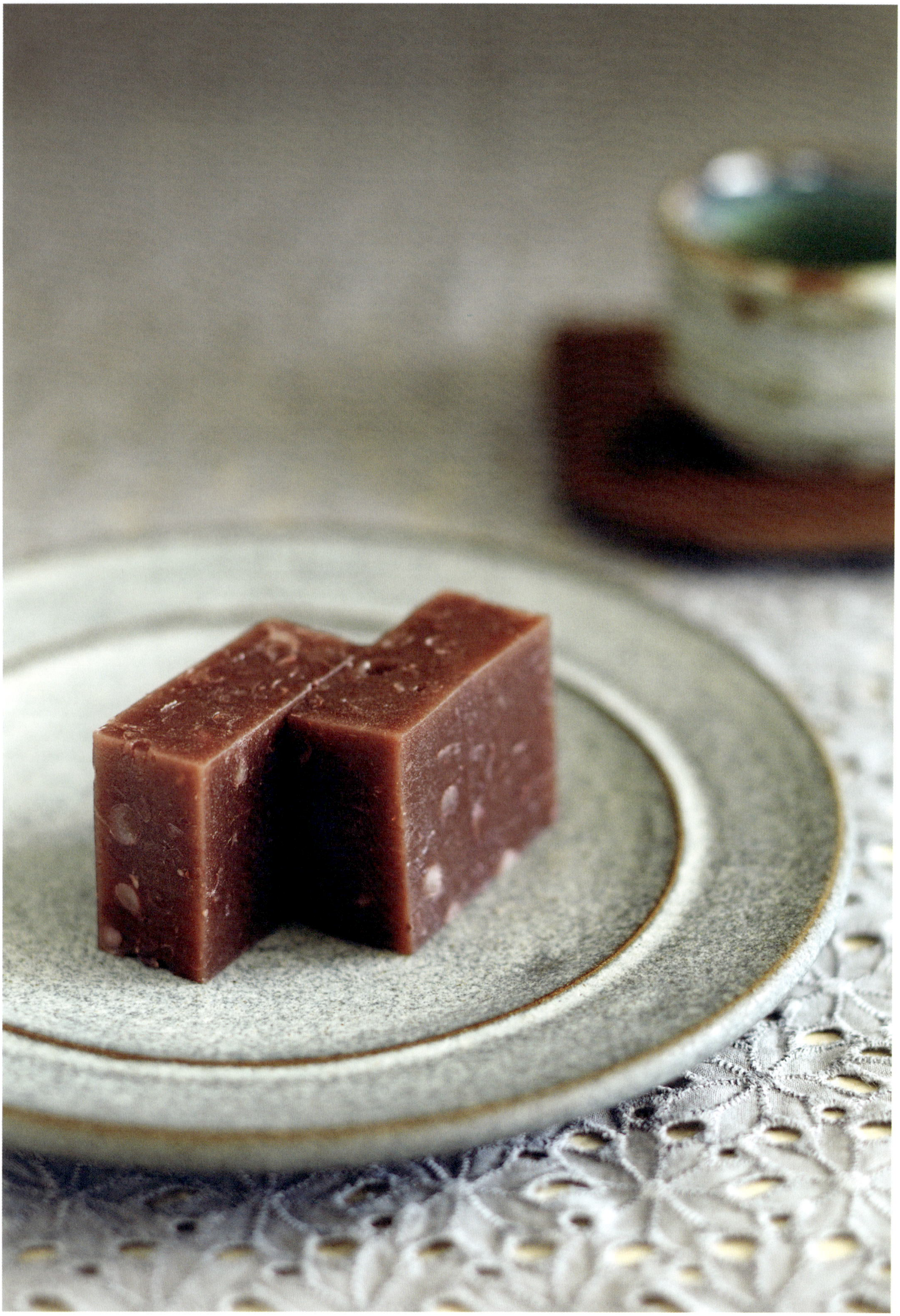

Nishiki-koji, or Kyoto's *daidokoro* (kitchen) as the locals call it, is an elbow-to-elbow landing strip of a food market. But oh the joy it contains within! A good Japanese market is a veritable sensory overload for the food-obsessed: the aroma of roasting green tea reminds me of fresh grass cuttings on a humid Sydney morning; the strangely addictive fishy scent of *oden* (hotpot of assorted ingredients in complex dashi), which used to trigger my gag reflex, is now as comforting as a lingering hug; sizzling yakitori's sweet, smoky perfume is distractingly alluring; the earthy funk from vats of autumnally shaded miso is bizarrely, yet undeniably, sexy; and the nasal-hair-spritzing pickle fermentations of *tsukemono* curiously reassuring.

New-season rice is graded like precious gems and beef, marbled to within an inch of its glorious life, taunts you like that lover you know is both so very good and so very bad for you. Actually, my 'wagyu friends' tell me it is only the external fat that is a no-no; the marbling is full of nutrients — enough information to justify my intake.

Pretty pink, lilac and mint-toned *wagashi* (tea ceremony sweets) cavort with handsomely lacquered *senbei* (rice crackers). Flaxen, just-from-the-fryer tempura and croquettes crackle and shine as they come up for air. Shimmering handmade tofu and milky wet layers of *yuba* (soy milk skin) offer a sensuous awakening. Inviting mountains of fish paste forms, such as *chikuwa*, *hanpen* and *satsuma-age*, nudge up against their vegetarian competition — multicoloured *nama fu* (fresh wheat gluten) and *mochi* (glutinous rice cakes).

Live sea creatures perform in tanks, begging to be taken home like puppies at the pound, while shavings of *katsuobushi* (shaved dried, smoked bonito) dance in the slightest breeze. Shoots, roots, leaves and fungi, gigantic red Kyoto carrots, overgrown strawberries and grapes on steroids vie for attention alongside their Lilliputian counterparts: raisin-sized potatoes (actually the 'seeds' of *nagaimo*, a mountain yam), perfect micro tomatoes, and *edamame* (fresh soy beans), still bristling on the vine.

I always feel like I've done a round in a boxing ring at Nishiki, but it's always worth it. Tokyo's Tsukiji (fish market) is, however, a far more dangerous escapade — and that's just crossing the car park, where there is a very high chance of being run over by fishermen on high-speed forklifts. If you do make it into Tsukiji's inner sanctum, you will be rewarded with a seriously mind-boggling selection of both live and barely dead marine life, and a mild drenching of blood, guts and melted ice. But rest assured the gleaming market is scented only with saltwater and sweet, fresh fillets. Kyoto's vast wholesale market further west is far less stressful to navigate, but you still need your wits about you, and the sensibility to ignore the stares, as the market folk rarely witness *gaijin* in their 'hood.

I took leave of Nishiki, forgoing baby octopus lollipops in favour of freshly cooked, glistening *satsuma-age* (fish paste cakes; page 152). I also snaffled a variety of pickles. After exiting the market's eastern jaws, I spent considerable time pondering exactly what I'd do with a *keitai* (mobile phone) strap, decorated with a miniature Japanese food icon — before outlaying a small fortune on several handfuls of the bizarre things, which I decided would be best used as Christmas tree decorations. I was later told by a friend who studies tea ceremony — upon seeing his gift to me of a cherrywood tea scoop being used as a chopstick rest — that finding new uses for things is part of the teachings of *chado* ('the way of tea'), which allowed me to feel adamantly Zen about my frivolous purchase.

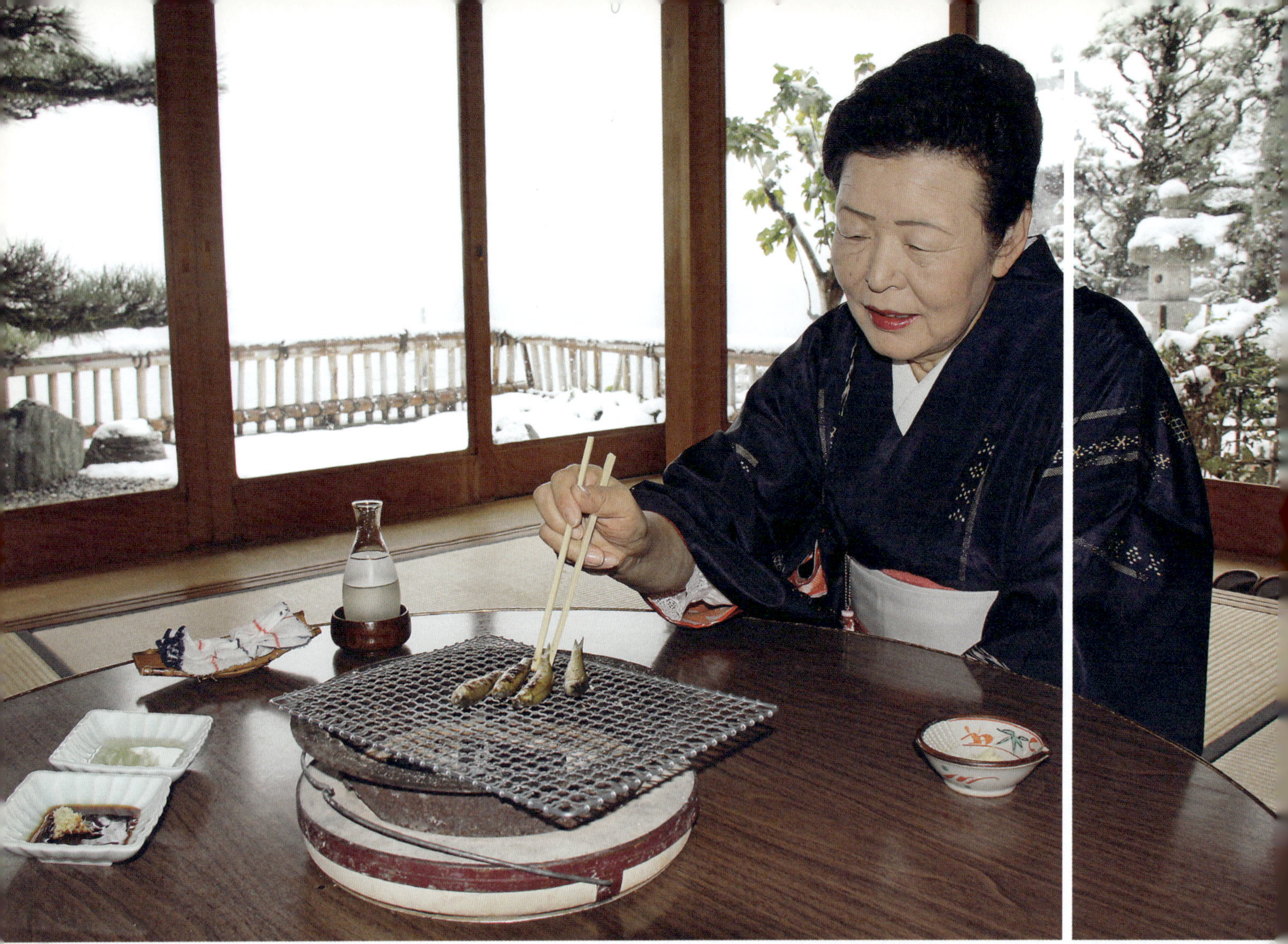

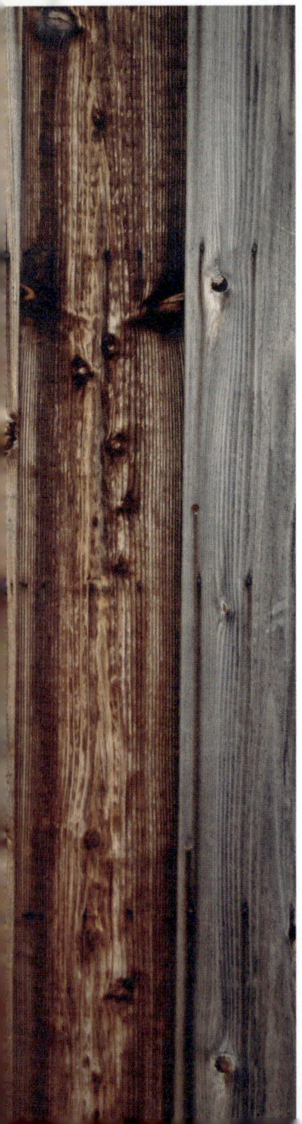

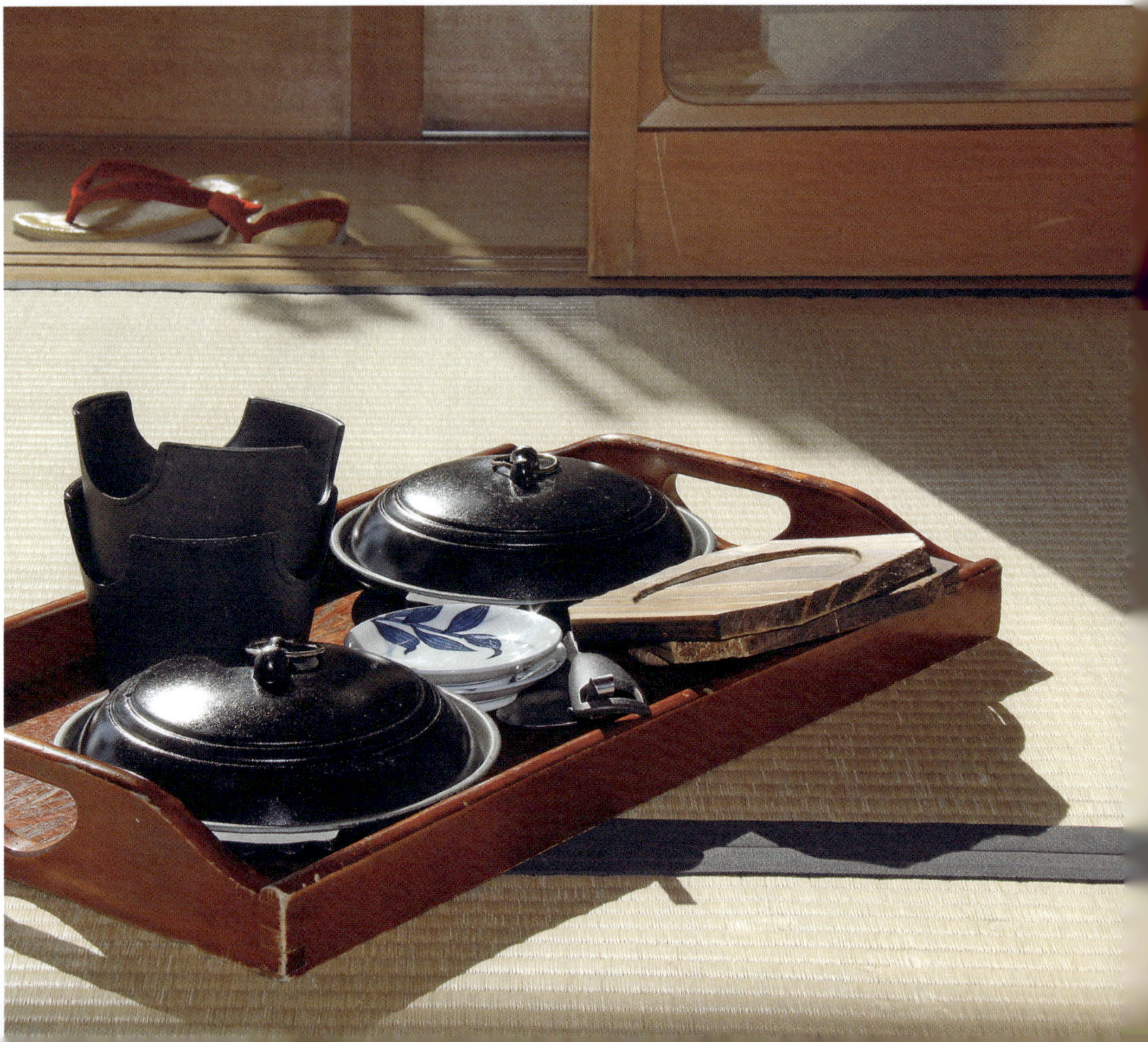

The Japanese possess an ongoing spirit of recognition and appreciation for things that – though seemingly small – are often so momentous.

satsuma-age

fish paste cakes
MAKES 12 PATTIES

Named after the town of Satsuma in southern Japan, *satsuma-age* traditionally contain bamboo shoots and carrot, but also common is the addition of *gobo* (burdock), lotus or *edamame* (fresh soy beans). Sweet potato, rehydrated shiitake mushrooms, octopus or prawns (shrimp), and flavourings such as ginger, shiso, *aonori* (seaweed), yuzu (Japanese citrus), chilli, curry and garlic can also be added for variation. I have even sampled bacon and buttered-potato flavours!

As with *chikuwa* and *kamaboko*, *satsuma-age* are a variation on the *surimi* (fish paste — think imitation crab!) theme. I keep some *satsuma-age* in the freezer for adding to *nabe* hotpots, soups or even stir-fries.

400 g (14 oz) fish fillets, preferably from two different fish — either both white fish, or one white and one oily (such as cod, whiting, snapper, haddock, hake, sardines, mackerel), depending on your taste
4½ tablespoons *katakuriko* or potato starch
2 tablespoons sake
1 tablespoon caster (superfine) sugar
1 egg white
2 teaspoons usukuchi shoyu (light Japanese soy)
½ carrot, finely grated
50 g (1¾ oz/⅓ cup) roughly grated bamboo shoots
1 spring onion (scallion), very finely chopped
vegetable oil, for deep-frying
1 teaspoon fine sea salt
shoyu or lemon wedges, to serve (optional)
grated wasabi, fresh ginger or daikon, to serve (optional)
karashi (Japanese mustard) or hot English mustard, to serve (optional)

Working quickly, chop the fish and blend until smooth in a food processor. Add the starch, sake, sugar, egg white and shoyu and blend until just combined.

Remove to a chilled bowl and stir in the carrot, bamboo shoots and spring onion until well combined. Cover and refrigerate for 30 minutes, or up to 2 hours.

When ready to cook, one-third fill a deep-fryer or large saucepan with oil and heat to 170°C (325°F), or until a cube of bread dropped into the oil browns in 20 seconds.

Add the salt to the fish mixture, combining well. Using lightly oiled hands, shape 2½ tablespoons of the mixture at a time into oblong shapes, measuring about 9 x 7 cm (3½ x 2¾ inches), and 1 cm (½ inch) thick. (Traditionally you would smear a thickness of 1 cm/½ inch over the back of a bamboo rice paddle and scrape it off into the hot oil, so you can also try this method if you like.)

Deep-fry the fish cakes in batches for 3½–4 minutes, or until puffed, deep golden and cooked right through — you will only fit a few in the fryer at a time.

Drain on kitchen paper and serve immediately with shoyu, if desired, and your choice of other condiments for mixing with the shoyu.

Alternatively you can cool the fish cakes, then refrigerate or freeze them to use in *nabe* (hotpots), soups or however you wish. The fish cakes will deflate on cooling.

mutsuki / ichigatsu – january / the 1st month

tsukemono

Apart from adding colour, texture and aroma to a meal, pickles have a cleansing effect on the palate. These crunchy condiments, particularly daikon, are believed to aid digestion. One or more vegetable pickles — such as cucumber, eggplant (aubergine), daikon, ginger, plum, garlic, cabbage, bamboo root, lotus root, burdock or turnip — are offered at every Japanese meal, often at the end of a *kaiseki* or formal meal. Being salty, pickles are also eaten as a snack with beer — a refreshing alternative to peanuts.

Specialist pickle shops can be found on practically any street corner in Kyoto, and might offer less common items such as eggs or even fish. You'd be hard-pressed to find even a tiny village in Japan without a local pickle vendor. Many Japanese have access to a small garden plot, even if they are not growing produce for sale, and as such are keen preservers — a habit formed in leaner times.

Often flavoured with *umami*-laden ingredients such as kombu (dried kelp) and shiitake mushrooms — and sometimes *katsuobushi* (shaved dried, smoked bonito) and/or aromatics such as dried citrus peel or shiso leaves — the highest-grade pickles are often packaged as beautifully as an expensive silk scarf, and taken as gifts when visiting friends, family or colleagues. Travellers regard regional pickles as a wonderful prize to take home from any trip.

There are six basic pickling agents: salt (*shio*), rice bran (*nuka*), miso, vinegar (*su* or *zu*), rice mould/culture (*koji*) and sake lees (*sake kasu*).

Nuka zuke and *miso zuke*, the two most popular forms of pickles, usually take months or even years to mature. However, their flavours are complex and mellow and they last a very long time if stored properly.

Sokusekizuke (quick pickles) and *ichiyazuke* (overnight pickles) can be as simple as packing vegetables in salt (*shiozuke*) and allowing the natural liquid in the vegetables to leech out, making its own pickling brine, or steeping grated or finely sliced vegetables in a vinegar solution for a few hours or overnight (*namasu*), as in the *kohaku namasu* recipe on page 104.

In the case of *miso zuke*, a quick and rather satisfying version can be achieved by submerging an ingredient in miso for a few days only. However, these fresh pickles do not last more than a few days after they have 'ripened'.

Here are two quick recipes to get you started, but I do encourage you to do some research and experimenting if you have the option of serious pickling production and storage, as the flavours cannot be replicated in a quick pickle.

takuan

pickled daikon
MAKES ABOUT 2½ CUPS

Takuan is the best-known Japanese pickle to foreigners, commonly found as yellow half-moon slices in the refrigerated section of Asian grocery stores. Traditionally fermented in *nuka* (rice bran), it takes months and sometimes years to achieve the final outcome — eventually turning the pickle from white to a yellowish-brown, with a delicious mellow flavour. It also requires the right climate, some tending and a large well-ventilated space (such as a garage), as the results are rather odorous for weeks on end — particularly in the warmer months. Unless your neighbours are truly sympathetic to your pickle-making plight, true *takuan* is not really a viable option for preparing at home.

Many commercial varieties are aged for shorter times and tinted with yellow food colouring. As this is not desirable in my world I have included a quick and easy daikon pickle recipe. It only needs to rest for a few days, but it will last for a few weeks if stored properly: namely sealed in the fridge, opened only occasionally, and with very clean utensils used to remove the pickle — never double-dip or return unused pickles to the jar.

1 whole daikon, about 750 g (1 lb 10 oz); see Note
2 strips of kombu (dried kelp), each about 1 x 4 cm (½ x 1½ inches)
2 dried red chillies, or 2 thick slices of fresh ginger (optional)
3½ tablespoons fine sea salt
75 g (2½ oz/½ cup) *kurosato* (Japanese black sugar) or dark brown sugar
125 ml (4 fl oz/½ cup) rice vinegar

Peel the daikon and cut into rounds 5 mm (¼ inch) thick. Cut each round in half to form two half-moons. (Alternatively, you can use a mandoline to slice the daikon into very thin rounds — these pickles can be used to wrap other ingredients to be enjoyed as *zensai*, a type of hors d'oeuvre that are great for entertaining.)

Place the kombu and chillies or ginger in a 1.5 litre (52 fl oz/6 cup) pickle bin, or divide them between two 750 ml (26 fl oz/3 cup) jars with lids. Using very clean hands, tightly pack the daikon into the containers. If using the pickle bin, screw the press as tightly as you can.

Put the salt, sugar, vinegar and 375 ml (13 fl oz/ 1½ cups) water in a saucepan and stir over high heat until the sugar has dissolved. Allow the liquid to just start to simmer, then remove from the heat and immediately pour it into the jars, filling them right to the brim. Use a clean spoon to help press down the daikon pieces if they start to rise up.

Seal the jars and allow to cool. Refrigerate for 3 days, gently shaking the jars several times a day.

To serve, use very clean lacquerware chopsticks or a pickle fork to place a small amount of pickles in small individual bowls for each diner. Replace the lid on the pickles and return to the fridge. The pickles will last about 2–3 weeks unopened, and about 1 week once opened.

Note: If your daikon has fresh green leaves attached, don't throw them away. You can sauté them in sesame oil, then drizzle with shoyu and mirin, or use them in the *ohitashi* recipe on page 79.

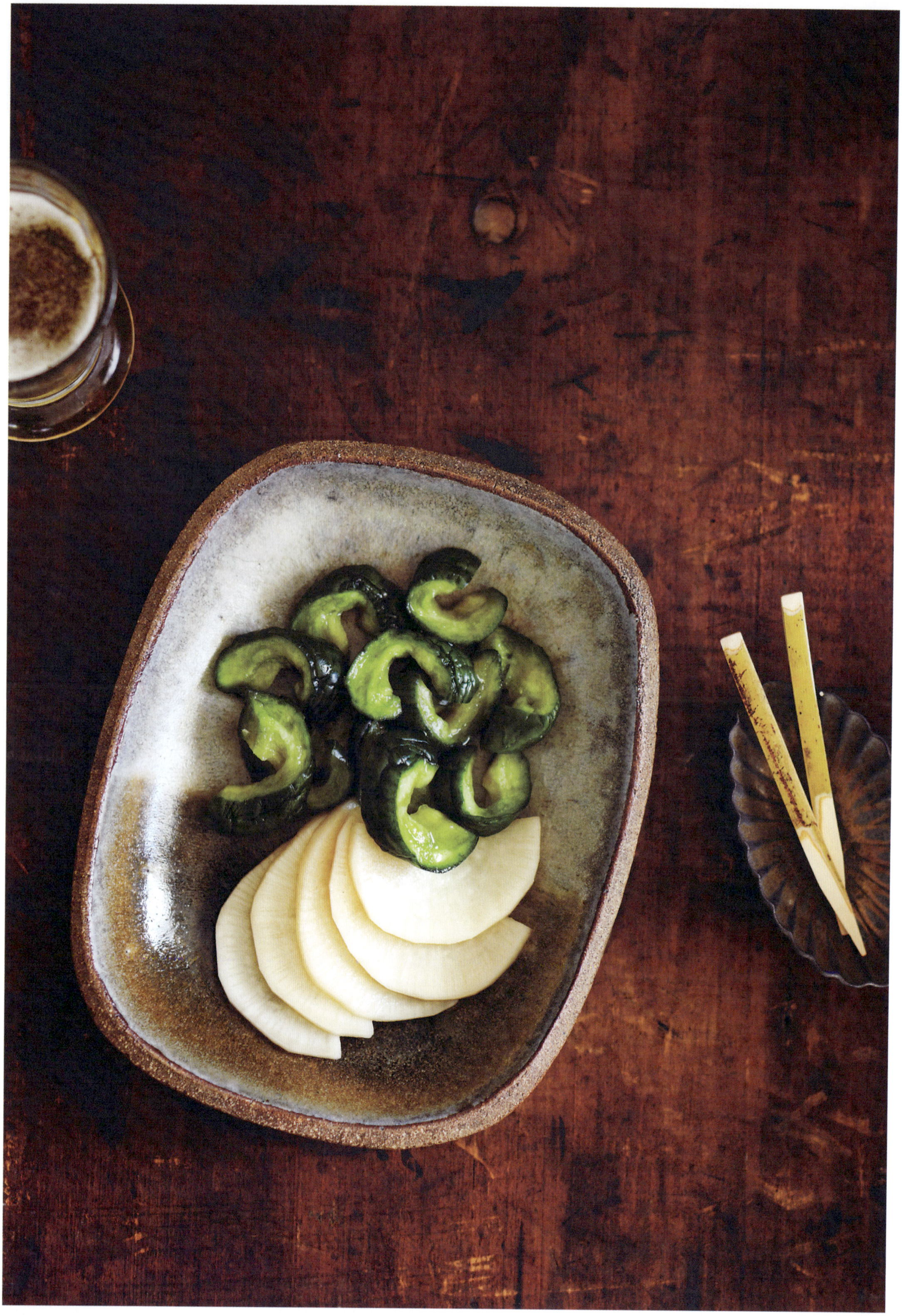

Cutting food into half-moons is popular in Japan, for aesthetic as well as practical reasons. It is mainly used for irregular-shaped vegetables that need to be cooked in simmered dishes. Japanese daikon, for example, has a very wide and a very thin end, so when the wide end is cut into half-moons, it cooks in the same time as full-moons cut from the daikon's thin end. This way no bits are wasted and there is a uniform texture. Try this with carrots too.

kyuuri miso zuke

cucumber pickled in miso

MAKES ABOUT 1½ CUPS

250 g (9 oz) *kyuuri* (Japanese cucumbers) or Lebanese (short) cucumbers
20 g (¾ oz) coarse sea salt
450 g (1 lb/1½ cups) miso paste — I like to use a combination of saikyo (sweet white miso) and aka (red miso), but you can experiment with your own choice for a range of flavours
aromatics (optional; see Note)

Cut the cucumbers in half lengthways. If using Lebanese cucumbers, use a small teaspoon or melon baller to scoop out the seeds. Cut the cucumbers on a slight angle into slices 1 cm (½ inch) thick, discarding the very ends.

Sprinkle half the salt in a wide, 1 litre (35 fl oz/4 cup) ceramic or glass container. Top with the cucumber slices, then sprinkle with the remaining salt.

Cut a piece of very thick cardboard just slightly smaller than the container rim, so it fits neatly inside. Place the cardboard in a suitably sized plastic zip-lock bag, squeeze out the air and seal, then sit it on top of the cucumbers.

You now need to press the mixture down with 3 kg (6 lb 12 oz) of weight, such as a similar-shaped container filled with about 3 litres (105 fl oz/12 cups) water. You could also use a few large tins of food or even a few house bricks — as long as they are very clean and sealed in a clean plastic bag so they don't taint or react with the salt.

Allow the cucumbers to sit for 8–12 hours at room temperature (unless the weather is particularly warm, in which case move them to the fridge), to extract as much liquid from the cucumbers as possible.

Rinse the cucumbers very well, then drain well. Reserve the cardboard in the plastic bag, but give the bag a good rinse.

Squeeze out any excess water from the cucumbers by pressing the slices between layers of extremely clean tea towels (dish towels).

Spread half the miso over the base of a very clean, small, but wide ceramic or glass container. Scatter the cucumber slices over the top. Press them down to submerge them in the miso as much as possible. Spread the remaining miso over the top, to cover the cucumbers completely. Place the cardboard in the plastic bag on top and press down slightly. Leave it on top and cover the container tightly with a lid or layers of plastic wrap.

Refrigerate for 48 hours for the pickles to mature.

To serve, pick out the desired quantity of cucumbers using a clean pickle fork or a skewer and rinse well before eating. If you prefer a less salty pickle, you can soak the cucumbers for 15 minutes or longer, changing the water halfway.

The remaining pickles will last another few days in the miso. Once the pickles have been consumed, any remaining miso can be added to soups or stews.

Note: A little finely grated fresh ginger, dried or fresh yuzu zest, shiso powder, *katsuobushi* (shaved dried, smoked bonito) or other flavourings can be added to the miso for variety.

MISO ZUKE VARIATIONS

Celery: Rinse, dry and cut celery into short lengths. Submerge the celery in the miso — there's no need to salt it first. Seal and refrigerate for 48 hours. Rinse very well before serving.

Garlic: Boil peeled garlic cloves for 3 minutes and dry with a clean tea towel (dish towel). Halve the cloves lengthways and submerge them in a jar filled with aka (red) miso — each bulb of garlic needs about ½ cup miso. Smooth over and press a round of baking paper on top to stop them drying out, then seal and refrigerate for at least a week to mature. This pickle will last up to a month in the fridge; the flavour matures further with time. Take out what is needed with a skewer or pickle fork and rinse before serving. Normally, fresh garlic becomes toxic after a few days out of its skin, but the high quantity of salt in the red miso keeps it safe longer. The residual miso makes a delicious miso soup.

Tofu: Cut firm tofu into slices 1 cm (½ inch) thick and submerge in your choice of miso. Cover and refrigerate for 24–48 hours. For a saltier, more savoury flavour, choose aka (red) miso, shinshu or hatcho miso; for a sweeter, more mellow result, use white or saikyo (sweet white Kyoto-style) miso. You can also add your own choice of seasonings — finely grated fresh ginger, shiso, *shichimi togarashi* (seven-flavour spice mix), sesame oil, sake or mirin, to develop your own tofu 'cheese'. Before serving, scrape off the excess miso and carefully rinse the tofu — the texture will be more fragile and creamy. Enjoy with rice, in a salad, on a cracker or as a nibble with drinks. You can eat it cold, or grill (broil) or pan-fry it if you prefer it warm.

zenbu zen 160

It was a short and fascinating walk from the station through the streets of ancient Nara to find Sekigawa-san's humble abode. The internal walls of Sekigawa-san's home were overly fragile and the floorboards grunted and groaned. Like most traditional Japanese houses it was really cold — most people in these parts seem to either suffer the cold or get used to it, as heating is kept to a minimum.

The monk's wife, cute as a button and neatly bound in kimono, proudly afforded myself and five of my new-found friends (Myong Hee, Kikuko, Misako, Mayumi and Yukari) a grand palace-sized welcome as she knelt in the *genkan* (entrance) — bowing deep throughout the extended duration of our footwear removal.

Once the seven of us were settled on the tatami upstairs, our host prepared the tea ceremony that would mark the start of our lesson in *shojin ryori* (Buddhist vegetarian cuisine — or more literally, 'dedicated person's food') and our formal *kaiseki* meal. In keeping with the Buddhist belief that no harm may come to animals, Zen Buddhists are strictly vegetarian. That is not to say that Buddhists never eat meat — it is sometimes a necessity in terrain that is hostile to vegetation, such as in the mountaintops of Nepal. I'm told Buddha himself also ate meat when in India, as he could not refuse anything on offer after seeing so many locals begging for food. Even today, as a rule, Buddhist monks are not permitted to decline an offer of food.

The tea ceremony was originally a monastic discipline, in keeping with the fundamental Zen philosophy of *wa-kei-sei-jaku*, or Harmony-Respect-Purity-Tranquility. It was developed, with the help of tea master Sen Rikyu, into an art form, and has consequently become an important custom through which all patriotic Japanese are able to demonstrate their understanding of the overall cultural 'code'.

Before imbibing matcha (a brew made from powdered green tea), one must first always consume a traditional Japanese sweet — often made with beans and flavoured with sugar. A tumble of pleasantly chewy little spheres made from rice powder, coated in *kinako* (roasted soy bean powder) and sugar, were not as sweet as some of the bean-based *wagashi* (tea ceremony sweets) I have consumed at previous tea ceremonies, and were deliciously moreish.

This important step, on the physical level, helps mellow any bitterness in the tea that follows, but on a spiritual level it enables one to taste both the sweet and bitter of life … 'as without one, how can you truly recognise the other?'

Looking official in his blue robes, Sekigawa-san slowly lowered himself into a kneeling position directly opposite me. With a slender bamboo tea scoop he transferred two dabs of matcha (green tea powder) into a ceramic tea bowl, then poured boiled and slightly cooled water onto it from a kettle that had been bubbling away on a kerosene heater beside him. He agitated the mixture with a fine bamboo whisk until the opaque green liquid was pale, thick and foamy on the surface — like crema on a good espresso. He rose, walked quietly to me and carefully placed the bowl, with the 'face' (the most decorative side) turned towards me, onto the table. As is customary, I admired the bowl, then placed it on the palm of my left hand, before rotating it three small clockwise turns so that the 'face' was respectfully facing away from me while I consumed its contents.

Although it was somewhat daunting to have all eyes on me, I excused myself, then drank in three large indoctrinated slurps, ensuring the tea was emptied on the last long sip. The vessel is communal, so the required etiquette is to then gracefully wipe once, with your thumb, where your lips have caressed the bowl. I returned the bowl counter-clockwise three times to its original position, before gently replacing it for collection — accompanied by a slight bow of the head. Boiled water was then poured over the whisk into the bowl and cleansed for the next guest.

Even without the ceremony, I have always enjoyed the comfort of matcha, but there is something exquisite about the formal observance. Watching the others deep in admiration of their tea bowl, heads solemnly bowing towards it before taking their first appreciative sip, was like taking part in a secret initiation ceremony — a rite of passage.

The ceremony over, our host gave a long, and what I can only presume was informative, talk on *shojin ryori*. Within the small, hushed room it would have been difficult for anyone to have translated for me, even at a whisper, but I did grasp the crucial bit: when he invited us to lift the paper coverings off our place settings to reveal our food trays.

In front of us were individual dishes containing three of the basic meal elements and cooking styles: *nimono* (a simmered food) of *kyo-yasai* (Kyoto vegetables); *aemono* (dressed food), in this case *shira-ae* (page 164); and *tsukemono* (pickles), of which you must retain at least one piece for cleaning your bowl at the end of the meal. The combination of several cookery methods is required for a balance of textures, flavours and colours, and it is common to serve three, five and sometimes seven dishes with rice.

Sake was poured while we ate, and I was taught that the cup should be placed on your left hand with your right underneath, sliding out and upwards in a slightly cupped position to say 'when' — so subtle and refined.

Rice was brought to the table and placed on our left, while shiitake dashi-based miso (page 29), laden with chunks of *konnyaku* (jelly from the devil's tongue root) and lots of vegetable peelings (as nothing is wasted), was placed on our right, providing the fourth *shirumono/suimono* (soup) component of the meal. A fifth component, *agemono* (fried food), came in the form of *kakiage* (shredded vegetables in tempura batter; page 165), which was placed in front of us on small plates lined with patterned rice paper. The leftover kombu from the dashi was also used in the *kakiage* in very fine slithers — adding an extra dimension of flavour and texture.

Zen Buddhist monks in training start the day simply with tea and rice. Lunch provides their one full meal, which needs to sustain them until dinner — always a light soup consisting of leftovers from lunch. *Kaiseki* loosely translates as 'pocket or bosom stone' — it was believed the monks would carry around warmed stones in their kimono over their stomachs to stave off hunger between the main meals.

The *kaiseki* set out before us was a well-considered hearty offering containing a very fine balance of cooking methods, flavours and textures. It looked very appealing and we were more than ready to tuck in. Before the meal could commence, we each removed seven grains of rice from our bowl using our *ohashi* (chopsticks) and placed them on our left palms, before transferring them to one side of our pickle dish — an offering in honour of those who have little or no food.

Officially one should eat in an anti-clockwise direction — you can start with whatever dish you choose, but you must finish everything in that bowl before moving on to the next. It is also courteous to eat everything presented to you.

Symbolically, tea was poured into our rice bowls to mark the end of the meal. We then wiped around the sides of the dish with our reserved pickle, which was trapped between the tips of two chopsticks, before scraping any remnants into the next, anti-clockwise, dish. This continued until we made it back to our rice bowl, where we cleansed it as best we could until all the sediment was sitting in the tea. We then drank the liquid and lastly ate the pickle slice. Each of our reserved seven grains of rice were then tipped onto a central plate and fed to birds or fish in the local koi pond.

Today, the multi-dish *kaiseki*-style meals are an extension of the formal tea ceremony — they almost always start and end with tea. Serving rice, pickles and tea also marks the end of most meals in Japan.

*

shira-ae

'white' tofu dressing
MAKES ABOUT 250 ML (9 FL OZ/1 CUP)

This creamy, non-dairy sesame dressing is particularly good tossed through lightly blanched greens, but also pairs well with a number of other vegetables after they have been simmered until tender in dashi — such as pumpkin (winter squash), carrot, turnip, shiitake mushrooms or burdock root. It is also great with fried eggplant (aubergine).

275–300 g (9¾–10½ oz) block of silken tofu
2 tablespoons toasted sesame seeds
1 tablespoon walnuts, toasted and chopped, plus extra to garnish (optional)
1 tablespoon caster (superfine) sugar
1½ teaspoons shoyu
1½ teaspoons mirin

Wrap a double thickness of clean, dry cotton tea towel (dish towel) or several layers of kitchen paper around the tofu block and place it on a small baking tray.

Place another similar-sized tray on top, then weigh it down with a container filled with water — or a few tins of tomatoes! Allow to sit for 1 hour, or until the towel is soaking wet and the tofu is about half its original size. You may need to replace the tea towel or kitchen paper during this time.

Unwrap the tofu — the block should be about one-third the size you started with, as the water will have been soaked up by the towels.

Finely grind the sesame seeds and walnuts using a *suribachi* (ridged Japanese mortar and wooden pestle). Crumble in the tofu and add the sugar, shoyu and mirin. Grind until you have a smooth, creamy dressing.

Toss with your favourite cooked vegetable and sprinkle with extra chopped toasted walnuts if desired.

Note: Drain your cooked vegetables well before dressing. If using leafy greens, make sure you squeeze out any excess liquid after they have been blanched, then chop into short lengths.

kakiage

vegetable fritters
MAKES ABOUT 12 LARGE FRITTERS

30 g (1 oz/1 cup) leafy carrot tops (greens), picked from baby (Dutch) carrots
4 baby (Dutch) carrots
75 g (2½ oz) burdock root, preferably fresh
½ leek, white part only (optional; see page 167)
half the kombu reserved from making kombu dashi (see page 29)
vegetable or sesame oil, for deep-frying
good-quality, fine-textured sea salt, to serve (see Notes)
lemon wedges, to serve (optional)

BATTER
50 g (1¾ oz/⅓ cup) plain (all-purpose) flour
55 g (2 oz/⅓ cup) *katakuriko* or potato starch
¼ teaspoon bicarbonate of soda (baking soda)
1 teaspoon sea salt
1 small egg yolk
125 ml (4 fl oz/½ cup) iced water

Rinse the carrot greens and set aside on kitchen paper or a clean tea towel (dish towel) to dry. Cut into 3 cm (1¼ inch) lengths. Cut the carrots into very fine julienne.

Peel and very finely julienne the burdock and place in a bowl of water with a little rice vinegar to prevent discolouration and to eliminate any bitterness.

Cut the leek, if using, and kombu into very fine julienne by hand. Combine all the vegetables in a bowl, mixing well.

One-third fill a deep-fryer or wok with oil and heat to 170°C (325°F), or until a cube of bread dropped into the oil browns in 20 seconds.

Meanwhile, make the batter. Sift the flour, starch, bicarbonate of soda and salt into a bowl and set aside.

Lightly mix the egg yolk and iced water in a bowl. Tip in the flour and mix with chopsticks just to combine. Add the vegetables and combine well with the batter, which should be slightly runny.

Carefully drop 1 tablespoon of the mixture into the oil at a time and use a wire-mesh strainer to quickly drag back the spreading edges of the batter to retain a circular shape. You will likely only fit 2–3 fritters in the oil at one time. Cook, turning halfway through, for about 5 minutes, or until crisp, golden and cooked through. Drain well on kitchen paper.

Ideally, serve immediately, or keep warm while you cook the remaining fritters. Serve with a tiny mound of good-quality salt

Notes: For added flavour you can mix some matcha (green tea powder), ground sansho, *yukari* (red shiso powder), curry powder or grated yuzu zest through your little mound of accompanying salt — or even some dried, salted *sakura* (cherry blossom) petals if you can find them.

If you prefer to serve your *kakiage* with the popular tempura-style dipping sauce instead of salt, gently heat 250 ml (9 fl oz/1 cup) niban dashi (see page 29) with 60 ml (2 fl oz/¼ cup) shoyu and 2 tablespoons mirin. Just before serving, mix in a little finely grated daikon and fresh ginger.

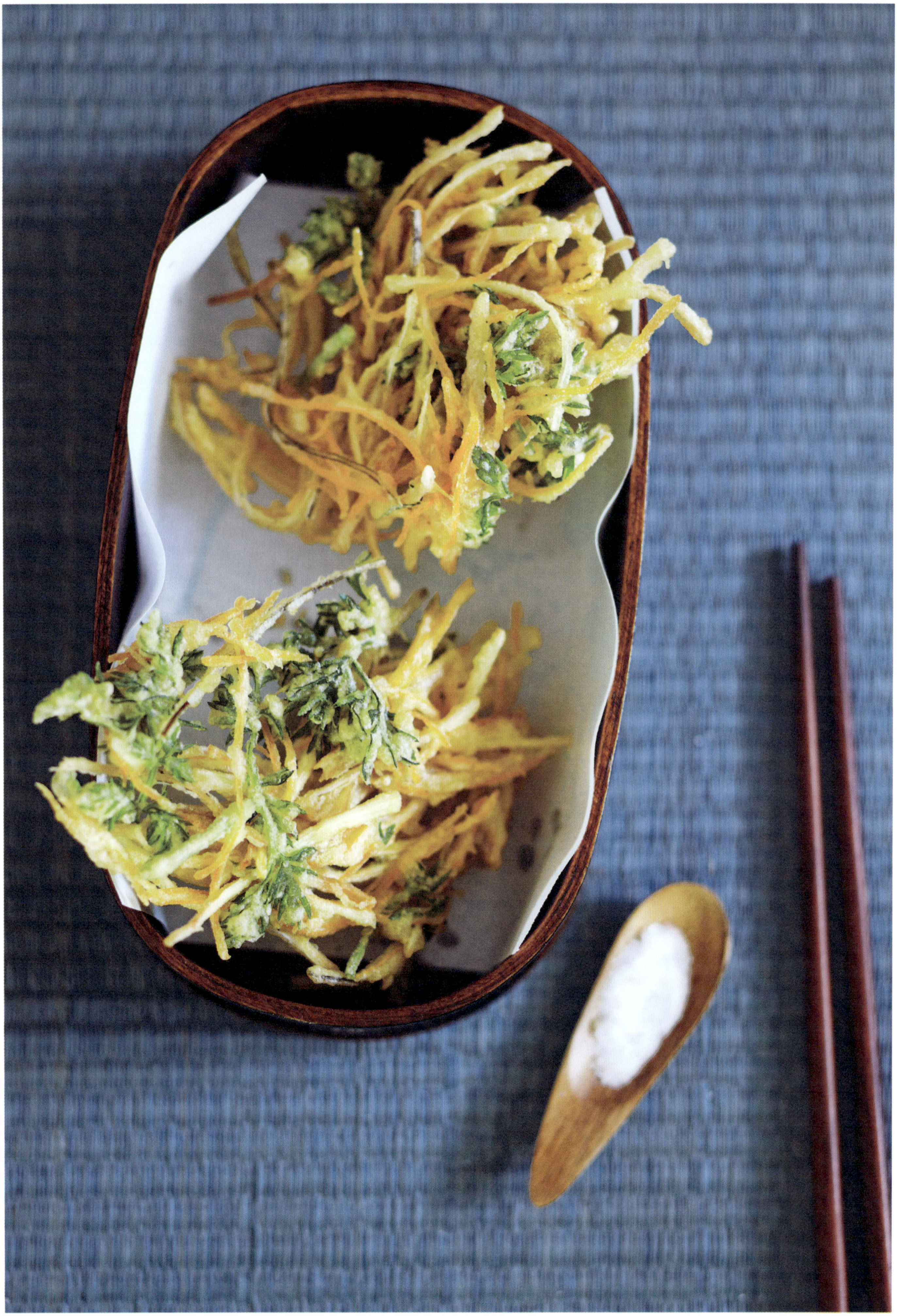

Leek is not normally permitted in *shojin ryori* cooking as, like onions and garlic, it is believed to be a stimulant. However I really love the flavour it adds, so I have made them optional. On that topic, you can also add a few finely chopped raw scallops, prawns (shrimp) or squid to the vegetable mixture for a non-vegetarian option – again, it won't be appropriate for *shojin ryori* cuisine.

After lunch, Sekigawa-san bashfully agreed to demonstrate his musical prowess. He then proceeded to whip the ceremonial cloth from his *koto* — a harp-like instrument, shaped like an electric keyboard — and promptly rammed talon-like picks onto his fingertips to warm us up for the main event. I adore the soft, twangy pluckings of the *koto*, but Sekigawa-san is master of the *biwa* — a type of guitar with a banjo-esque sound that you might have heard in the background of a classic recording for *kabuki* (classical Japanese dance-drama).

I'm not sure what led to it, but suddenly the girls were modelling his rope-like *obi* (sash), tying it in knots of some cultural significance and giggling like schoolgirls. By the corner altar, where our host had been praying when we arrived, stood a long thin wooden plank inscribed with *kanji* characters. Curious, someone asked after its purpose and he explained that in *zazen* training (a sitting form of Zen sect meditation that can last hours at a time) the monks tend to drift off. The 'stick' is used to give them a short, sharp smack between the shoulder blades and many trainees request it if in need of 'refreshment'.

Myong Hee suggested it might help my stiff neck and shoulders, but I was reluctant. When Myong Hee further provoked me with a casual 'Why not, it's an experience?' I gave it a shot, sensing a challenge. It was highly stimulating and painless and I instantly felt the energy flow more freely throughout my body as Sekigawa-san whacked me. I let out a long, loud spontaneous laugh before detecting what appeared to be a look of hurt on my aggressor's face: I hoped I hadn't offended him with an inappropriate response.

Suddenly recalling why I was there, Sekigawa-san pulled out his collection of food 'mooks' (magazine-style books, especially popular in Japan), including several by Mari Fujii, the *shojin ryori* expert I was hoping to meet in Kamakura.

*

I dressed for dinner, and for the first time since arriving in Japan, slipped into my heels as I left the apartment. I'd carried them with me so I was determined to give them at least one outing!

We entered through the gate of a nondescript building, along a short path and into a beautifully designed modern restaurant space. It was like lifting up a veil: it is rare to truly see what is before you in Kyoto until you start to peel back the layers, a notion that applies to most aspects of Japanese society.

Our modern *kaiseki* included, among other things, an eclectic and overly rich combination of *fugu shirako* (poisonous puffer fish sperm sac) croquettes, wagyu with *uni* (sea urchin) and mascarpone, abalone, *fugu* sashimi with fried chips of its skin, foie gras with truffles and — my nemesis — the raw guts of *namako* (sea slug), which tastes like I imagine pond scum might! But who am I to judge? I spent the remainder of the night and the next day purging my system of its toxic overload — but not before I had taken off my heels and placed them neatly on the shoe rack in the *genkan*.

*

169 **mutsuki / ichigatsu** – january / the 1st month

The protective layers I had built around myself were starting to crack; it felt as if I was standing on the edge of a precipice, ready to fall, yet fearful of letting go.

But, after five weeks in Kyoto, I was also feeling more grounded. Having had some time for reflection, I felt peaceful and more open and willing to accept and make changes for the better in my everyday life. My need to stop, on a daily basis, to notice the beauty in things became apparent. After nine months of hacking and wheezing, I finally stopped coughing. I was beginning to lose weight and felt my legs toning from the long daily walks investigating the endless fascinations of my new town.

Shiatsu therapist Bridget Scott met me outside Shisendo Temple and led me through a winding warren to a peaceful tatami room sheltered by a grove of slender bamboo. Sunlight, peeking through nature's green skyscrapers, tickled my nose as I lay swaddled in an indigo woollen blanket, my head resting on a nuggety, buckwheat-filled pillow. The room slowly filled with the soothing aroma of woody incense and I melted into a deep relaxation. An elderly neighbour practised her angelic *koto* and I was pinned down by the sudden desire to stay safe in that blissful nook for all eternity.

Bridget, a British expat and long-term Kyoto resident, studied shiatsu under her master for nine years before he would deem her qualified. This kind of extended learning is common in Kyoto: even after you have practised for decades, you never quite shake off your *sensei* (teacher). Bridget is brilliant at her craft and highly intuitive. I formed an immediate respect for her and, as such, was quietly alarmed when she said she found it difficult to get a clear reading from my meridians. Before I knew it, the hour was up and Bridget gently reported that my body showed signs I was holding on to some trauma. I briefly touched on recent events in my life, and with an empathetic sigh she assured me there was no place like Japan for 'facing your stuff'. She said being outside your usual comfort zone with little support, huge cultural differences, and limited language skills can provide the perfect environment in which to get in touch with yourself again. Overcome with emotion, I poured my heart out to this compassionate woman.

It transpired that the multi-talented Bridget was also a dancer, skilled in both traditional *nihon buyoh* (Japanese classical dance) and the avant-garde *butoh* — a seemingly schizophrenic combination. Bridget is a constant source of inspiration to me: one of those honest, down-to-earth characters full of joy, effortlessly loved by all who meet her and a considerate friend. As is common for foreigners in Kyoto, she also teaches English at a local university — the same university my young friend Emilee attends. Emilee's mum Amanda knows Kathy — a friend of both Bridget and her close friend Mark. And, coincidentally, the three of them are good mates with Michiko, whom I ran into (at Mark's place!) after 17 years and who has since put me back in touch with her sister, who I'd met in Tokyo when I was 20. There it was again, in all its glory — the continuing cycle of *go-en*.

In Kyoto, there are far fewer than 'six degrees of separation' among the locals. Both the expat and Japanese communities will tell you it is impossible not to run into someone you know because Kyoto is a 'small town'. That might be the case when comparing it with the 13 million residents of Tokyo city, but with a prefecture population of about 2.7 million living in very close proximity (about 1.5 million within the compact city area itself) it certainly isn't small by international standards. Yet Kyoto somehow manages to retain a charming country-town-like atmosphere. Still, having people you have merely walked past once in a restaurant stop you in the street or at a festival for a chat is, indeed, a little surreal.

*

After a late-night introduction to single-malt scotch by Sydney friends passing through Kyoto, I woke a little under the weather for my dear friend Lindy's arrival.

I was excited to have a friend from home staying and, after a long orientation march around 'my' town, we retreated into the architecturally stunning Kyoto Station building, where we settled on a *kushiyaki* restaurant (specialising in skewer-grilled food), with a bird's eye view of the nightscape. We wolfed down a variety of morsels on sticks from the woodfired grill, the highlight being *butabara kushiyaki* (succulent pork belly skewers; page 173), simply salted and grilled to perfection.

*

zenbu zen 172

butabara kushiyaki

grilled pork belly skewers
MAKES 12 SKEWERS

This recipe relies on two elements. The first is good-quality pork, which is very easy to find in Japan — it simply melts in the mouth and has the kind of flavour that has you absent-mindedly licking your lips in remembrance of that first juicy bite. Do your best to source flavoursome, untainted meat. The second is your heat source — the dish is particularly good cooked on a chargrill as long as the heat isn't too high, as that little bit of smokiness adds to the overall flavour. For home use I have given instructions for cooking it under a hot grill (broiler), as you would in a Japanese kitchen. However, they mainly use gas grills, so if you have an electric grill try cooking it on a barbecue instead.

The accompanying *bainiku*, a purée made from umeboshi (Japanese pickled plums) is optional.

350 g (12 oz) piece of boneless pork belly
5 pencil-thin leeks or thick spring onions (scallions), white part only
sesame oil, for brushing
sea salt, for sprinkling
lemon wedges, to serve

BAINIKU (PICKLED PLUM PURÉE) — OPTIONAL
4 plump umeboshi (Japanese pickled plums), soaked in water for 20 minutes to extract a little salt (see Note)
½ teaspoon honey, or to taste
1 shiso leaf, finely shredded, or some finely shredded basil or mint optional)

Soak 12 short bamboo skewers in water for 2 hours. Place the pork in the freezer for the same amount of time, which will make it a little easier to slice.

To make the *bainiku*, remove the stone from the soaked plums and discard. Grind the flesh in a small *suribachi* (ribbed Japanese mortar and wooden pestle) until smooth — if you don't have a *suribachi*, chop and crush the plums with the flat side of a heavy knife until a paste forms. Add the honey and shiso, if using. The paste should still be quite tart, but feel free to add a little more honey if desired. Set aside.

Using a very sharp knife, cut the skin from the pork belly and discard, leaving most of the fat on the meat. Cut the meat into slices 7 mm (³⁄₈ inch) thick, then cut each slice into 2.5 x 2.5 cm (1 x 1 inch) squares.

Cut the leeks into 2.5 cm (1 inch) lengths — you will need 24 pieces. Blanch in boiling water for 1 minute, then drain well and cool slightly.

Drain the bamboo skewers. Starting with a piece of pork, thread three pieces of pork and two leek pieces onto each skewer, alternating the pork and leek.

Preheat the grill (broiler) to very high. Very lightly brush the pork with a little sesame oil and season with salt. Grill (broil) the skewers for 2–2½ minutes on each side, or until the pork is cooked through and lightly golden.

Serve immediately with lemon wedges, a Japanese beer and the plum purée, if desired.

Note: Umeboshi are easily obtainable at Japanese grocers and good supermarkets. They can be eaten just as they are, as a salty snack with drinks, or soaked in water to remove some of the salt, then added to other dishes for a subtle plum flavour.

We spent the next few days ticking off a few classic tourist spots, including gleaming Kinkakuji ('The Golden Pavilion') — escorted by volunteer guides (students eager to practise their English) — and Arashiyama for a caffeine-led sprint through the bamboo forest, and a fantastic 'modern' *ochazuke* lunch (rice with green tea and sometimes dashi; page 176). Lindy quickly became hooked on one of my own many addictions — real *warabi mochi* (page 182), a traditional sweet made from the starchy *warabi* root, covered in thick black sugar syrup and *kinako* (roasted soy bean powder). However, she scoffed so much of it that she can no longer hear the name mentioned without turning as green as the confection.

A sweet old man who works at the Shisendo Temple is always up for a scrambled battle of linguistics, and during our visit he shyly presented us each with a five-yen coin. With the word for 'five' translating as *go* and the abbreviation for yen being *en*, the name of the coin becomes *go-en* — the same as the common Japanese term that loosely translates as 'natural connections'. The coin's lucky nickname — plus the fact it has a hole in the centre, making it a circle — means the coin is often given as a sign of 'fortunate connection', either with a red and white ribbon attached, or in a tiny envelope. It seemed the concept of *go-en*, of natural connections being made, was being thrust on me on an almost daily basis.

Having some time off from researching and writing gave me a chance to process the events of the past six weeks. Looking back made me realise just how fast the weeks had flown and how I wished I had more time. How magnificent it would be to have a whole year studying the seasons in Japan — but alas, I would have to reconvene with reality all too soon.

✻

At Nagoya Station, Lindy and I met up with our Sydney friend Shaun, a Japanese-trained sushi master en route to the *kura* (brewery) of boutique sake maker Kozaemon-san. In Mizunami, a small town in Gifu prefecture, we stopped off to tuck into the regional specialty: *miso-katsu* — with *katsu*, in this instance, being a shortened version of *tonkatsu* (page 42), smothered in a thick miso gravy — and a comforting bowl of *tonjiru* (hearty pork, vegetable and miso soup; page 181). Both dishes went down a treat that chilly day, and well and truly lined our stomachs for the afternoon's sake tasting.

✻

Bamboo ties in beautifully with the Buddhist ideal of nothing being wasted. The densely growing evergreen shoots to the sky, forming shade and cool in the heat and humidity of a Kyoto summer, and is used as nature's sacred barrier against evil around certain temples. In season, the fresh shoots are cooked and eaten, and the excess is preserved. The stems and pulpy cross-sections are used everywhere from house construction to sake vessels, tea whisks, baskets and food packaging.

ochazuke

rice with tea
SERVES 4

Most commonly served as a snack, often late at night due to its reported success to fend off a hangover the next day, *ochazuke* is a simple dish of rice with hot green tea and sometimes dashi or water poured over — much as you might irrigate a bowl of cereal with milk.

Furikake are dry seasonings that are sprinkled over the rice for added flavour, and might include nori flakes, toasted sesame seeds, dried shiso, *katsuobushi* (shaved dried, smoked bonito) or similar. Pickles, particularly umeboshi, are added for saltiness and texture.

Originally said to have been served to samurai as a light but sustaining meal before battle, *ochazuke* has evolved to become a more substantial light meal by being topped with anything from flakes of grilled (broiled) fish (salmon and salmon roe; a cousin to *oyakodon*, page 208), to an egg — a healthful breakfast alternative perhaps?

Other toppings include leftover simmered protein dishes such as chicken and bamboo shoots, or my personal favourite, *gyuuniku to gobo no nimono* (simmered beef and burdock root), which I have included here. For this version, I prefer to use dashi rather than tea, but the choice is yours.

GYUUNIKU TO GOBO NO NIMONO (SIMMERED BEEF AND BURDOCK)

- 100 g (3½ oz/1 cup) finely shredded or shaved burdock root (see Notes)
- 2 teaspoons sesame oil
- 1 slender leek, white part only, cut into matchsticks
- 2 tablespoons sake
- 2 tablespoons mirin
- 80 ml (2½ fl oz/⅓ cup) usukuchi shoyu (light Japanese soy)
- 1½ tablespoons sugar
- 400 g (14 oz) very thinly sliced marbled beef, cut into matchsticks
- ½ teaspoon finely grated fresh ginger

OCHAZUKE

- 740 g (1 lb 10 oz/4 cups) hot cooked white or brown rice (see Notes)
- 1 spring onion (scallion), green part only, thinly sliced on the diagonal
- 1.5 litres (52 fl oz/6 cups) hot ichiban dashi (page 26) or niban dashi (page 29), or your choice of freshly made tea (see Notes)
- *furikake* (seasonings), to serve (optional; see recipe introduction)
- *tsukemono* (pickles), such as pickled ginger, umeboshi or pickled cucumber (page 158), to serve (optional)

First, make the *nimono*. Put the burdock in a small saucepan and cover with water. Bring to the boil and cook for 5 minutes, or until the burdock is just tender. Drain and set aside.

Heat the sesame oil in a frying pan over medium–high heat. Add the leek and sauté for 2 minutes, then add the burdock and sauté for 1 minute further.

Add the sake, mirin, shoyu, sugar and 1½ tablespoons water. Stir until the sugar has dissolved, bring to the boil, then reduce the heat to a simmer. Add the beef and ginger and move the beef around the pan for a few minutes until it changes colour. Simmer for 3–4 minutes, or until the beef is tender and most of the liquid has evaporated. Season with a little sea salt to taste.

Divide the hot rice among four deep bowls, then top with the *nimono*. Sprinkle with the spring onion.

Serve the dashi or tea in a beaker or individual teapot for each diner to pour over their rice. Serve with *furikake* for sprinkling over, and pickles for crunching on at intervals, if desired.

Notes: Burdock root is seasonal, but it is available frozen (julienned) from Asian food stores. It is ready to cook with as it is — just thaw it before cooking for this particular recipe. If using fresh burdock root, scrape the skin off it, then whittle off the burdock into fine shreds like you are sharpening a pencil with a knife, the old-fashioned way. Soak for 10 minutes in a bowl of cold water with a tablespoon or so of rice vinegar to remove any bitterness and to stop it browning. If using frozen burdock root, this step is not necessary.

Reheated leftover rice is commonly used for this dish, to avoid wastage.

If using tea instead of dashi, choose from *sencha* (green leaf tea), *genmaicha* (green tea with toasted brown rice), or either *mugicha* (roasted barley tea) or *sobacha* (roasted buckwheat tea) — both deliciously earthy, non-caffeinated alternatives.

Variation: Add some leftover vegetables such as *edamame* (fresh soy beans, removed from the pod), or chopped mizuna or other leafy greens.

Freshly grated wasabi can be served on the side to spice up a more simple *ochazuke*.

Legend has it that *yamabushi* (mountain monks) are closely connected to the divinities by proximity of their mountaintop homes, and are therefore afforded certain powers with which to return, at intervals, to lower ground to heal and bless the townfolk. Channelling Buddha's voice through their conch-shell horns and chanting holy incantations, they roam the streets in single file and may, for a small fee, bless your home or business dwelling.

mutsuki / ichigatsu – january / the 1st month

zenbu zen 180

tonjiru

hearty pork, vegetable and miso soup
SERVES 4–6 AS PART OF A MULTI-DISH MEAL

You can easily double this recipe to serve four as a main course soup.

300 g (10½ oz) pork belly on the bone, skin removed if desired
2 teaspoons sesame oil
1 leek, white part only, thinly sliced
150 g (5½ oz) daikon, cut into 1 x 2 cm (½ x ¾ inch) rectangular strips, about 5 mm (¼ inch) thick
150 g (5½ oz) burdock root, shaved or julienned (see Note)
1 small carrot, cut into 1 x 2 cm (½ x ¾ inch) rectangular strips, about 5 mm (¼ inch) thick
150 g (5½ oz) konnyaku, cut into 1 x 2 cm (½ x ¾ inch) rectangular strips, about 5 mm (¼ inch) thick (optional)
1.5 litres (52 fl oz/6 cups) niban dashi (page 29)
4 tablespoons miso — I use 3 tablespoons saikyo (sweet white) miso, and 1 tablespoon aka (red) miso
thinly sliced spring onions (scallions), to serve (optional)
shichimi togarashi (seven-flavour spice mix), to serve (optional)

Cut the meat from the bone, reserving the bone. Cut the meat into rectangular strips about the same size as the vegetables.

Heat the sesame oil in a large saucepan over medium–high heat. Stir-fry the pork bone and meat strips for a few minutes, or until they all change colour.

Add the vegetables, konnyaku and dashi and bring to the boil. Reduce the heat and simmer for about 45 minutes, or until the pork is tender.

Remove and discard the bone, then stir in the miso until it has dissolved in the soup. Serve in small bowls, sprinkled with spring onion and shichimi togarashi as desired.

Note: If using fresh burdock root, see the Notes on page 177 for preparation instructions. Frozen burdock root can be used instead.

warabi mochi

bracken starch dumpling
SERVES 8

Real *warabi mochi*, only available in Japan, is made from the starchy *warabi* root and has a green tinge. As the starch is very expensive, *warabi mochi* is often made instead with a blend of starch or *kuzu* — both readily available in Japanese grocery stores.

Texturally *warabi mochi* is very soft, gelatinous and chewy. It is usually served coated in *kinako* (roasted soy bean powder) and drizzled with *kuromitsu* (literally 'black nectar'), which is made from *kurosato* — an unrefined and reportedly 'healthy' black sugar.

KUROMITSU
100 g (3½ oz/½ cup) *kurosato* (Japanese black sugar) or dark brown sugar
55 g (2 oz/¼ cup) caster (superfine) sugar

WARABI MOCHI
80 g (2¾ oz) *warabimochi-ko* (*warabi mochi* starch) or *kuzu*
45 g (1½ oz/¼ cup) *kurosato* (Japanese black sugar) or dark brown sugar
50 g (1¾ oz/½ cup) *kinako* (roasted soy bean powder), plus extra for sprinkling

First, make the *kuromitsu*. Place the sugars in a saucepan with 170 ml (5½ fl oz/⅔ cup) cold water. Stir with a metal spoon over medium–high heat until the sugar has dissolved. Allow to come to the boil without stirring, then reduce the heat to a simmer and cook for 8 minutes or until slightly syrupy (it will thicken on cooling). Set aside.

To make the *warabi mochi*, put the starch and sugar in a saucepan with 310 ml (10¾ fl oz/1¼ cups) water. (If using *kuzu*, crush any larger granules with the back of a spoon to help them dissolve more readily.) Whisk until the mixture is well combined, smooth and runny.

Stir over medium heat for 15 minutes, or until the mixture becomes very thick, sticky and translucent — it will first look like clear lumps in a milky liquid, then turn into a cloudy mass and eventually a translucent paste. Use a wet spatula to scrape the sticky mixture out of the pan and into a large bowl of iced water. Leave until cool enough to handle.

Liberally dust a work surface with some of the *kinako*. Lift the *mochi* out of the water and allow any excess water to drip off. Place it on the dusted surface, then coat the top with most of the remaining *kinako* — use your hands to spread it all over, flattening out the *mochi* to a thickness of 1.5 cm (⅝ inch). Cut with a knife into 2 cm (¾ inch) squares, then sprinkle the cut edges with the remaining *kinako*, ensuring the *mochi* are completely covered.

Place a few pieces on a small serving dish and liberally sprinkle again with a little extra *kinako*, if desired. Serve with the *kuromitsu* for drizzling over — as much or little as desired.

This dish is best eaten with small flat bamboo picks for cutting through the *mochi*.

Note: *Kuromitsu* is used in a variety of Japanese desserts and confections. I sometimes use it to sweeten coffee, and it is used in the matcha latte on page 265 and the *houjicha* tea ice cream on page 225.

This recipe for *kuromitsu* makes about 170 ml (5½ fl oz/⅔ cup). You won't need the whole quantity for this recipe. The remainder will keep in a clean, well-sealed jar in a cool, dark place for several weeks.

You can also flavour the *mochi* mixture with a little grated yuzu zest or matcha (green tea powder), or even finely ground coffee. Matcha can also be added to the *kinako* for coating the *mochi*.

mutsuki / ichigatsu – january / the 1st month

The grand 100-year-old brewery was young compared with the age of the business itself, which had been in the Kozaemon family for 300 years. The tatami 'party room', decorated with handpainted screens and elegant *ikebana* (flower arrangements), possessed a slightly warped view through century-old glass onto the family's traditional garden, which made it look even more beautiful — like a magnificently framed watercolour.

While his younger brother remains confined within the *kura* (brewery) as *toji* (master brewer), Kozaemon-san, or Kozi, as he shall now be known (no one escapes a nickname from Aussie friends!), represents the business by travelling around the globe, introducing his wares and meeting like-minded, food- and drink-obsessed folk.

We whiled away the afternoon sluicing our gullets with more than 60 varieties of Kozi's artisanal sake, grateful for having consumed such a robust lunch. Kozaemon uses more than 10 different types of rice from different regions of Japan — but uses only one variety in each sake to best appreciate its distinct flavour. Kozi explains that different grades of sake relate to the degree of polishing the rice receives. The core of the rice is the most pure tasting, as it is not as tainted by proteins and fats as the outer layers can be, and therefore makes for the most refined sake. However, the more you polish, the more rice you need to make a particular volume of sake. When you consider you could end up using twice as much rice per bottle, it is easy to calculate how production costs might affect the end price.

Of course, there are many other contributing factors when it comes to making excellent sake. Trust me, sakes can vary significantly, and if you seek out the good stuff, you will be rewarded.

As a rough guide, look for the following words on translated labels.

Junmai – pure sake – containing only rice, water and *koji* (the mould that aids fermentation of the rice). The rice is polished down by at least 30 per cent, and it has a reasonably full flavour.

Honjozo (sometimes *honjozukuri*) – a small amount of distilled alcohol is added to the mix to help increase the yield, lighten the flavour and stop the sake spoiling.

Ginjo – one of the highest grades of sake and the grain must be polished down by at least 60 per cent. Within this category sits the king of sakes, *dai-ginjo*, where as little as 30 per cent of the original grain remains after polishing. If no alcohol is added in the production of these sakes, they are labelled *Junmai-ginjo* or *Junmai dai-ginjo* respectively.

Nama zake – an unpasteurised sake that must be refrigerated so it doesn't go off. It often has a lively, slightly tangy spritz to it, tingling on the tongue a little like a sparkling wine. If it does go off, you will recognise an overly funky, yeasty aroma and flavour and high acid, which is likely to turn you off drinking it anyway.

Nigorizake – noticeable for its cloudy white colour and thicker texture; it fortunately tastes better than it looks. A little sake *kasu* (or lees, the leftover compacted rice after the pressing) is left in during the filtering process, or added back to clear sake. The *kasu* is also used to thicken soups and stews during winter, adding a yeasty, slightly sour, sake-like flavour.

As with winemaking, all sorts of permutations can come into play. For example, some sake is aged in cedar barrels, which imparts a slightly woody essence into the alcohol. You will sometimes find sake served in *masu* (square cedar cups) to enhance the effect. Be warned though — the aroma of the cedar can override delicate sake, so save the cedar cups for the cheaper stuff. Usually you will be served sake in either *tokkuri* (small flasks) with small ceramic cups called *ochoko*, or in taller glasses called *guinomi*, which are often filled not only to the brim but so it overflows onto a small dish below — demonstrating generosity and abundance. Once you open a bottle of sake, it will start to deteriorate, so keep it refrigerated and don't leave it hanging around too long. Unlike wine, sake doesn't generally age well. However, if stored expertly, *koshu* (aged sake) can develop interesting sherry-like characteristics, including colour.

We enjoyed both cold and warm sake that day. You often hear people say you should only ever heat low-grade sake, to mask its inferior quality. But Kozi assured me that most of his sake, including *umeshu, yuzu shu* and *kabosa* (Japanese citrus), can be enjoyed either chilled in summer or warmed in winter. It is really about personal preference. However, he advised not to heat any sake above 40°C (104°F) as it could ruin the delicate flavours and cook off some of the alcohol. Heaven forbid! Most sake has an alcohol content a little higher than wine, but people report feeling more 'stoned' than giddily drunk after imbibing a few glasses. By the end of that afternoon I was certainly intoxicated but, to my mind at least, still relatively coherent ...

We sloshed our way deep into the mountains, to a local restaurant in a small log cabin permeated with charcoal age. A spritely couple in their sixties manned the grill, while their son ran the floor. The ingredients for the menu had been foraged in the mountains that day, and the specialty of the house was a long, squiggly, starchy root, the forebearer of the more readily available cultivated *nagaimo*. It is apparently only detectable when it sprouts through the earth with potato-like seeds attached (sold as 'micro potatoes' in the markets).

The first course was raw potato, ground to a sticky paste, wrapped in nori and dipped in shoyu and wasabi; it tasted much cleaner than I'd expected. They deep-fried the same dish and presented it with a potato *kakiage* (page 165) and three of the 'micro potatoes' threaded on a toothpick. It tasted soooo good — but a seasoning of *ajinomoto* (MSG) will do that to just about anything!

Warm homemade tofu with nori and *shichimi togarashi* (seven-flavour spice mix) felt wholesome and nurturing, as did an earthy miso soup brimming with wild mountain mushrooms, including rare white *maitake* and others I'd never laid eyes on before.

A cold slop of raw potato ground until foamy was poured over rice, then mixed together into a wallpaper-paste-like goop that even the strongly constituted Shaun-san struggled with. I forced it down with the promise it was good for digestion, and when a tingling, slightly itchy sensation buzzed around my lips my hosts assured me it was a 'good sign'.

As a special treat, two small dishes were brought to the table. Kozi tried to cover them up with his hands. When I enquired why he was being so mysterious, a fit of giggles erupted from the restaurant's owners. With a wide, cheeky grin, Kozi revealed a tumble of crisp, deep-fried giant bees. At about 6 cm (2½ inches) in length, they

Small statues at temples most commonly depict the beloved Jizo-san: the guardian of travellers and children. Jizo flits between earth and the spirit world, guiding souls on the journey to their resting place. Coins, commonly *go-en* or *gojuu-en* (the five-yen and 50-yen coins, their central hole making a connective 'circle') are placed in close proximity to the statues, in the hope the deities will answer prayers and ease almost any kind of suffering for both the living and the deceased.

looked more like killer wasps to me. I was assured their lethal stingers had been removed and, as they'd had a heavy dousing of MSG, they were as moreish as salt and pepper prawns. Apparently they would make us 'strong'!

Even more potent was the yellowing moonshine *shochu* stored in a four-litre glass jar with a sludge of giant bees on the bottom. The 'cold and flu tonic' looked gruesome and packed a punch, but the flavour was pleasantly honey-like.

*

Although waking up grumpy from having consumed an incomprehensible amount of sake, and compounded by a near-sleepless night on beds made of bricks, Lindy and I soon found something to smile about. Shards of pale morning sunlight pierced through the steam in the *kura* (brewery), transforming it, in my mind's eye, into a scene from a Turkish bath-house full of buffed, half-naked young men … running, lugging, lifting and climbing, pounding, stirring, pouring and mixing. Lindy and I could barely contain ourselves: our eyes transfixed on the scene, and mouths agape, we absent-mindedly elbowed each other. A good sign I was on the mend.

A minimum of commercial equipment is used at the Kozaemon *kura*: manpower is king and the brewers' refined collective senses of sight, touch, taste and smell are put to the test on an hourly basis during sake-making season. The steamed rice is carried, by hand, up feeble wooden ladders in heavy tubs to a place high in the cavernous *kura*. To send it via mechanical chutes — as is done in larger-scale manufacturing — would decrease the temperature too quickly and damage the premium product that can only be achieved using traditional methods. The rice is then tipped into a large humid bed, where it is tucked in with sheets to retain the heat, before spores of natural yeast are allowed to flutter down from the ancient eaves to start the fermentation process and development of *koji* (rice culture).

While many large modern factories are air-controlled and can therefore produce sake year-round, sake is traditionally made in winter — after the September/October rice harvest and the subsequent party at which the rice is blessed. Talk about a steep learning curve. I had become fascinated with the silvery drop.

During the train ride to Kanazawa, four of us sipped on yuzu sake and peach juice, and crunched on thin rice crackers flavoured with lobster. Like kids on a school trip we took silly photos of each other and our 'teacher' *sensei* Kozi, who had adopted the traditional pose of sleep. He later told me that a recent theory behind Japanese falling asleep on public transport (and anywhere else for that matter) is that mothers strap their babies to themselves while performing their daily chores and the babies are naturally rocked to sleep by the movement. The Japanese believe a catnap to be hugely beneficial, even if just for 5 minutes, and don't think twice about nodding off in public.

Kanazawa in western Japan is highly regarded for its cuisine. That night we enjoyed a magnificent *kaiseki* (formal, multi-dish meal) as an ode to the end of winter. While it was all stupendous, the highlight for me was the local dumpling specialty, *ebi manju* (page 188).

*

ebi manju

prawn and taro dumpling
SERVES 4

Manju, or dumplings, are often served as a sweet, but this savoury version is something you may come across during a *kaiseki* meal. I recommend trying it as a lovely starter at a Japanese-themed dinner party — the recipe can easily be doubled, but you may need to use two deep frying pans for the final cooking stage.

Instead of prawn (shrimp) meat, you can also use crabmeat in these dumplings. You can make them vegetarian by substituting finely sliced shiitake mushrooms for the prawn, and using shiitake dashi (page 29) for the dashi.

400 g (14 oz) taro, lotus root, or *ebiimo* if available (see Note)
2 teaspoons *katakuriko* or potato starch
½ teaspoon sea salt
½ teaspoon caster (superfine) sugar
1 egg white
35 g (1¼ oz/¼ cup) chopped cooked prawn (shrimp) meat
1 tablespoon finely chopped spring onion (scallion), plus extra to garnish
⅛ teaspoon finely grated fresh ginger, plus extra to garnish
1 teaspoon sake

ANKAKE SAUCE
250 ml (9 fl oz/1 cup) dashi
1½ tablespoons usukuchi shoyu (light Japanese soy)
2 tablespoons mirin
2 teaspoons caster (superfine) sugar
2½ teaspoons *katakuriko* or potato starch

Bring a wide pot of water to the boil. Line a bamboo steamer basket or a wide colander with baking paper.

Peel and roughly grate the taro, then spread it out over the steamer basket. Place the basket over the boiling water and steam, semi-covered, for 20–30 minutes, mixing and mashing together regularly to promote even cooking. The taro is ready when it squishes together easily into a pliable, slightly sticky mass. Note that the cooking time can vary depending on the type of taro you use.

zenbu zen

Using a large *suribachi* (ribbed Japanese mortar and wooden pestle), grind the taro to help bring it together. While it is still hot, add the starch, salt and sugar and mix until very well combined. Allow to cool very slightly, but while the mixture is still just warm, mix in the egg white — it will be a little difficult to combine at first, but will come together well.

In a small bowl, mix together the prawn, spring onion, ginger and sake until well combined.

Using wet hands, divide the taro mixture into four equal amounts and shape into smooth balls. Taking one at a time, flatten each into a disc in the palm of your hand — it should be about 1 cm (½ inch) thick and 8 cm (3¼ inches) in diameter. Put one-quarter of the prawn mixture in the centre, then fold the edges over to cover, using wet hands to help seal it back into a dumpling shape or a slightly flattened ball. Place the dumpling, seal side down, in a small ceramic or lacquerware rice bowl. Repeat with the remaining taro and prawn mixtures.

Put the bowls in a large, deep-sided frying pan and add enough boiling water to come halfway up the sides. Place over high heat and bring to the boil, then reduce to a rapid simmer. Loosely cover with a sheet of foil, leaving air pockets on either side for the steam to escape, so as not to cause too much condensation. Cook for 20 minutes — by this stage the dumplings will have puffed and grown slightly, and be heated all the way through.

Meanwhile, place all the sauce ingredients in a small saucepan with 2 tablespoons water. Stir over medium heat for about 10 minutes, or until the sauce boils and thickens.

When the dumplings are cooked, remove the bowls from the water and wipe around the outer edges to remove any drips. Evenly ladle the sauce over the dumplings, so that it comes about two-thirds up the side of the dumplings.

Garnish with extra spring onion and a tiny dot of extra ginger. Eat with a spoon!

Note: If available, fresh lotus root (*renkon*), lily bulb (*yurine*) or *ebiimo* can be used in place of taro. *Ebiimo* ('prawn potatoes') are a cross between taro and potato, and are particularly creamy in texture and taste. They take their name from their distinctive stripy skin and slight curve, and are also called *kyo-ebi-imo* when grown in Kyoto.

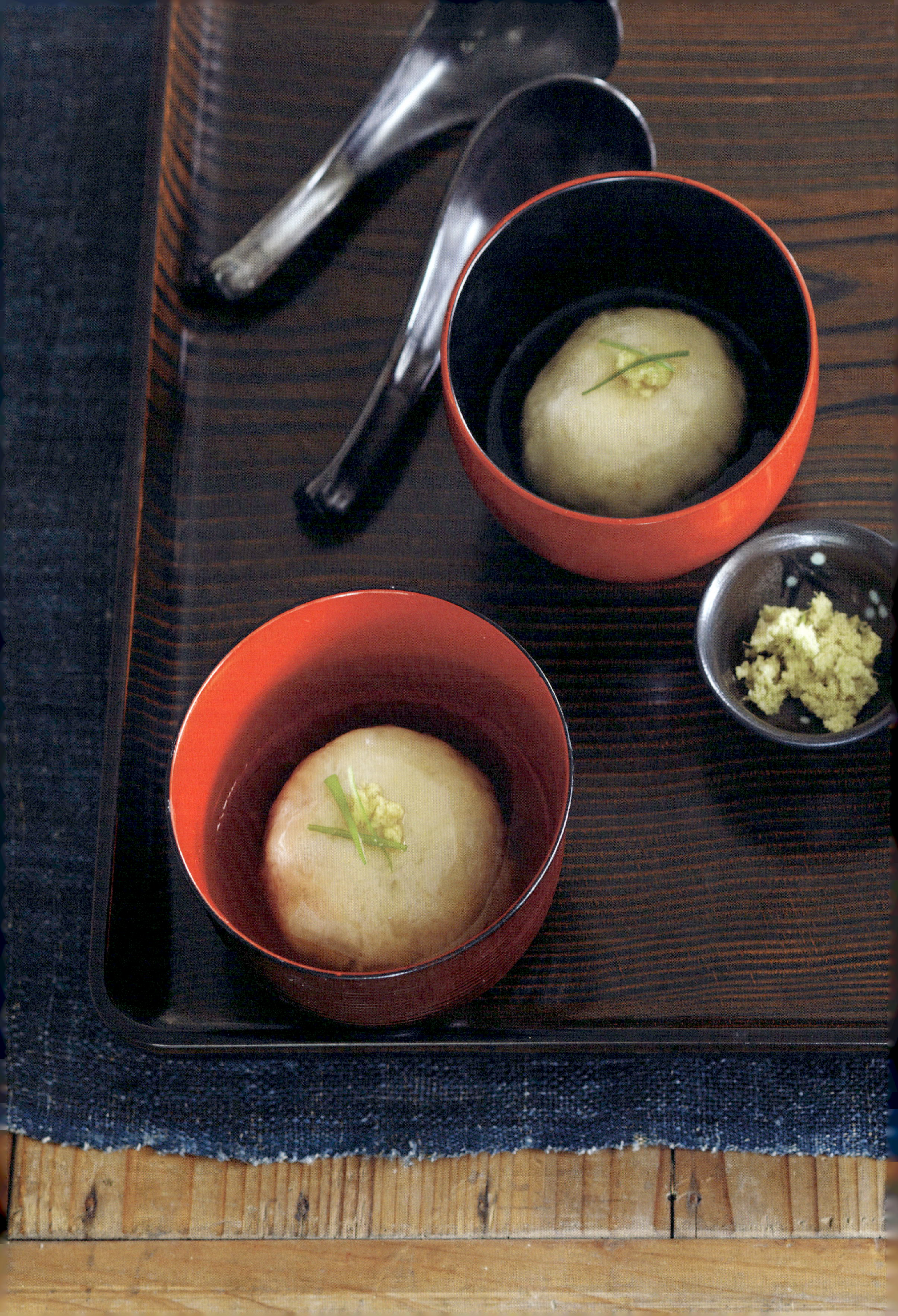

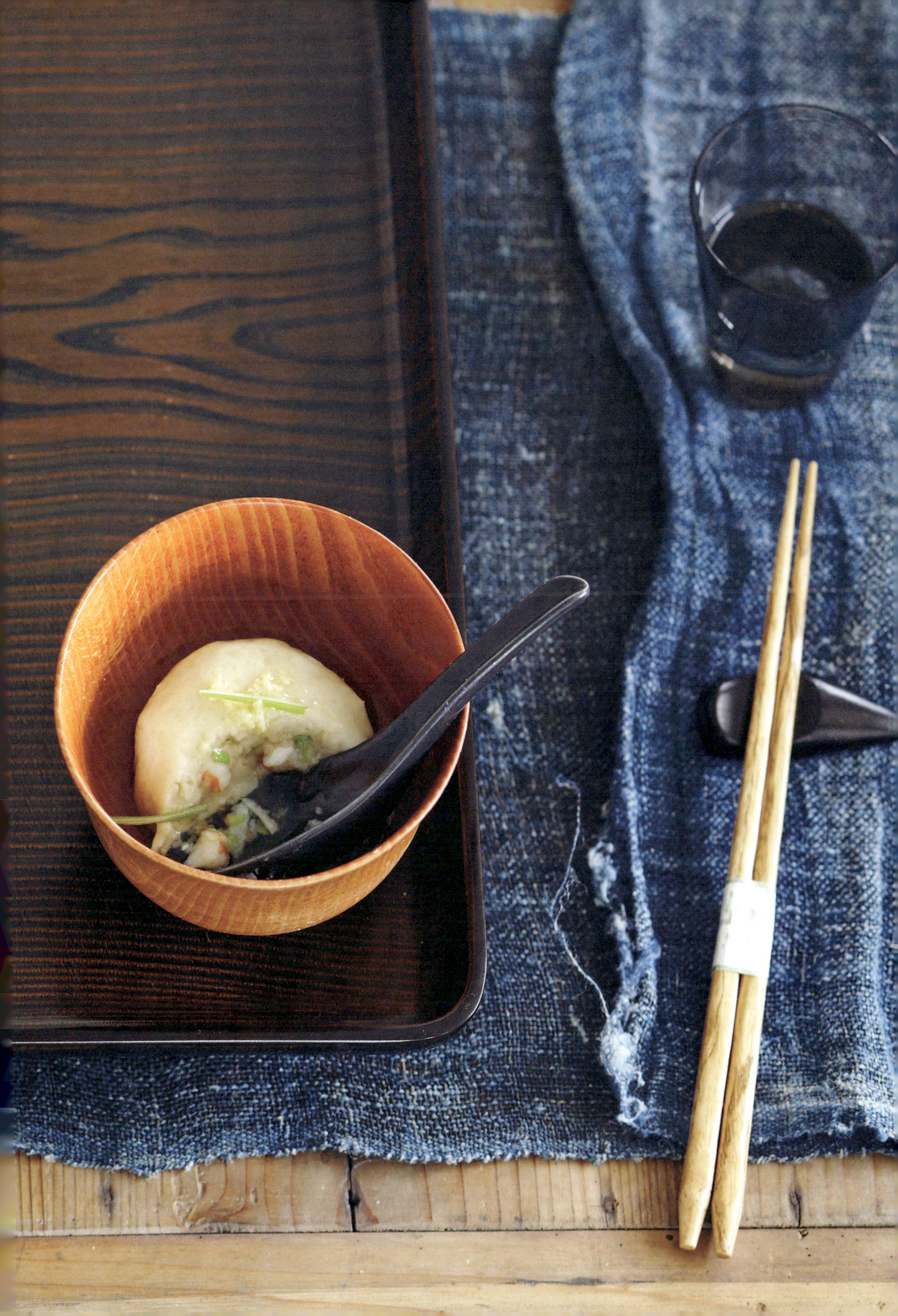

A brisk jaunt around the famous Kenrokuen Garden, complete with snowball fight, was followed by a stroll in one of the most beautifully kept traditional districts outside Kyoto. We stopped for *wagashi* (tea ceremony sweets) in a famous teahouse before Lindy and I excused ourselves from the group to board our train to the Japanese Alps. Our destination: Takayama, a luminous winter wonderland.

'WELCOME JANE LAWSON' read the banner hung outside our *ryokan* — for no reason other than we were *gaijin* in a town still relatively low in non-Japanese tourists. We explored the well-preserved streets lined with local arts, crafts and foods, before retiring to our stunning and spacious tatami room on the river, where for two nights we dined like queens on elegant regional *kaiseki*. We retired on our final evening feeling very Zen.

That peaceful feeling was shattered during the night when Lindy became violently ill. The sound of her rich and repetitious hurling kept me awake for several hours and so, unable to assist, I popped an emergency Valium. I awoke early in the morning to find both Lindy and her futon missing. On closer inspection, I found them located by the bathroom door.

Sick as a dog, she dragged her pale self to the train along with the makeshift sick bucket I had crafted from a large plastic sweets jar — a pretty gift from our inn. The stench of the smoke leaching out of an adjoining carriage made us both wretch like cats with tandem fur balls.

By the time we arrived at our hotel in Tokyo, it was my turn to cling to the ceramic in the palatial bathroom that accommodated me for the next 12 hours while I purged the offending fresh-water river fish parasite from my system.

*

If you only ever make one trip to Japan, be sure to book a night or so in a *ryokan* (traditional inn) – they are sometimes more expensive than a neighbouring hotel, but the experience cannot be compared. Sleep on futon bedding on a tatami floor, wear a *yukata* and dine in your room on a sumptuous Japanese feast. Kyoto's refurbished *machiya* or old merchant houses are also a magnificent and atmospheric way to experience an authentic Japanese dwelling.

消火器

kisaragi/nigatsu

FEBRUARY | THE 2ND MONTH

CHAPTER 4

THE 2ND MONTH

Being the height of winter in Japan, it is not surprising that Kisaragi is known as the 'month of wearing extra layers'.

february

kisaragi / nigatsu

Oni wa soto fuku wa uchi ('Out with demons, in with happiness'), I chanted absent-mindedly as I waved goodbye to Lindy a few days later. I hope she didn't misinterpret my sentiments!

Setsubun, translating as 'parting of the seasons', is best known as the signal to winter's end and the start of spring, and also roughly marks the start of the New Year in accordance with the Old Chinese Calendar. Although the Japanese have adopted 31 December as New Year's Eve, they also still recognise Chinese New Year in February. A raging bonfire at nearby Yoshida Shrine marks the occasion annually, and thousands line up to cast into it talismans and fortunes from the past year, or other burnable 'waste' they wish to cut ties with. The energy is palpable as the various wares perish in the flames, lifted to the gods in plumes of smoke and ash. The Japanese possess an ongoing spirit of recognition and appreciation for things that — though seemingly small — are often so momentous.

Sardines are also used to chase away bad spirits. Their stench is said to turn demons away. They are either burnt outside homes or simply hung at the front door in threat, alongside a branch of dangerously spiky holly — the combination translated as *hiiragi iwashi*. People scatter soy beans around the house while repeating the aforementioned chant — and, for protection, you are supposed to eat the same number of beans as your age. Kids chase around the streets wearing *oni* masks while pelting each other with extra beans and squealing with delight. Displays of gifts or foods shaped like cavemen's clubs (also handy for beating off demons) and many types of bean sweets line the walls of every second shop, but are removed the minute the event is over.

My local supermarket was selling deep-fried *tai yaki* — fish-shaped pancakes filled with red bean paste. Although tempted, I instead purchased some 'rock' weapons made from spongy cake nuggets made with *kurosato* (Japanese black sugar) and sweet potato chunks. I also picked up a 20 cm (8 inch) long *futomaki zushi* (a thick sushi roll), which, for luck, I would eat, in silence, all in one go, for lunch, while facing 'the lucky direction'. Exactly which direction that is provokes much dissent: some believe it to be 'south-east', while others insist the direction changes annually. Downing the roll is said to ensure good health, longevity and success in business.

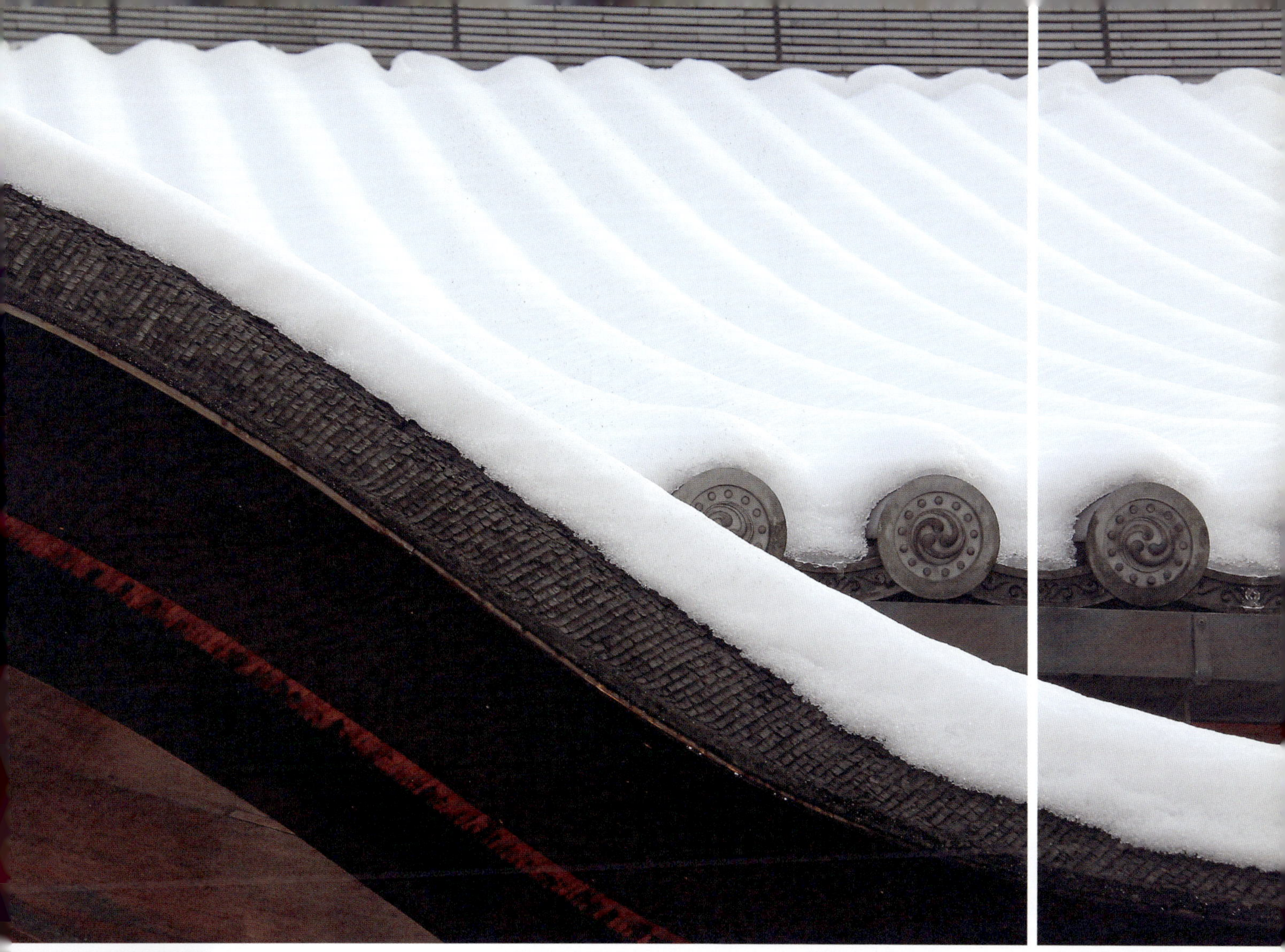

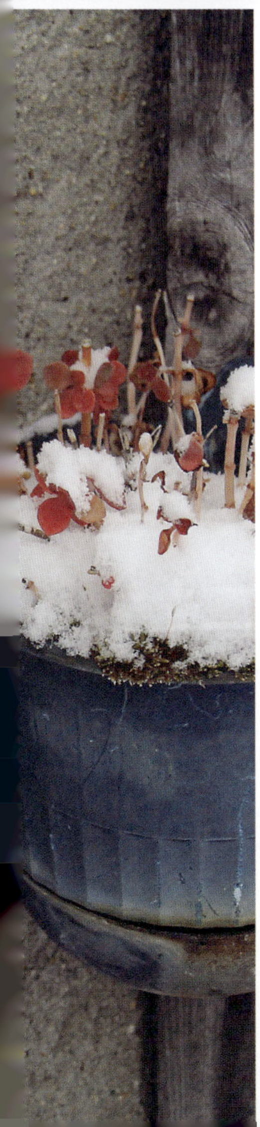

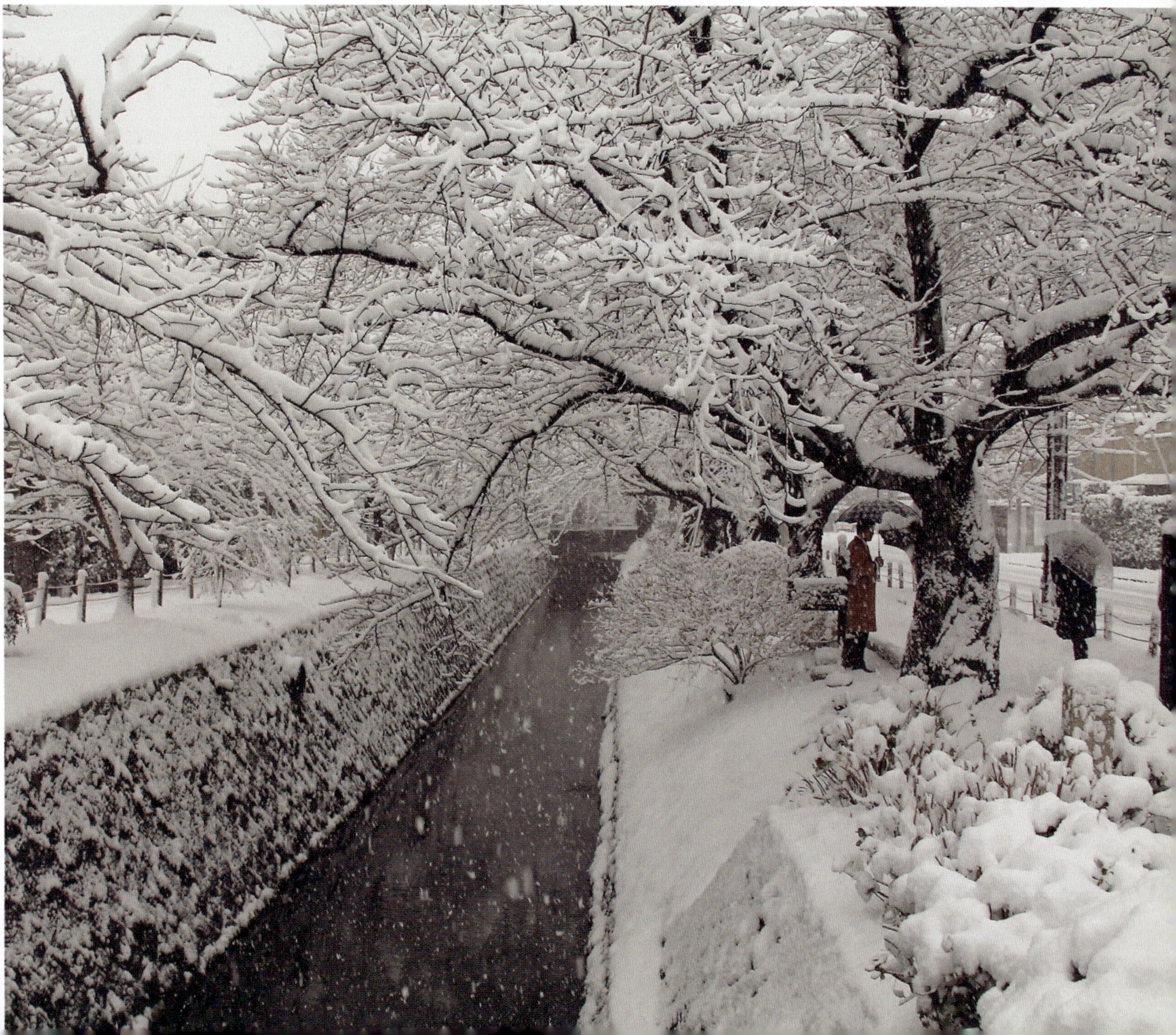

I was delighted to see the arrival of several short-seasoned spring vegetables, all fairly new to me. *Urui* (the shorter, more marketable name for *oobagibooshi*), also called plantain lily, looked a little like a thin, silky leek, but with elegantly sculptured lily-like tops, while the leaves of the *kuushinsai* (Chinese spinach or morning glory) looked more like those of a succulent or sea vegetable, with the occasional bean-sprout-like nodule, perched on the tips of thin mizuna-like stems.

I also gathered a range of mushrooms, including the funkily aromatic *maitake*, smelling more strongly than shiitake, and I looked forward to assessing how much more *umami* (the so-called 'fifth taste') could be packed into *umami*-laden miso soup.

In homage to a day dedicated to beans, I also picked up a container of *daizu no gomoku-ni* (soy beans and vegetables; see recipe opposite) — one of my favourite *obanzai* (home-style) dishes.

*

At home, I scattered soy beans, demanding all evil spirits to flee, while sweetly inviting gods of happiness and luck to be with my friends and me for the coming year. Witnessing yet another ending and beginning had put me further in touch with my emotions: it was as though this country was standing behind me, tapping me on the shoulder at regular intervals to say, 'Hey, enjoy the journey. Don't rush it. Recognise where you are at and embrace all before moving forward.'

*

Feeling energised after several days' rest, I decided to climb Mount Kurama. Now when I say climb, I mean take a cable-car part of the way and then walk up the perfectly accommodating paths higher into the mountain to reach the stupendous temple at its summit. Regardless, it did test my lung capacity, which had nevertheless improved dramatically since my arrival.

A loud, sharp crack, followed by a rustling through the trees, piqued my paranoia, as I imagined angry brown bears somersaulting down the hill in search of a meaty snack. The son of an acquaintance had recently been attacked while jogging in the Japanese countryside. He lost the tip of a finger and a nipple — neither of which I was willing to relinquish.

Yet the chanting emanating from the temple was more songlike than I was used to, and I stood transfixed by the voices as I swayed on the spot, in unison with the appreciative giant lanterns that lazily circled back and forth in the breeze. I let myself go with it, breathing in the view, loving it and myself with every inhalation and exhalation. On eventual retreat, I was awarded a fluttering of snow, which had developed into an impressive white storm by the time I reached the base of the mountain.

I drifted home, carried by a lightness of being, to a pot of aromatic and warming *shogacha* (see page 204) and a few well-deserved *kinako* truffles (page 203).

*

daizu no gomoku-ni

simmered soy beans and vegetables
SERVES 8–10 AS PART OF A MULTI-DISH MEAL

This popular and very typical example of *obanzai* (home-style cooking) is a wonderful side dish for any Japanese meal. As it keeps for about 5 days in the fridge, it is also particularly good for *osechi* (New Year's holiday food), where most of the cooking is done ahead of time so the cook — most often the mother — can enjoy the festivities with the family. It is also popular during *Setsubun*, the end of winter and the start of spring, in keeping with the bean theme outlined earlier.

200 g (7 oz/1 cup) dried soy beans
3 dried shiitake mushrooms
½ large carrot
100 g (3½ oz) burdock root
150 g (5½ oz) *konnyaku*
750 ml (26 fl oz/3 cups) dashi of your choice
60 ml (2 fl oz/¼ cup) sake
60 ml (2 fl oz/¼ cup) mirin
2½ tablespoons shoyu
2 teaspoons caster (superfine) sugar
2 tablespoons dried hijiki seaweed (optional)

Put the beans in a saucepan, fill the pan with cold water and bring to the boil over high heat. Remove from the heat and allow to cool to room temperature, then transfer the beans and liquid to a large bowl. Fill to the top with fresh cold water, then cover and refrigerate for 12 hours.

Drain and rinse the soaked beans, discarding the soaking water. Place the beans in a saucepan with 2 litres (70 fl oz/8 cups) cold water. Bring to the boil, then immediately reduce the heat to a simmer. Cook for 50–60 minutes, or until just starting to become tender.

The actual cooking time for dried beans depends greatly on their age and quality, so use your own judgment to assess when they are ready. Skim off any foam that rises to the top while they cook.

Meanwhile, soak the mushrooms in 750 ml (26 fl oz/ 3 cups) boiling water for 50 minutes, or until tender. Drain the mushrooms, reserving the soaking liquid, which will be used as stock.

Cut the mushrooms, carrot, burdock and *konnyaku* into small, neat, squarish pieces about the same size as the beans.

Drain and rinse the soy beans. Place in a saucepan with the vegetable and *konnyaku* pieces, dashi, sake, mirin, shoyu, sugar and seaweed, if using. Bring to the boil over high heat, then reduce the heat to a simmer. Cover and cook for 2 hours, or until the beans are tender and most of the liquid has been absorbed.

Rest the beans for 1 hour, then gently reheat the dish before serving. This dish can be refrigerated for up to 5 days, and the flavours will continue to develop during this time.

Notes: You can substitute one of the vegetables in this dish with lotus root or bamboo shoots, and use the kombu left over from making kombu dashi (page 29) instead of the hijiki.

If you are short on time, you can use 2½ cups pre-cooked tinned soy beans instead of dried beans.

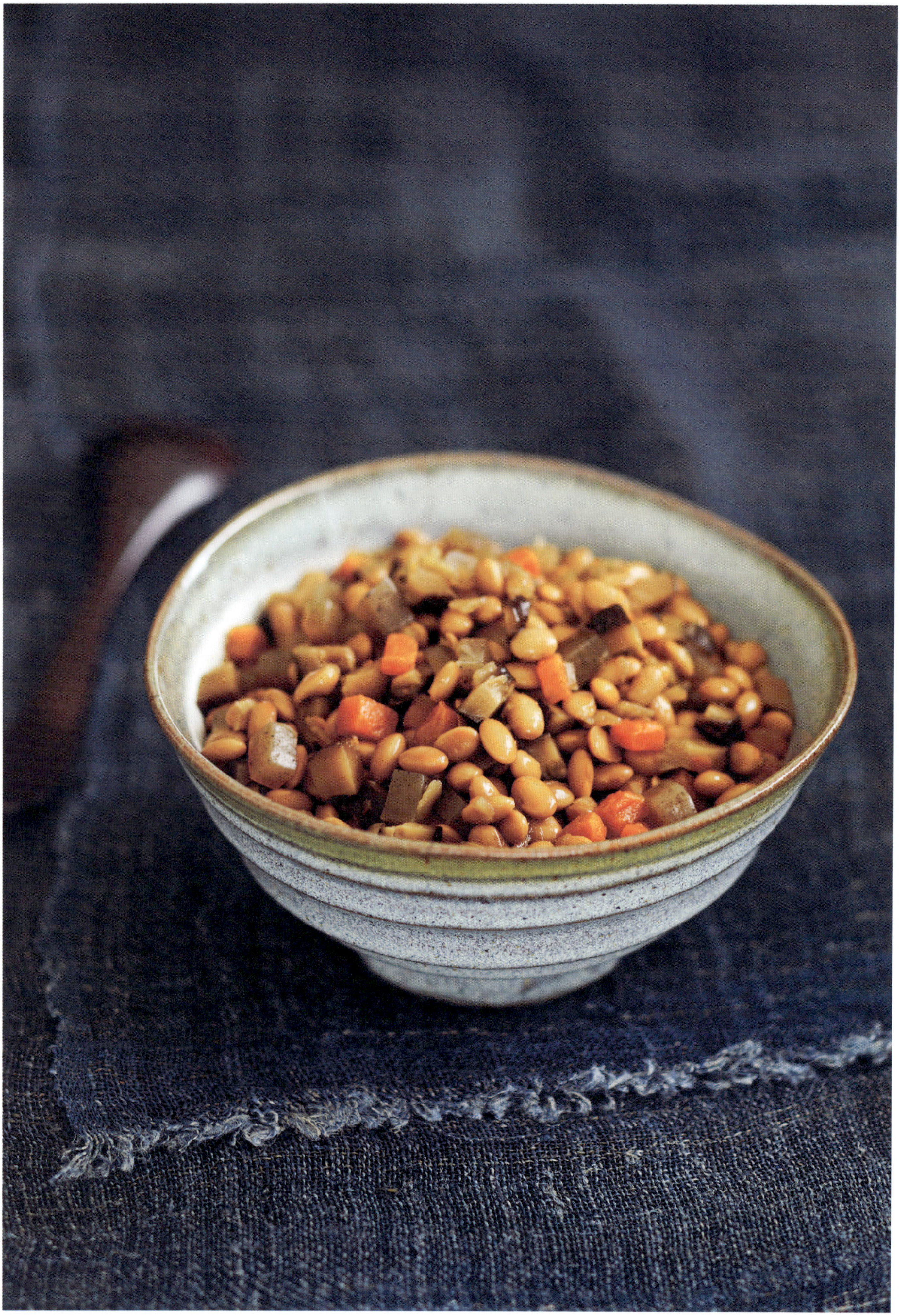

Soy beans and their by-products (shoyu, tofu, *yuba*, etc) are such an important part of the Japanese diet that it is reflected in their name: in the word *daizu*, the particle *dai* means 'great' or 'important', and *zu* simply means 'bean'. Curiously, the fresh version of the soy bean has a different name — *edamame*, or 'branch' or 'stalk' beans.

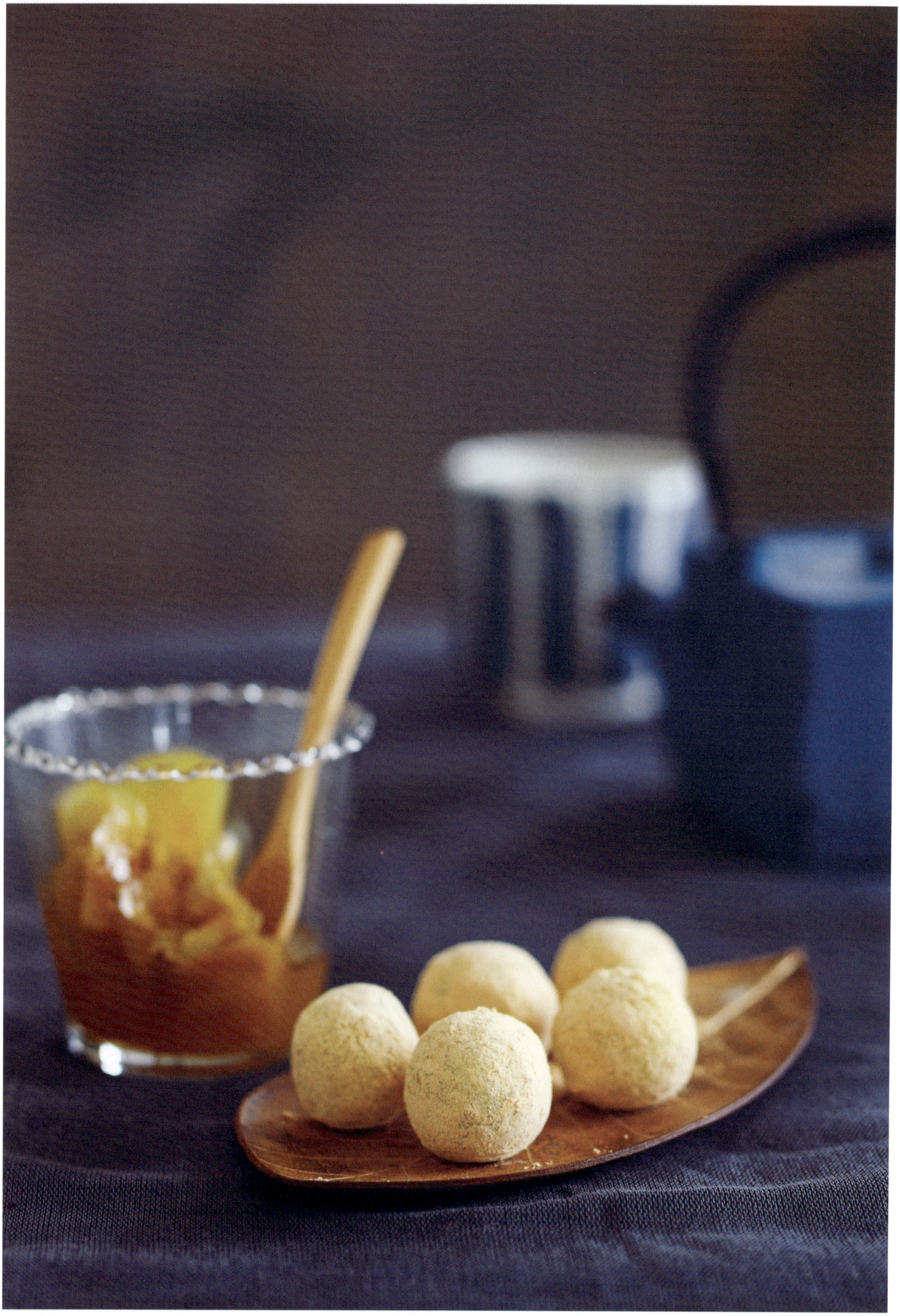

kinako shiro torafuru

kinako and white chocolate truffles
MAKES 24

200 g (7 oz/1⅓ cups) organic or couverture white chocolate melts (buttons)
2½ tablespoons cream
2 tablespoons unsalted butter
a few drops of pure vanilla extract
1½ teaspoons organic maple syrup
30 g (1 oz/¼ cup) walnuts, toasted and finely chopped
50 g (1¾ oz/½ cup) *kinako* (roasted soy bean powder)

Place the chocolate, cream and butter in a saucepan over very low heat. Stir with a metal spoon until the chocolate has almost completely melted, then remove from the heat and stir until it is smooth and runny.

Stir in the vanilla, maple syrup and walnuts, combining well. Pour the mixture into a non-metallic container, then cover and refrigerate for 2 hours, or until firm.

Roll heaped teaspoons of the mixture into neat balls between your hands. Tip the *kinako* onto a plate and roll the chocolate balls in it, coating well. Place on a tray lined with plastic wrap, then cover and refrigerate for 1 hour, or until ready to serve.

Remove the truffles from the fridge just a few minutes before you wish to serve. They store well for up to a week — if you don't eat them in one sitting! Great with green tea or coffee.

Finally! The snow fairy had waved her magic wand during the night and Kyoto, all dressed in white, was a sight to behold. I ran out to frolic in it, adoring the way the thick snow muffled the sound of my dancing footsteps. I happily allowed the drifting flakes to settle on my hair and shoulders — no protective parasols for me! I was practically skipping over the red wooden bridge on Jingu Michi (Shrine Street) when Myong Hee, husband Bob and sculptor friend Yutaka-san came into view, waving me over to join them for breakfast. In the golden glow of an airy café, we scoffed down croque-monsieurs (grilled ham-and-cheese sandwiches) and multiple coffees while mulling over art, shiatsu, *hari* (acupuncture) and food. We talked about trusting our intuition and about how our individual journeys ultimately connect to everyone else's — which got me thinking about my quest just to 'be' as much as possible and allow life to lead me, rather than the more controlling behaviour I was used to.

I am all for planning when needed, but to truly succeed in this extremely fulfilling and enriching lifestyle one must be prepared and ready to 'let go', which involves trust. But even 'being open' and 'letting go' involves some form of practice and learning. I was still struggling with my workload and how and when I should stop. Only time, patience and the willingness to adapt would teach me how to find the balance. I was desperate to take some time out then and there, but felt pressured by planned outings, friends coming to stay, a trip to Kamakura followed by a lengthier trip to Hokkaido, and a jaunt back to Australia to moderate at a food festival before returning to Japan for a further month. All of which I had manifested for myself ...

✽

shogacha

ginger tea

MAKES 375 ML (13 FL OZ/1½ CUPS)

Originally a Korean invention, this tea is now very popular in Japan, especially with young Japanese. It is the first thing I reach for when I come through the door on a freezing cold day in need of an instant warm-up, or when I have the sniffles. It also aids queasy tummies as ginger can counteract nausea. *Yuzu cha* — yuzu tea made by cooking down yuzu rind in sugar — is also a wonderfully aromatic winter drink.

500 g (1 lb 2 oz) fresh ginger root
500 g (1 lb 2 oz/2¼ cups) caster (superfine) sugar
1 tablespoon *kuromitsu* (page 182) or honey (optional)

Peel the ginger, then use a mandoline or very sharp knife to slice it as thinly as possible. If you don't want big pieces of ginger in your cup when you drink the tea, you might like to further chop the slices into smaller pieces.

Put the sugar, *kuromitsu* or honey and 500 ml (17 fl oz/2 cups) water in a large saucepan and stir over high heat until the sugar has dissolved.

Bring to the boil, add the ginger and stir with a metal spoon just to combine. Return to the boil, then reduce the heat to a simmer and cook for 1 hour, stirring only if absolutely necessary to stop it sticking, until the syrup is thick and deep golden — a little like jam. If you stir too much the syrup will crystallise — this makes no difference to the flavour, but it does make it more difficult to remove the syrup from the jar when it firms up.

Pour the hot syrup into a 375 ml (13 fl oz/1½ cup) sterilised jar and seal. Turn the jar upside down to help kill off any bacteria that has settled in around the rim and allow to cool to room temperature.

The syrup will keep in the refrigerator for several months, as long as only clean spoons are used to remove the mixture from the bottle.

To use, place approximately 2 teaspoons of the mixture in the bottom of a tea cup or mug. Fill with boiling water and stir to dissolve the syrup. Enjoy hot.

You can also spread it over toast like honey, or spoon it over ice cream or pancakes instead of maple syrup.

Feeling exhausted again, I calculated the energy needed to adhere to all my commitments and wasn't sure I'd built up enough reserves. I was internally processing a lot of information, and when it finally registered that this struggle and confusion was all indeed part of my learning process, and that I just needed to go with it, the burden was instantly released. I felt as though tiny helium balloons suddenly attached themselves to my small but weighty shackles and transported them to elsewhere in the universe. I happily let them fly.

After breakfast Bob (until recently an 'alternative therapy' sceptic) left for his next *hari* session like a little kid frantic to get back to his computer game: his enthusiasm was infectious. Meanwhile, Yutaka, Myong Hee and I visited the city museum where Yutaka's art students were exhibiting their major works: blue plastic octogenarians; giant wooden bat skeletons; suspended resin clouds with descending raindrops; and a short-skirted Japanese schoolgirl climbing through a Buddhist altar as she symbolically moved from one world to the next. The quirky, energetic works from the young Japanese artists were intriguing and it was clear, more than ever, that the Japanese see things through very different lenses. While inevitably taught certain styles, I suspect that the Japanese appreciation of the aesthetically pleasing or unique stems from an ancient cultural base carried deep within their cellular memories.

We lunched in a 450-year-old former temple on superb *oyakodon* (page 208). On the side were small bowls of smoky-brothed soba noodles, topped with crunchy pebbles of tempura batter and finely shredded pencil-thin leek. Although it was an incredibly rustic setting, with an atmosphere thick with ghosts, a table by the door was completely covered in colourful *anime* and *manga* characters, an old stereo pumped out cool jazz, a lifetime's collection of kewpie dolls nestled in a corner, and in one dark alcove rested a beautiful, if somewhat creepy, traditional doll next to a photo of what appeared to be a departed family member. The decor was a little eclectic, but it seemed to work — a 'look' that only the Japanese could pull off with style.

With his *gaijin* passenger in mind, Yutaka kindly drove us to a lookout with an eagle's eye view over Kyoto. On a clear day you can apparently make out the skyscrapers of Osaka, but on this day, the scene was covered with a mist that seemed to be making its way towards us. Within minutes the city was covered with a white screen, and before we could blink we were under attack from a horizontal snowstorm.

It was strangely confronting, unexpected and wild, and while the men scurried to the warm car, Myong Hee stood tall, like a mystical mountain goddess, her hands elegantly sheltering her face while the gentle flakes whipped and whizzed around her flowing winter coat.

*

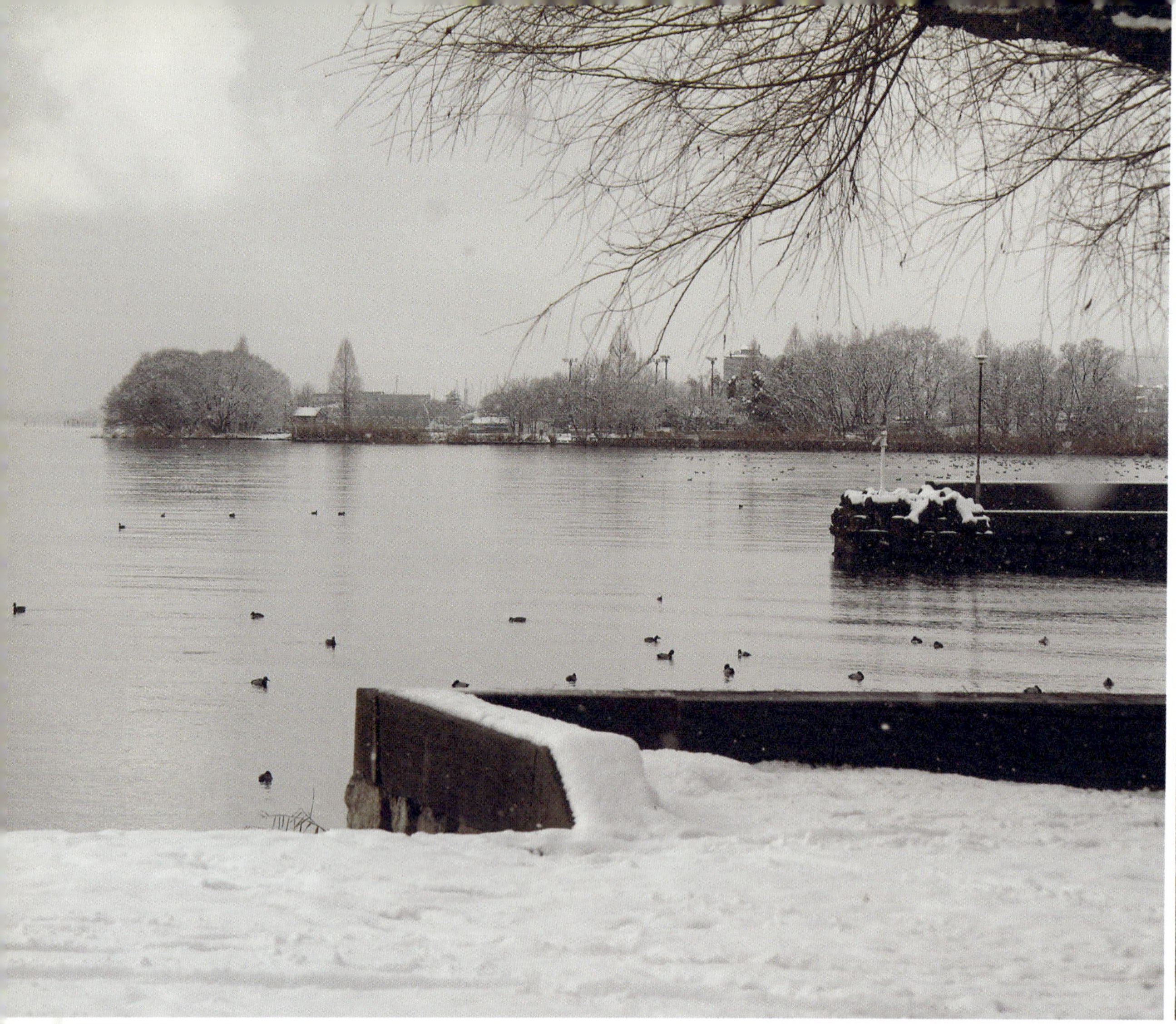
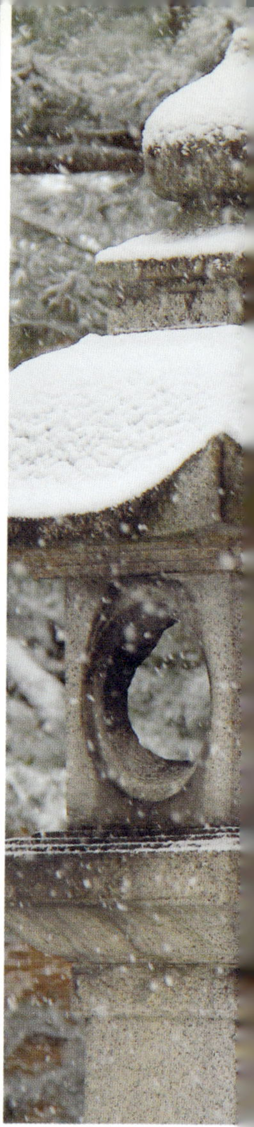
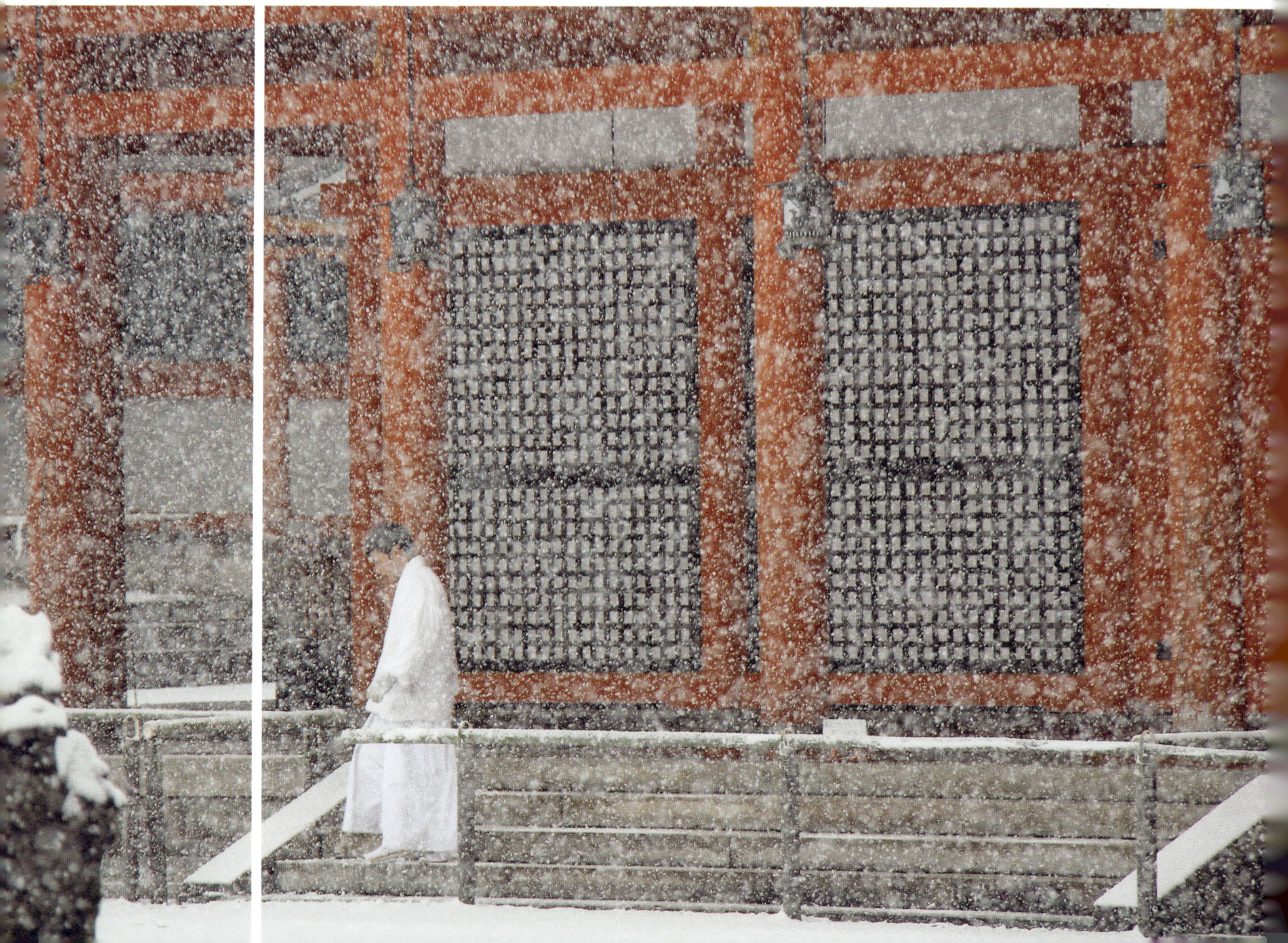

I was truly comforted by the snow and, in an unexpected form of meditation, examined the detail and unique patterns in the individual flakes I collected as they paraded by the window on a daily basis. I was moved by the beauty, fragility and poignant message they conveyed – exquisite and fleeting, forming the perfect metaphor for freefalling with grace in a life all too short.

oyakodon

'parent and child' rice bowl
SERVES 4

Oyako, meaning 'parent and child', is a rather fitting name for this particularly comforting dish — *don* being the short version of *donburi*, or rice bowl. However, the title is attributed to the combination of chicken and egg. In northern Japan you can also find salmon and salmon roe under the same name, but for me it has nothing on this dish, which is the kind of one-bowl meal you crave on a cold, dreary day, or if you are feeling less literally 'under the weather'.

Katsudon is another typical *donburi* using the same eggy onion sauce from this dish, minus the chicken, poured over strips of *tonkatsu* (fried pork cutlet; page 42) on rice.

Oyakodon is quick to make as long as your stock is prepared, so keep some on hand in the freezer, or use a good-quality store-bought alternative. The tori dashi (chicken stock) recipe here is more rich than standard dashi and is infrequently used in Japan — but it works well for regional or seasonal versions of certain dishes like this wintry *oyakodon*, other chicken-based *nabe* (hotpots), and the soup curry on page 241.

This recipe makes more stock than you need here, but it freezes well, so store it in batches for making *oyakodon* in a hurry. If you prefer, niban dashi (page 29) can be used instead.

TORI DASHI (CHICKEN STOCK)
15–20 g (½–¾ oz) piece of kombu (dried kelp)
750 g (1 lb 10 oz) chicken wings, chopped
250 ml (9 fl oz/1 cup) sake
1 thick slice of fresh ginger (optional)
½ large leek, white part only, cut in half
2 large handfuls *katsuobushi* (shaved dried, smoked bonito), about 40 g (1½ oz)

60 ml (2 fl oz/¼ cup) shoyu
2 tablespoons mirin
2 tablespoons sake
1½ tablespoons caster (superfine) sugar
1 brown onion, sliced into thin wedges
500 g (1 lb 2 oz) skinless, boneless chicken thighs, cut into 2.5 cm (1 inch) pieces
3 eggs, lightly beaten
1 spring onion (scallion), thinly sliced on an angle
a handful of *mitsuba* (Japanese trefoil) or flat-leaf (Italian) parsley leaves
6 cups (about 1.1 kg/2 lb 7 oz) hot freshly cooked rice

To make the tori dashi, put the kombu and 3 litres (105 fl oz/12 cups) cold filtered water in a large pot and set aside for 1 hour. Place the pot over high heat and bring just to the boil. Immediately remove the kombu and reserve for using in *tsukudani* (pages 113–115) or *kakiage* (page 165). Set the broth aside.

Meanwhile, place the chicken wings in a large frying pan over medium–high heat and cook for 25–30 minutes, turning occasionally, until golden all over. Place the wings in a colander and pour boiling water over to remove the excess oil. Remove any cooked-on bits from the base of the pan and reserve.

Add the wings to the kombu broth with the reserved pan crumbs, sake, ginger and leek. Bring back to the boil, then reduce the heat to a simmer. Skim off any foamy residue from the surface and cook for 2 hours, to obtain a nice rich chicken flavour.

Add the *katsuobushi* and turn off the heat. Allow the flakes to swim into the water, then strain the whole lot through a colander lined with muslin (cheesecloth), into a large bowl. Cover and refrigerate overnight.

When ready to cook, scoop the fat layer off the stock. The stock will be slightly jellied in texture, but will melt easily. You will only need 500 ml (17 fl oz/2 cups) for this recipe, but the rest will keep in the fridge for several days, or in the freezer for up to 2 months.

To make the *oyakodon*, pour 500 ml (17 fl oz/2 cups) of the stock into a large, deep-sided frying pan and add the shoyu, mirin, sake and sugar. Place over medium–high heat, stir until the sugar has dissolved, then bring to the boil.

Add the onion and cover with the lid. Cook for about 5 minutes, or until the onion is starting to soften. Add the chicken thighs, then cover and cook for 5–6 minutes, or until the chicken is just cooked through.

Pour three-quarters of the egg over the mixture and very gently swirl it into the liquid using chopsticks. Replace the lid and cook for 10 seconds.

Pour the remaining egg over, sprinkle with the spring onion and *mitsuba*, then immediately cover and remove from the heat. Allow to settle for 10 seconds, then use a wide, flattish ladle to divide the mixture among four deep bowls of hot rice.

Serve immediately. The egg should still be a little runny on top — it will continue to cook with the residual heat.

Note: If you are home on your own, you can easily make a quarter quantity of the *oyakodon* in a small frying pan, which makes it easier to serve, as it simply slides out of the pan across the top of the rice in your bowl.

Even the view from the entrance that leads into a Japanese garden, temple, shrine or other place of importance can be a sight to behold — the gate performing the function of a picture frame. Windows are also strategically placed in buildings to highlight a specific scene. I suspect that is one reason I have in recent times become rather drawn to photographing doors, gates and window frames — perhaps as a symbolic link to Kyoto's spiritual world.

211   **kisaragi / nigatsu** – february / the 2nd month

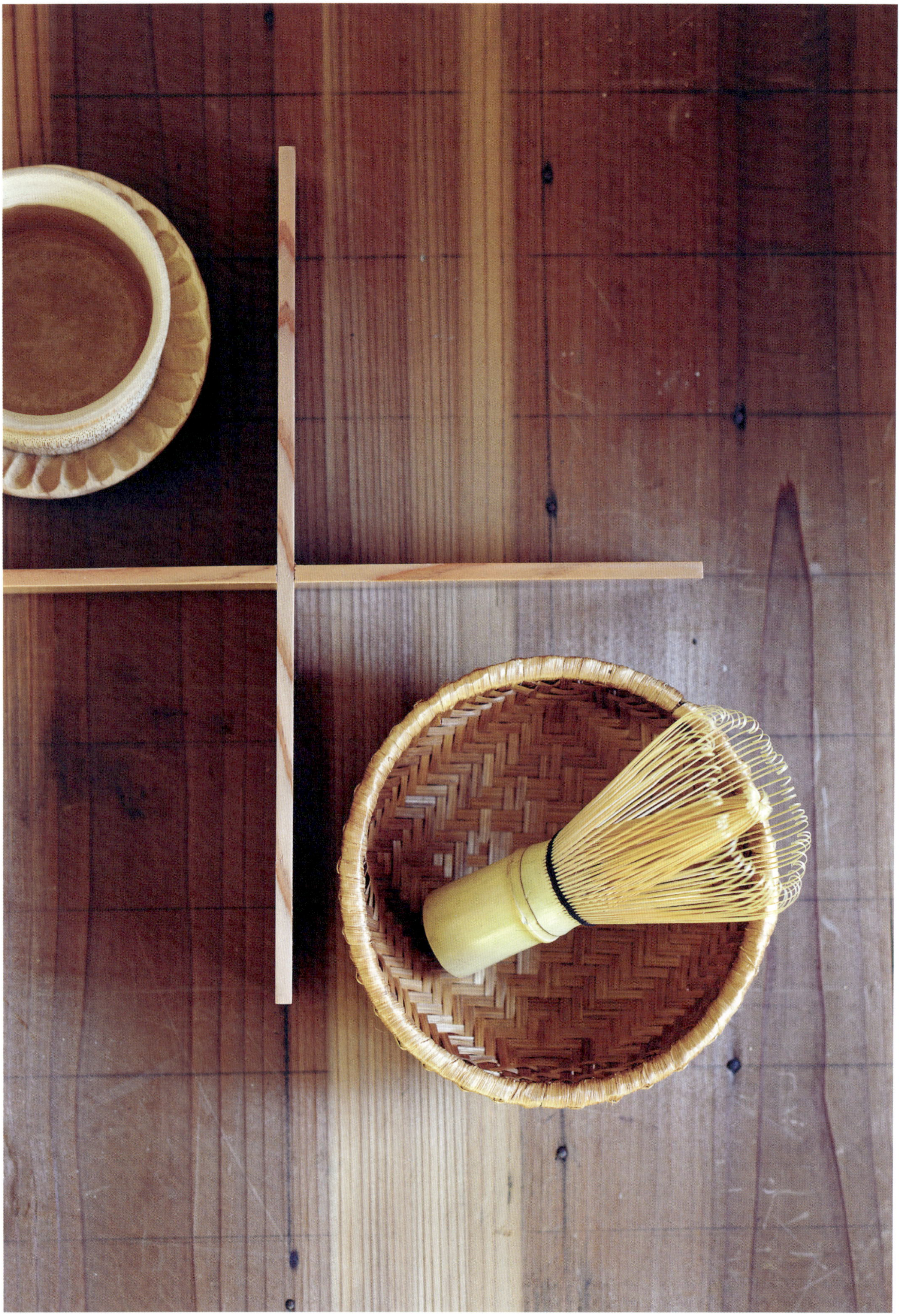

Perhaps I'd been spoilt, but I was growing tired of paying exorbitant prices for average *kaiseki*. I lunched at a well-known *ryokan* (traditional inn) and, while locked away in a private room with a view of a peaceful garden, I sat through eight lacklustre courses on exquisite, centuries-old ceramics. If you are not discerning enough with your research, food in Kyoto can become rather repetitive after a while. While I deeply respect tradition, it is rather tedious to consume the same dishes over and over if they are not technically spot-on; as pretty as a meal might be, it can be a very expensive letdown if the flavours are dull or flat.

Was the shine simply wearing off? After all, it no longer excited me putting out the garbage early on a frosty morning to outwit the crows (who, given the opportunity, would scavenge through the contents and scatter it all over the road). Nor did I relish essential chores such as washing the sheets or brushing my teeth. Shockingly, they had become just as mundane as they had been back in Sydney. I was no longer super ecstatic about every single new thing I fell across … just every second thing.

After persistently engaging my suspicious elderly neighbours with polite greetings, they finally deemed it appropriate to bestow on me the greeting '*ohayoo gozaimasu*' of a morning, almost running me down to do so. It was a monumental indicator that I was becoming accepted into the community. Little did they know I was soon to abandon them for the seductive lower land of the Gion (the best known of Kyoto's geisha quarters), although I hoped one day to return.

*

Hallelujah! Faith was restored when I met Bridget and her Japanese-cuisine-obsessed partner, Tad, for lunch at Touzentei, a small restaurant on Shinmonzen Dori.

The walls were adorned with stunning handmade paper printed with sleek modern adaptations of traditional Japanese patterns, and the food was very much in keeping with the thread of lacing a traditional base with a considered, contemporary edge — a manifesto I connect with.

Everything about this place possessed subtle, wonderful angles. Individual interpretations of dishes retained an apparent respect for their origins, but were handled with a fresh approach. The clean, precise flavours drove me wild. Even the rice topped with *chirimen jakko* (minuscule dried sardines with sansho) had been executed with great care. The sashimi seemed fresher than I had eaten in weeks. My tastebuds were doing the happy dance, screaming out for more.

In a meal with many highlights, the *chawan mushi* (page 214) with a fine wakame glaze was the hero: both the texture and flavours made me swoon.

*

chawan mushi

steamed savoury custard cups
SERVES 4

Named after the *chawan* or tea cups they are cooked in, these savoury custards are exquisitely silky and comforting. The dish is in fact referred to as a soup, as the eggs and stock do separate slightly, leaving the flavoursome stock at the base of the cups. The wakame *ankake* topping is not commonly added, and for a plain *chawan mushi* can be omitted.

In winter I prefer to serve these immediately, as soon as they are cooked; in summer, omit the wakame sauce and serve either warm or chilled.

You can also cook this in smaller cups for dinner parties, or in one large bowl for family dinners — adjust the cooking time accordingly. Serve as a starter or as part of a multi-dish Japanese meal.

4 small eggs
560 ml (19¼ fl oz/2¼ cups) niban dashi (page 29)
2 teaspoons shoyu
2 teaspoons mirin
2 teaspoons sake
100 g (3½ oz) cooked prawn (shrimp), crab or lobster meat, chopped (see Note)
1 tablespoon ginko nuts (sold in small tins or vacuum packs in Asian grocery stores)
1 spring onion (scallion), thinly sliced on the diagonal
8 *mitsuba* (Japanese trefoil) leaves, or flat-leaf (Italian) parsley leaves

WAKAME ANKAKE SAUCE (OPTIONAL)

1 tablespoon small wakame (seaweed) pieces
125 ml (4 fl oz/½ cup) ichiban dashi (page 26)
2 teaspoons sake
2 teaspoons usukuchi shoyu (light Japanese soy)
¾ teaspoon caster (superfine) sugar
¾ teaspoon *kuzu* or arrowroot

Crack the eggs into a bowl and lightly mix with chopsticks or a fork. Add the dashi, shoyu, mirin and sake and a pinch of sea salt and mix until just combined. Don't whisk the mixture or your custard will be full of bubbles. Strain through muslin (cheesecloth) or a very fine sieve into a jug.

Half-fill a saucepan or wok, large enough to support a bamboo steamer, with water. Bring to the boil, then reduce the heat to a light but steady simmer.

Meanwhile, divide the seafood, ginko nuts, spring onion and *mitsuba* among four *chawan* (deep, large Japanese tea cups with lids), or small deep bowls.

Carefully ladle three-quarters of the egg mixture into the cups; reserve the rest of the egg as you will need it shortly. Put the bamboo steamer over the simmering pot, then carefully place the cups, without their lids, in the steamer base.

Wrap a clean tea towel (dish towel) or a double layer of kitchen paper around the steamer lid — this will absorb moisture in the steam, stopping any drips from the lid landing on the custards. Place the lid on the steamer and steam for about 12 minutes, or until the surface of the egg is starting to set. Carefully pour the remaining egg into the cups and cook for a further 3 minutes, or until the tops are set.

Meanwhile, to make the sauce, rehydrate the wakame by soaking it in cold water for 10 minutes — it will need to be softer than usual, hence the longer soaking time. Drain the wakame, then grind using a *suribachi* (ribbed Japanese mortar and wooden pestle), or process with a hand-held stick blender, until you have a very fine paste.

Put the dashi, sake, shoyu, sugar and *kuzu* in a small saucepan. Crush the *kuzu* with the back of a spoon and stir over high heat until the sugar has dissolved. Bring to the boil, then whisk in the wakame paste.

Remove the custard cups from the steamer and gently ladle the sauce over the top of each custard. Cover with the cup lids, if using them, to keep warm.

Serve with a small spoon for eating the custard, solids and soup in the base of the cup.

Note: Instead of prawn, crab or lobster, you could also use small pieces of lightly cooked chicken, *unagi* (grilled eel), clams (vongole), scallops, *kamaboko* (cooked fish paste cake), shiitake mushrooms, cooked carrot or bamboo shoots, or other seasonal vegetables such as *yurine* (lily bulb).

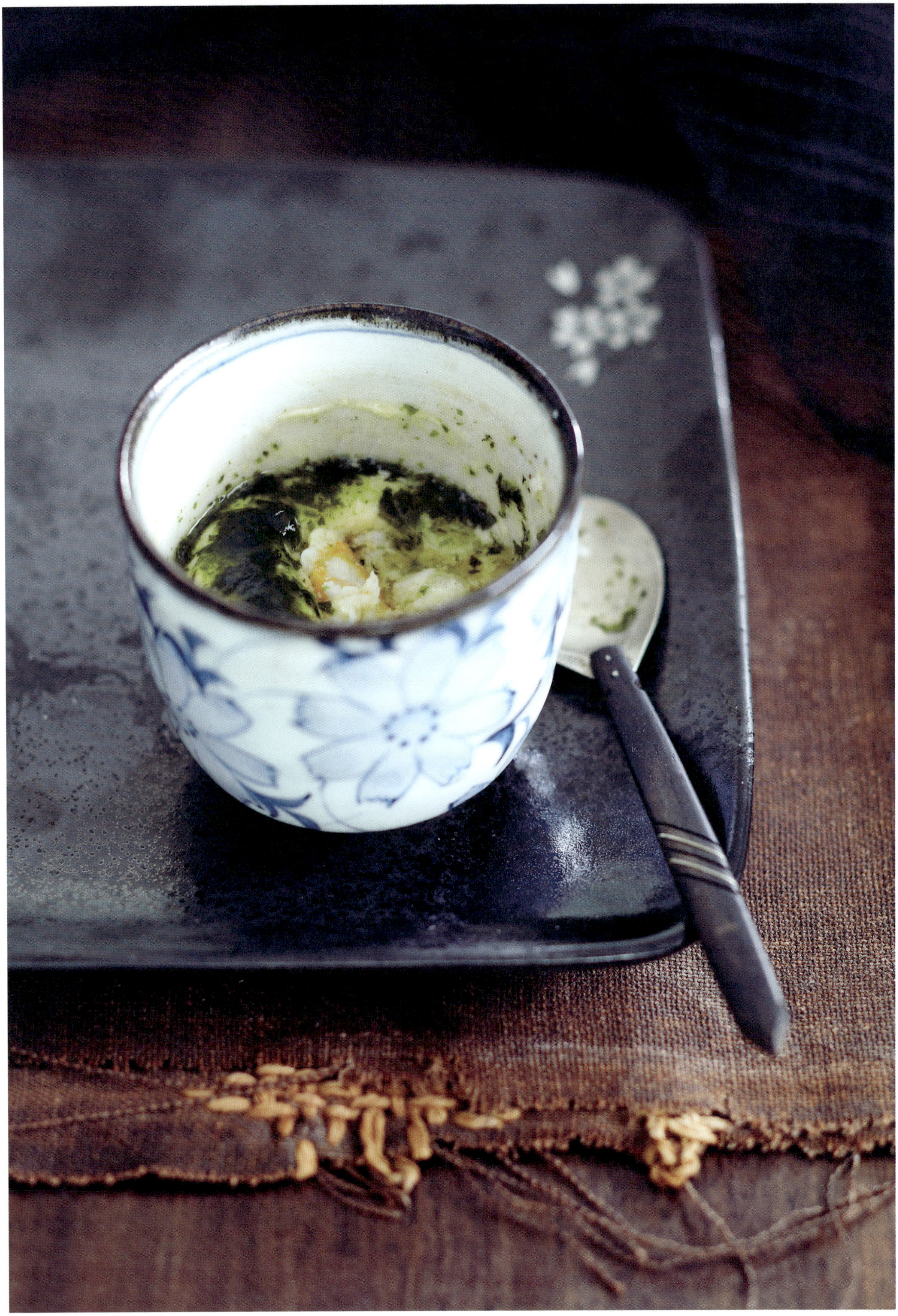

kisaragi / nigatsu – february / the 2nd month

tai to tamago okayu

rice gruel with snapper and yuzu
SERVES 4–6 AS PART OF A MULTI-DISH MEAL

There are three types of rice gruel or soup served in Japan: the first two, *okayu* and *ojiya*, are closer in texture to Chinese congee, to which they are related. *Okayu* is made with uncooked rice, and *ojiya* with leftover cooked rice left unrinsed.

In the third type, *zosui*, leftover cooked rice is rinsed to remove the excess starch, making a lighter, thinner gruel or soup.

My preference fluctuates between the three depending on my mood. If it's really cold I choose hearty, comforting *okayu* or *ojiya*, and if I need something lighter on my tummy I go for *zosui*.

The choice is yours of course, so prepare this recipe, inspired by the Yuzuya *ryokan*, as you wish.

300 g (10½ oz/1½ cups) white rice — or 740 g (1 lb 10 oz/4 cups) leftover cooked rice if making *ojiya* or *zosui*

3 litres (105 fl oz/12 cups) ichiban dashi (page 26), niban dashi (page 29) or kombu dashi (page 29) — depending on the depth of flavour you prefer

185 ml (6 fl oz/¾ cup) mirin

1½ teaspoons sea salt

1 whole fresh yuzu (optional)

350 g (12 oz) snapper fillets, skin on, cut into 3 cm (1¼ inch) squares

1 tablespoon wakame (seaweed), soaked in water for 2 minutes to partially rehydrate it, then drained

2 eggs (optional)

1 spring onion (scallion), thinly sliced

a handful of whole *mitsuba* (Japanese trefoil) or flat-leaf (Italian) parsley leaves

60 ml (2 fl oz/¼ cup) usukuchi shoyu (light Japanese soy)

2 tablespoons fresh or bottled yuzu juice or lemon juice

one or more of the following *furikake* (condiments): toasted sesame seeds, nori or *katsuobushi* (shaved dried, smoked bonito) flakes, or finely grated fresh ginger, to serve (optional)

Put the rice and dashi in a *donabe* or large flameproof casserole dish over high heat and bring to the boil. Add the mirin and salt and return to the boil. Skim off any foam from the surface, then reduce the heat and simmer for 1 hour if using uncooked rice, or 40 minutes if using leftover cooked rice, stirring regularly. The rice should become very soft and the soup thick.

(If using a whole fesh yuzu, run a small sharp knife lightly around the circumference and following the line, peel off a thick strip of skin. Place the yuzu in the centre of the *donabe* about 10 minutes before the end of the rice cooking time.)

Gently stir the snapper into the rice. Cook for 1 minute, then stir in the wakame.

Crack an egg, if using, in two opposite sides of the *donabe*. Turn off the heat and allow to sit for a minute — the egg whites will just start to cook a little around the edges.

Swirl the egg through the rice with chopsticks. Sprinkle the spring onion and *mitsuba* over the top and serve at the table with a ladle for scooping into small individual bowls. Just before serving, use the back of the ladle to press down on the yuzu, squeezing out some of its juice and fragrance into the rice.

Combine the shoyu and yuzu juice in a small jug, and have condiments available for each person to season their dish.

Variations: If you are under the weather and desiring something very simple but nurturing, simply make the soup up to the point where it softens and thickens, and omit the rest of the ingredients.

This dish is very versatile. Instead of snapper you could use other fresh or leftover ingredients, such as chicken, prawns (shrimp), fish paste cakes such as *kamaboko, chikuwa* or *satsuma-age* (page 152), Japanese mushrooms such as shimeji, shiitake or enoki, as well as miso, bamboo shoots and Asian greens.

One of my favourite versions includes chicken, bamboo shoots, shimeji mushrooms and leek, using tori dashi (page 208) or shiitake dashi (page 29).

A version using shiitake dashi (page 29) and a variety of Japanese mushrooms makes a great vegetarian *okayu*.

I was sad to leave my safe house in Okazaki, but took a deep breath and, with running mascara, headed south to 'the Gion house' for the next part of my adventure. The *machiya* (traditional townhouse), with tatami throughout, had been breathtakingly renovated. It was a little expensive, but I wanted to experience living somewhere reeking of history and in a neighbourhood where I could literally bump into whispering *maiko* (apprentice geisha or *geiko*) when stepping from my front door.

My friend and colleague Kay arrived from Australia earlier than expected and we spent hours catching up. I was surprised to be impervious to mention of office politics and saw it as a positive sign of moving on.

Kay seemed distracted on a stunningly beautiful morning walk to Kiyomizu Temple and I pondered whether work pressure might have been preventing her from taking it all in. I need not have worried: she is so incredibly sharp that she takes in so much more than seems possible, even during the most difficult of times. She made completely astute commentary about her surroundings and, sensing the Kyoto calm, instantly liked my temporary adopted home.

We stopped for lunch at Yuzuya, a gorgeous inn, and feasted on an astonishing selection of Kyoto *obanzai* (home-style dishes) in tiny portions, followed by a supremely comforting and nurturing rice hotpot with snapper, yuzu and eggs (page 218).

*

Several luxurious days were spent wandering with no specific aim in mind except to relax and absorb the surrounding beauty. We ducked in and out of quaint stores purveying various collectables: delicate papers and handicrafts, antique fabrics, prints, ceramics and other treasures all oozing potently ancient energy — yet by Japanese terms, many of the items would have been considered yesterday's trash. We refuelled in cafés from the ethereal to the bohemian, talking each other's ears off and walking until our feet ached.

While Kay was winding down, I took the opportunity to contemplate where I had come from and to — easily making comparisons now that someone who had witnessed my 'crash and burn' was now seeing me so much more at peace. Although I felt my mojo slowly returning, I was still far from the end of the journey. For the first time in too long, I felt beautiful and happy and was in no rush to go home.

*

It is not uncommon to find swirls of wispy cloud encircling the surrounding mountain peaks of the sacred district of Ohara, but the breathy formations seemed particularly heavenly and welcoming that day. Although renowned for its small but stupendous local farmers' market, the country village is infinitely more famous as the home of the serenely beautiful Sanzen-in Temple.

We quietly padded over the dwelling's tatami and out onto the open decking, where we slowly breathed in the unadulterated air. We gazed upon a frozen ballet of elegant budding cherry trees and listened to the sweet symphony of melted trickling snow and twittering hatchlings.

Kay was visibly moved and without a doubt under Sanzen-in's glorious spell. The spiritual essence of the villa-like temple is always palpable and guaranteed to draw an audible gasp from the lips of every first-time visitor. Those who make the return pilgrimage elicit a more obvious and grateful exhalation.

We slowly wandered about the grounds, snapping images that would never fully capture the experience. Rudimentary stone carvings of chubby, happy children lolled in the moss as we passed a makeshift teahouse, prompting a local to gently tap us on the shoulder, recommending we return to sample the tea. We sat peacefully on the red-cloaked benches, sipping on *kombu cha* — a savoury kelp tea laced with *ume* (plum) and gold leaf, in contemplative, involuntary meditation.

*

I awoke from one of those nightmares you can't shake. If I understand correctly, dreaming about water is somehow representative of one's emotions, so I couldn't help but wonder about the significance of a tidal wave that would wipe out life, as we know it ...

Of course, this came during a period in which I had been thinking about Dad more than usual and the memories of him taking his last gasping breath in our arms were painful — they had been 'silent' for some time.

This revival of grief was so intense I had sobbed mournfully into the dark for hours, hoping Kay couldn't hear me. It had now been 11 years since my father died and although my heart was suddenly aching, I was certain this release of residual grief, perhaps having been put on hold through other distractions in my life, was a very good thing.

It was Kay's last day in Kyoto so we took a final stroll together. In an antique shop on Shinmonzen Dori my eyes were drawn to a 180-year-old Edo-period plate. I instantly fell in love with its crackled bronze glaze, hand-etched plum blossom branch and ancient black *kanji* (calligraphy), which the shopkeeper translated as something like: 'In the spring and cold you must come.' It was destined to be mine!

After working up an appetite 'geisha hunting' — an addictive pastime in which one 'respectfully' rumbles with other tourists in an attempt to capture that elusively 'clear' shot of the ghostlike chameleons shuffling to appointments in firm-fitting kimonos — we scuttled off to dinner at Gion's sensational Kezako.

The meal commenced with its signature dish of foie gras, wrapped in sweet, funky *narazuke* (an amazing daikon pickle made with sake lees) and concluded with a dessert containing yuzu miso ice cream (see page 224) — a touch of pure genius, suitably fitting to farewell my brilliant friend.

*

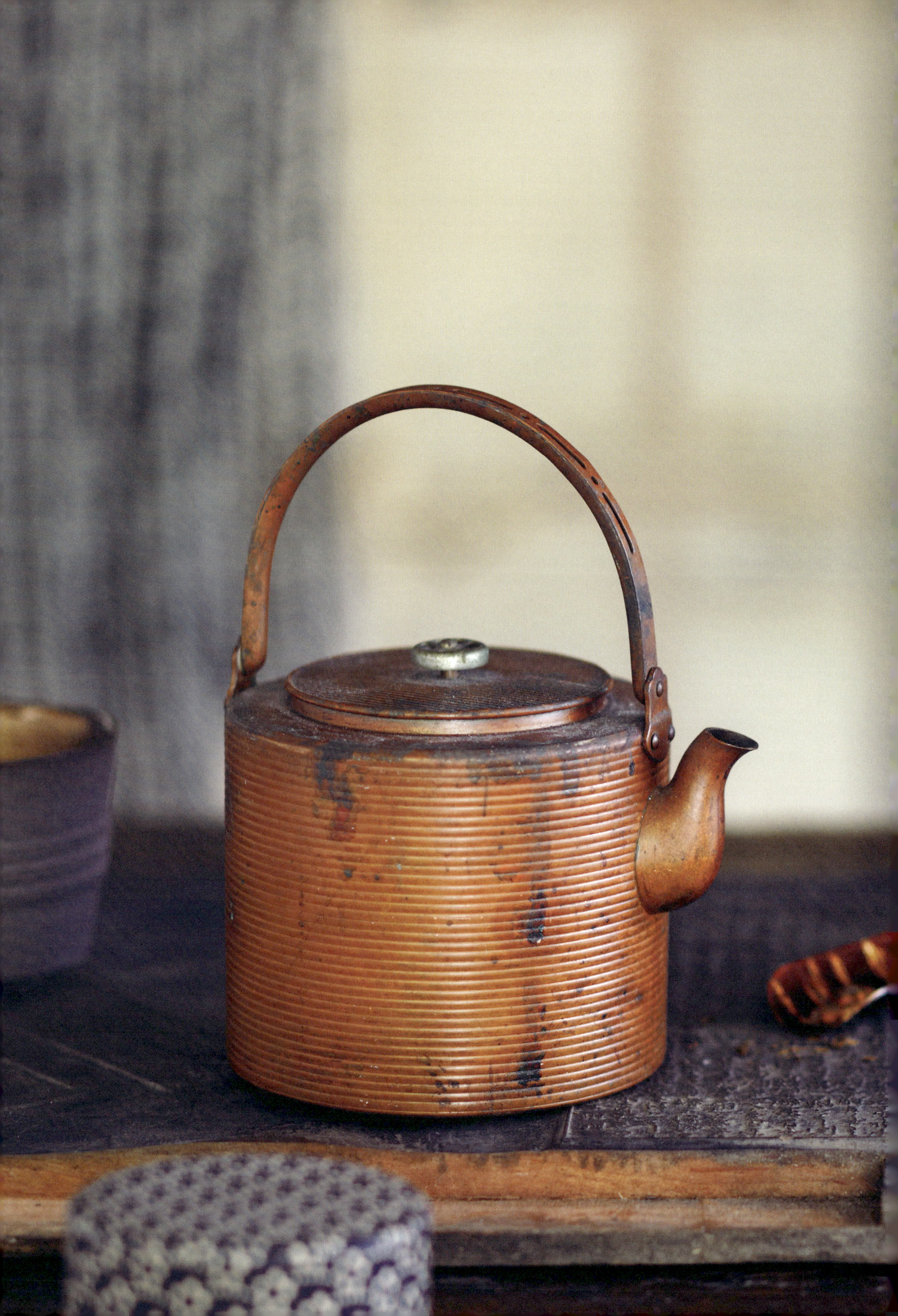

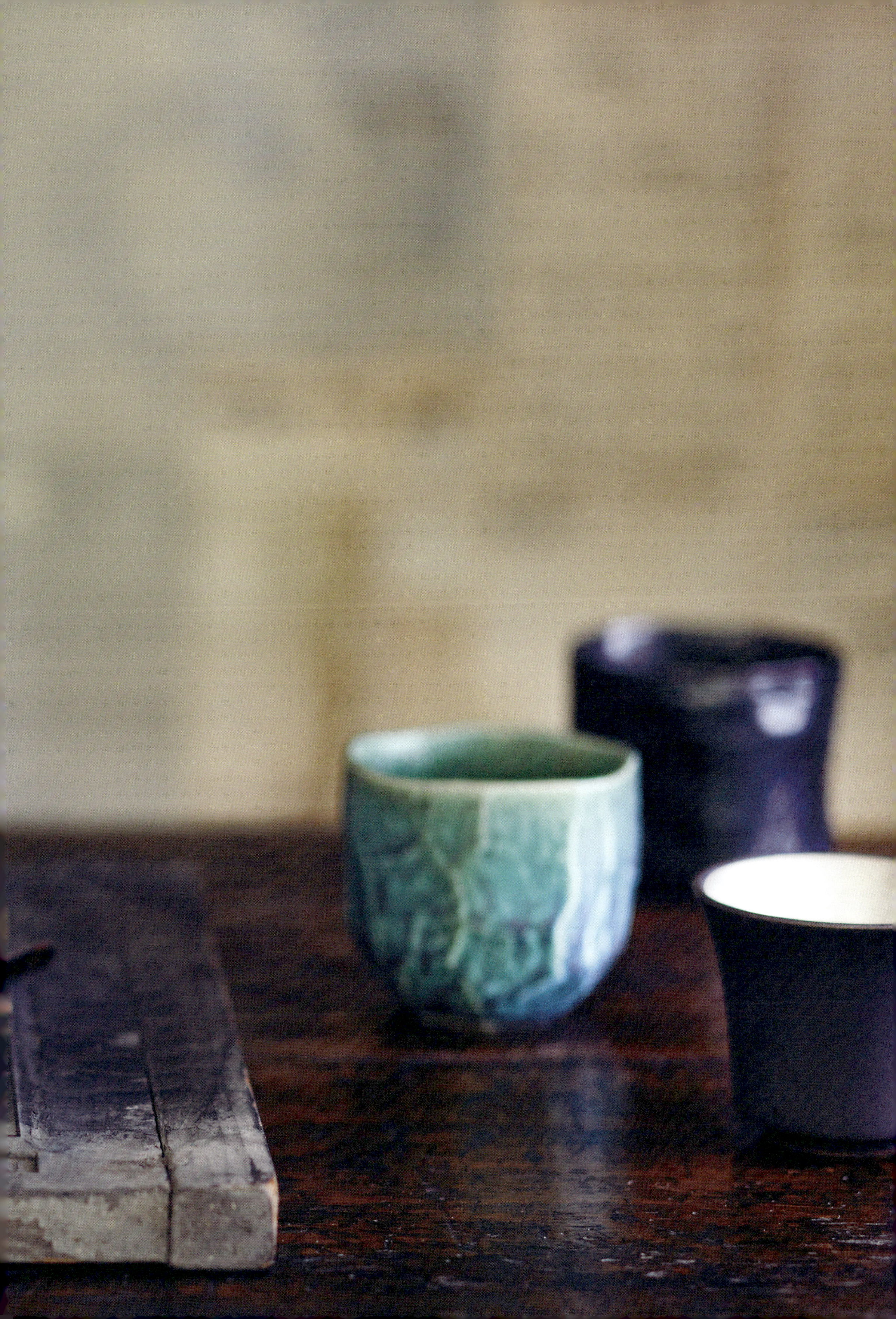

yuzu to miso aisu

yuzu and saikyo miso ice cream
MAKES 1.25 LITRES (5 CUPS)

The Japanese generally have a penchant for foods that may seem, er, somewhat curious to many of us — and ice-cream flavours are no exception.

While seaweed, soy, charcoal, wasabi, salad, garlic, curry and cypress may seem tame enough, the spectrum gets a little challenging at the other end: fried chicken, eel, squid guts and raw horse meat complete with chunks would not even tempt my adventurous palate (well maybe the fried chicken) ...

So while yuzu miso ice cream might sound a little odd, you can see it is tame in comparison. Actually it's delicious, and a perfectly complementary way to end a Japanese meal if a Western-style sweet is desired.

Not convinced? Try it for yourself. Remember saikyo miso is the sweetest of misos, with a creamy finish, and yuzu is, well, irresistible: a wonderful combination of sweet, tang, salty, creamy and *umami*. It is not a really sweet ice cream, but additional sugar may be added if desired.

500 ml (17 fl oz/2 cups) milk
375 ml (13 fl oz/1½ cups) cream
1 teaspoon finely grated yuzu or lemon zest
9 egg yolks
110 g (3¾ oz/½ cup) caster (superfine) sugar, or to taste
140 g (5 oz/½ cup) saikyo miso (sweet white miso)
1½ tablespoons fresh or bottled yuzu juice, or to taste
1 tablespoon good-quality sake

Put the milk, cream and yuzu zest in a saucepan over medium–high heat and bring just to the boil. Remove from the heat and set aside to infuse for 15 minutes.

Whisk the egg yolks and sugar in a bowl until creamy. While whisking, slowly pour the warm milk mixture onto the eggs, then strain into a clean saucepan. Stir over medium heat for 10 minutes, or until the mixture is just thick enough to coat the back of a spoon.

Remove from the heat, whisk in the miso, yuzu juice and sake and stir until smooth. Strain into a bowl, through a fine sieve.

Allow to cool slightly, then place a piece of plastic wrap over the surface of the custard and refrigerate until cold.

Churn in an ice-cream machine according to the manufacturer's instructions. Serve within 2–3 days.

houjicha to kinako aisu

roasted tea and kinako ice cream

MAKES 1 LITRE (4 CUPS)

I am a huge ice cream fan, so I couldn't help but start fiddling with other flavours while I was developing the yuzu miso ice cream opposite, and came up with this version, using beautiful *houjicha* (roasted green tea) and *kurosato* (Japanese black sugar) … Try this as an alternative to matcha (green tea) ice cream.

500 ml (17 fl oz/2 cups) milk
375 ml (13 fl oz/1½ cups) cream
1 vanilla bean, split open, seeds scraped and reserved
2½ tablespoons *houjicha* (roasted green tea)
9 egg yolks
185 ml (6 fl oz/¾ cup) *kuromitsu* (page 182), or instead use 100 g (3½ oz/½ cup) *kurosato* (Japanese black sugar) and 2 tablespoons honey
1½ tablespoons *kinako* (roasted soy bean powder)

Put the milk, cream and vanilla bean and seeds in a saucepan over medium–high heat and bring just to the boil. Remove from the heat, add the tea and set aside to infuse for 15 minutes.

Put the egg yolks, *kuromitsu* (or black sugar and honey) and *kinako* in a bowl and whisk until creamy. While whisking, slowly pour the warm milk mixture onto the eggs, then strain into a clean saucepan. Stir over medium heat for 10 minutes, or until the mixture is just thick enough to coat the back of a spoon.

Remove from the heat and strain into a bowl, through a fine sieve. Allow to cool slightly, then place a piece of plastic wrap over the surface of the custard and refrigerate until cold.

Churn in an ice-cream machine according to the manufacturer's instructions. Serve within 2–3 days.

While the winter peaks of the surrounding mountains are thick with powdery snow on an almost daily basis, there are only a handful of snowy days in Kyoto city. However, when the snowfall is enthusiastic enough to settle thickly, the contrast of dark wooded temple contours or vermilion *torii* against the pristine white snow is breathtaking and unforgettable. Even the most everyday items are transformed.

227 **kisaragi / nigatsu** – february / the 2nd month

Kamakura's salty sea air reminded me of home. To reach Fujii-san's house, Myong Hee, Mayumi and I had to scale a near-vertical staircase carved into the face of a sheer cliff: by the time I lugged myself to the top I was well and truly bemoaning the fact I hadn't checked in my suitcase at the station. My discomfort dissipated somewhat when awarded with a spectacular ocean view through scraggly, windswept trees and a welcome smile at the door.

Sweet, gentle Fujii-san sported a kind but impish twinkle in her eyes and I knew we were in for a treat. She seemed genuinely happy to have us in her home for the day and beckoned us to sit as she prepared a pot of flavoursome *kamairi-cha* — a pan-fried unfermented green tea.

Twenty-eight years prior, Fujii-san's late husband had introduced her to *shojin ryori* (Buddhist cuisine). At the time, he was a monk with the Zen Rinzai Buddhism sect and was so highly regarded for his cookery skills that he competed in the original series of *Iron Chef*. Only in Japan! After his death, Fujii-san continued to research various sects and develop her own style of cooking, eventually adding her own bestselling cookbooks to the bookshelf bearing her husband's lauded titles.

Although she was busy in the kitchen for most of the day, we managed to glean informative snippets from her as she darted in and out. She told me, in hushed tones of intermittent English, that to properly execute *shojin ryori*, the chief cook must possess *sanshin* or the three 'heart minds': being *daishin* (magnanimous mind); *roushin* (nurturing mind) and *kishin* (joyful mind), which would ensure they were able to properly sustain their Buddhist 'family'.

Emphasising the importance of seasonal ingredients, she added that she would never use a summer ingredient in winter. 'Why would you cool the body in winter by eating cucumber or tomato? You need roots and tubers for warming.' I certainly wouldn't argue with that. I was, however, curious to learn that onion and garlic were excluded from the cuisine long ago, as the ingredients were said to have 'stimulated' the monks.

She advised that *shojin ryori* was introduced to Japan by the Chinese in the thirteenth century as a segment of Zen Buddhism beliefs, and as such contains more fried foods than other Buddhist cuisine. To make their limited vegetables more interesting and substantial the Chinese, who were very poor at the time, fried them in oil to add texture, flavour and colour. Fried foods are particularly widespread throughout Japan today and, having perfected the art many centuries ago, you'd be hard-pressed to find a more perfectly fried morsel anywhere in the world.

Dish after spectacular dish drifted from the kitchen onto our tables: black sesame *gomadofu* (page 252) was topped with a spicy condiment of *yuzu kosho* (green chillies and yuzu zest). *Gobo* (burdock root) was tossed with a white tofu dressing for *gobo shira-ae*; see page 164 for the *shirae-ae* dressing. And *nagaimo yoromushi* — similar to *chawan mushi* (page 214), but using grated *nagaimo* (mountain yam) or sometimes daikon instead of eggs — was a first for me. It is regarded as a comfort food, particularly when convalescing.

Next was *rikyu-jiru kabu* — whole turnip, including its skin, cooked in a stock thickened with ground sesame and seasoned with *seri*, a leafy herb with a sharper flavour than the parsley-like *mitsuba* (Japanese trefoil). Sen Rikyu, a sixteenth-century Zen master of tea ceremony, couldn't get enough of the mighty sesame seed and, in his honour, *shojin ryori* dishes containing them are referred to as Rikyu-style.

Sautéed spinach and shimeji mushrooms were served chilled with a vinegar dressing and shredded nori. And the *awabi modoki* (fresh shiitake mushrooms stuffed with tofu; page 230) — named for the abalone it resembled, and served on a little fresh wakame seaweed salad — could indeed have been fished from the sea.

Koyadofu (from the Koyasan sect) is tofu that has been frozen, then dried, and eaten once it has been reconstituted by being simmered in liquid, commonly a mixture of dashi, shoyu and mirin. Dried foods are particularly popular in *shojin ryori*, as the nutrition and flavour levels are reportedly high due to their slow concentration by the sun. *Koyadofu* is the result of a happy accident involving tofu being accidentally left out in the snow, then eventually drying out in the sun. Fujii-san tells us it has 'sunshine power'.

The food kept coming: *daikon no fukii miso* (daikon topped with a combination of miso and bitter *fuki* leaves); rice with *kuromame* (black soy beans) and shiso; *renkon mochi* (lotus root dumplings) in soup; small dried fig, lotus and *kuwai* (arrowhead) tempura; and finally, a petite dessert of *nagaimo kintan* (yam jelly) with sweet kiwi fruit.

Fujii-san sat with us for tea and we chatted some more. We listened carefully as she compelled us with her passionate views about food. She was confident that until the end of the Edo period (1603–1868), although the Japanese were poor, they were nutritionally happy and proud. After the Meiji Era (1868–1912) and losing the war to the 'material world', Western foods flooded into Japan. She concurred with some of my other contacts that many younger Japanese started to embrace the foreign lifestyle, and because of this have 'forgotten how to live simply or realistically' and have also slowly lost their cooking skills — eroding the value of eating with family. She believed that many Japanese have become ill from a Western diet, acquiring dairy and wheat intolerances from eating foods that were never part of their ancestors' diet.

The afternoon certainly provided more 'food for thought' than I had anticipated.

*

229 kisaragi / nigatsu – february / the 2nd month

awabi modoki

mock abalone of tofu-stuffed shiitake
MAKES 8 PIECES; SERVES 4–8 AS PART OF A MULTI-DISH MEAL

This is my version of a recipe inspired by the incredible Mari Fujii.

300 g (10½ oz) block of silken tofu — organic if available
1 tablespoon mirin
1 tablespoon usukuchi shoyu (light Japanese soy)
1 tablespoon sake
1 tablespoon white sesame seeds, toasted
½ teaspoon finely grated fresh ginger (grated using a Japanese ginger grater)
½ teaspoon sea salt
8 fresh shiitake mushrooms, about 6 cm (2½ inches) in diameter, stems removed
katakuriko, potato starch or plain (all-purpose) flour, for dusting
1½ tablespoons sesame oil, for pan-frying
finely julienned mitsuba (Japanese trefoil), seri or shiso, to garnish (optional)

Wrap a double thickness of clean, dry cotton tea towel (dish towel) or several layers of kitchen paper around the tofu block and place it on a small baking tray.

Place another similar-sized tray on top, then weigh it down with a container filled with water — or a few tins of tomatoes! Allow to sit for 1 hour, or until the towel is soaking wet and the tofu is about half its original size. You may need to replace the tea towel or kitchen paper during this time.

Combine the mirin, shoyu and sake and set aside.

Finely grind the sesame seeds using a *suribachi* (ribbed Japanese mortar and wooden pestle). Crumble in the pressed tofu and continue to grind until the tofu is smooth. Stir in the ginger and salt until well combined.

Lightly brush the insides of the mushroom caps with starch or flour, then divide the tofu mixture among the caps and smooth over. Sift enough flour over the top of the tofu to lightly coat it.

Heat the sesame oil in a large frying pan over medium–high heat. When hot, add the mushrooms, tofu side up, and cook for 4 minutes. Carefully turn them over and cook for a further 4 minutes, or until a crisp golden crust has formed.

Quickly turn them over again so the mushrooms are tofu-side up. Carefully pour the shoyu mixture around the base of the mushrooms. Cook, shaking the pan occasionally, for about 1 minute, or until the liquid has almost evaporated.

Immediately serve the mushrooms on a platter, garnished with herbs if desired.

Variation: For an impressive vegetarian starter, heat some kombu dashi (page 29) and shiitake dashi (page 29) and thicken to a sauce-like consistency with *kuzu* or arrowroot. Add some rehydrated wakame (seaweed), then pour into wide shallow bowls and top each with two of the mushrooms.

231 **kisaragi / nigatsu** – february / the 2nd month

zenbu zen 232

During a much-needed post-lunch stroll along the beach I noticed a tsunami warning sign that prompted me to regale the group with my 'amusing' tidal wave dream. When another one of our group shared a similar dream from the same night, we silently glanced at each other before quickening our pace, heading inland.

Much later, during a sumptuous Italian feast in Kamakura, in vast contrast to the purity of the day, we all became Bacchanalian drunk. Myong Hee fell asleep completely upright, serviettes were twisted into moustaches, and my left hip gave way — but I managed to pour myself into a cab and hobble to my hotel room.

I spent the night writhing in pain, while passively smoking the festering air expelled from the night receptionist's lungs. By morning I was in a shocking state, yet I was given no concession — forced by my friends at breakfast to imbibe *ika shiokara* or, more poetically, 'raw squid strips in a sauce of its own fermented guts', together with milky sake containing the same bacteria as yoghurt. After my recent *namako* (sea slug guts) experience, which followed the river fish parasite incident, I had a sneaking suspicion that I would be reintroducing *shiokara* to the world at any time. My prediction proved to be correct during another smoky train trip home.

When I eventually slumped onto my futon, I felt haunted, not by the 150-year-old house I was living in, but by my own fear: I was afraid of continuing to repeat the same patterns and mistakes I had already made. Exactly what had I learnt here? I'd certainly had less rest than I'd intended. Introducing the word 'no' to my vocabulary would have been useful.

It was two steps forward, one step back. I had witnessed my guests absorb the 'Zen' of Kyoto and flitter back to Australia re-energised and indeed inspired to change their own lives. But was I achieving any such thing? I checked in with myself to find that while I still felt pressured and stressed to a certain degree, and tired from looking after everyone else but myself, I had to acknowledge that certain things were different: after nine months of hell, my cough had finally receded; my blood no longer boiled when something potentially infuriating occurred; and I was better able to let go of things, both metaphorically and literally, that I may normally have held on to for way too long. I even noted that I was eating more slowly, a considerable indication that everything was in fact slowing down just a little for me.

*

My shiatsu therapist, Bridget, advised that my suddenly super-sensitive bladder was a sign of being 'busy busy'. No surprises there.

When she touched certain points on my body, I became almost narcoleptic. At the end of the session, she cupped her hands over my eyes and, perhaps delusional with exhaustion, I had the most intense experience. Like an acid flashback, row upon row of tiny pencil-line Buddhas filled the void, as though someone accidentally leant on a keyboard of a cosmic computer.

This image was just as quickly replaced with a three-dimensional hexagon displaying a glowing white *kanji* (Japanese language character) pulsating as if to get my attention. I tried to focus on the *kanji* so I could look up its meaning when I got home, but when Bridget moved her hands to my ears, the light spread out golden and the message had been erased.

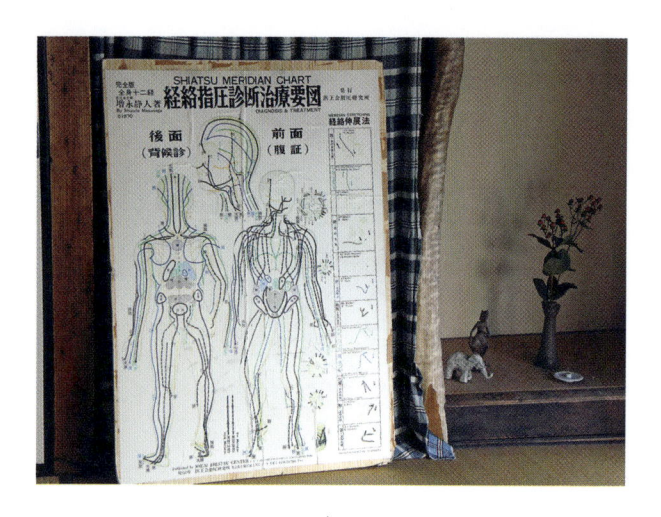

I was rather curious as to what was happening: shiatsu seemed to be having a profound effect on my mind and body, but Bridget was almost as perplexed as I was and sensibly suggested there was a lot going on in my system and that I should just stay and rest a while rather than moving anywhere too soon. I gratefully took her up on the offer, only departing the room when two stinkbugs arrived with my marching orders.

At home I slept as though I was drugged until it came time to heave myself out of bed and dress for dinner. I felt I had to go: it was in my honour and, of course, there is the Japanese rule of obligation to be adhered to.

Before leaving Australia I had confided in a friend, coincidentally Buddhist, that I was worried I might find myself a bit lonely in Japan. She responded by saying that the Buddhist belief is that you recreate your own little world wherever you are, and in some ways I feared I had done exactly that. I'm not seriously complaining. I knew how very fortunate I was to have made friends so quickly here, but right now I was in urgent need of peace, quiet and rest. Symptoms of stress and anxiety began to sneak up on me again. I had forgotten how debilitating it was and, although disappointed in myself for allowing it to happen again, I was appreciative of the reminder that my illness was very recent history. I really needed to employ every effort to just STOP!

*

The lack of knowledge from the ever-courteous station staff regarding the whereabouts of the *Twilight Express* platform was proof that the slow route to Hokkaido is not the preferred option for a tech-savvy generation. However, I was strangely happy to be making the old-fashioned journey.

I'd arrived early, feeling completely spaced out and disconnected. I watched the second hand of the station clock … tick … tick … tick …

Unable to move, and without reason to, I sat frozen, relishing the act of waiting and the prospect of doing absolutely nothing and speaking to no one for the next 23 hours. I was in dire need of time to myself and hoped that my Niseko host Ruskin — a friend of an acquaintance, who had been living and working on the mountain for a few years — would allow me to use a room in his spacious home as a safe place. That's a lot to ask of anyone, but particularly someone you had never met or even spoken with.

I spent the first six hours locked away in my tiny, protective sleeper cabin, staring out the window at the rugged countryside, watching wild waters crash against the shoreline before being surrounded by snow laid out as far as the eye could see. As we skated over the icy tracks, my brain was challenged by the split view of snowy mountains to my left and tumultuous grey seas on my right. When there was no longer enough light to see even a hint of a shadow, I set my iPod on shuffle and continued to block out the world before drifting off.

Dawn began to break just prior to leaving the coast of Honshu, Japan's main island, via a tunnel 400 metres below sea level (200 metres below the sea bed).

A stab of panic went through me. My anxiety levels shot through the roof in the seemingly endless tunnel while, at the same time, exhaustion attempted to pull me back into slumber. I had no real concept of time, but the longer it dragged on, the more delirious I became, until I finally yelled internally 'JUST LET IT GO' and, without exaggeration, we were out the other side within seconds.

Safely on Hokkaido, I noted my insanely desolate surroundings: snowy ghost towns so bleak and far-reaching that I wondered if I had somehow hopped on the wrong train and crossed over to Siberia.

Pulling into Sapporo, I received a concerned text from a friend. There had been an earthquake in Chile, resulting in tsunami warnings in Japan, particularly Hokkaido.

I switched on the TV in my hotel room: every station was broadcasting red alert warnings. I would be safe in Niseko, but a shudder went through my whole body as I recalled, once again, my recent tsunami dream.

Had my semi-conscious thoughts, in the deep-sea tunnel, about the potential destruction caused by a huge earthquake under the sea bed really been so ridiculous? I was not feeling particularly comfortable about making the return journey. But I would think about that later.

Right now I needed to switch off.

*

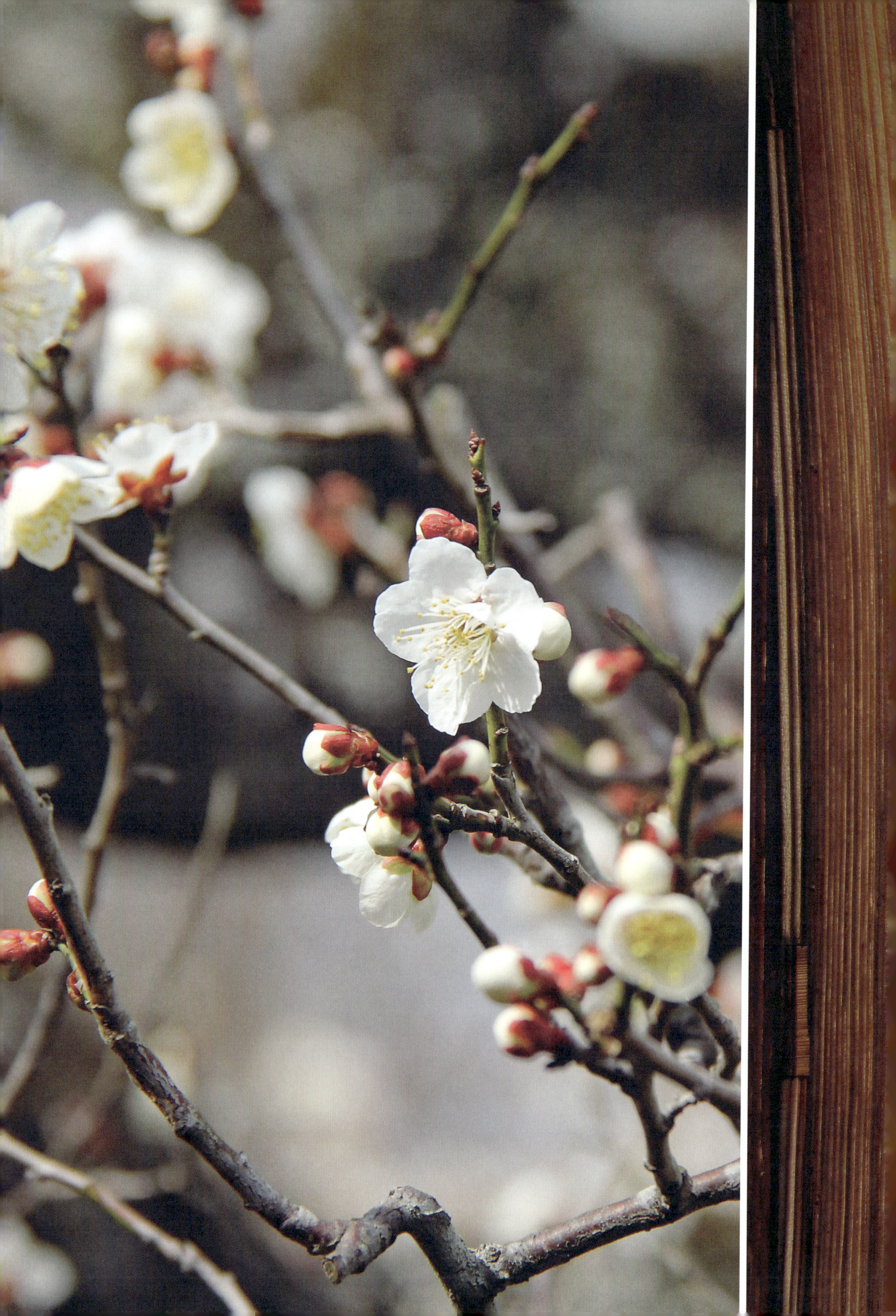

yayoi/sangatsu & uzuki/shigatsu

MARCH & APRIL : THE 3RD & 4TH MONTHS

CHAPTER 5

THE 3RD & 4TH MONTHS

The months when things grow luxuriously and the unohana blooms.

march / april

yayoi / sangatsu & uzuki / shigatsu

I arrived at Kutchan Station a little nervous about staying with a complete stranger. About a minute before my host was due to arrive, he sent me a text informing me he was running 15 minutes late, so I waited outside in the snow. It was bleak, but beautiful, and I enjoyed my first glimpse into a far more sparsely populated Japan.

About half an hour later, and starting to get a little chilled, I received a call to say that he was detained due to a 'domestic issue' and one of his boys would arrive soon to pick me up. Oh, and they were arranging some alternative accommodation ... just for one night, maybe ... I imagined a small avalanche taking out a bedroom or perhaps sewage flooding the house, before settling on a more likely scenario involving a female.

After waiting in the snow for an hour, I was feeling rather peeved by the time my chauffeur arrived, and was understandably cautious about getting into a vehicle with someone who was even more of a stranger than my host-to-be. Part of me wanted to return to Sapporo ... until the very handsome Paul hopped out of the car and I decided to take my chances. Warm and considerate, he was clearly attempting to make my transition into 'snow town' as smooth as possible. As he lifted my suitcase into the car, I casually asked him what the drama was. The softly spoken Kiwi cleared his throat before diplomatically replying: 'I think I'll let Ruskin explain that one to you.'

Pressing him further with a 'Sooo, I'm staying somewhere else tonight?' he cryptically responded that he was still working on that. I laughed nervously and asked if he realised how surreal this was for me? I was somewhere I had never been, in a car with a guy I didn't know from an axe murderer, who was supposed to be driving me to some dude's place whom I had also never met, but there was a secret 'situation' and no one knew where I was actually going to be spending the night.

He was silent, awkwardly searching for the right thing to say, so I quickly saved him by adding that my time in Japan had been very much about going with the flow, so I guessed that this was what I needed to do. He agreed it was 'probably the best approach'. He also revealed that, en route to lunch, we would pop into the supermarket to pick up some supplies, as he'd love me to help the two of them cook dinner for some guests that night. Yes, it crossed my mind that we were stocking up for a month in a remote shack where I'd be prepared for sale into slavery ... before lecturing my vivid imagination to pipe down.

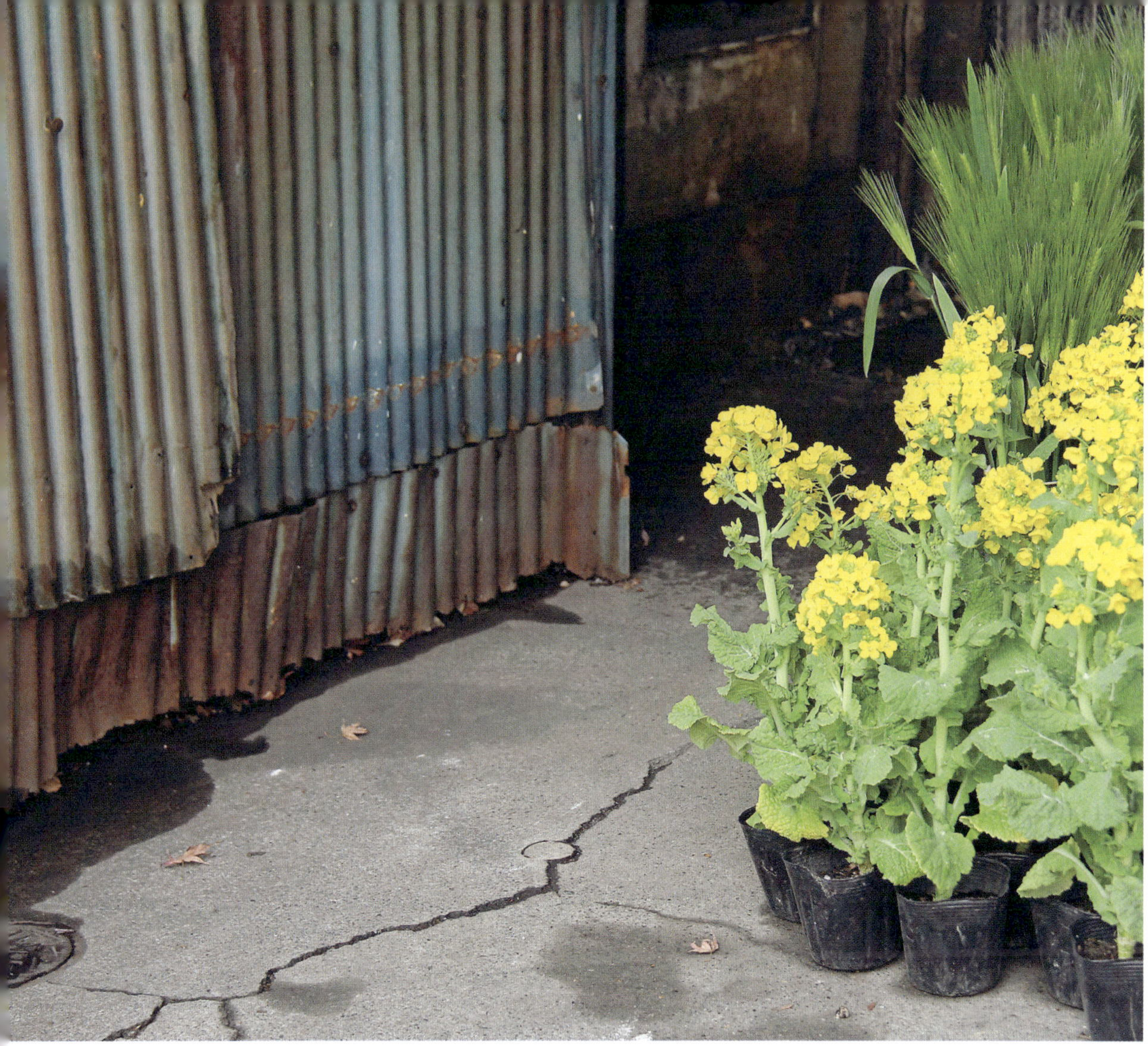
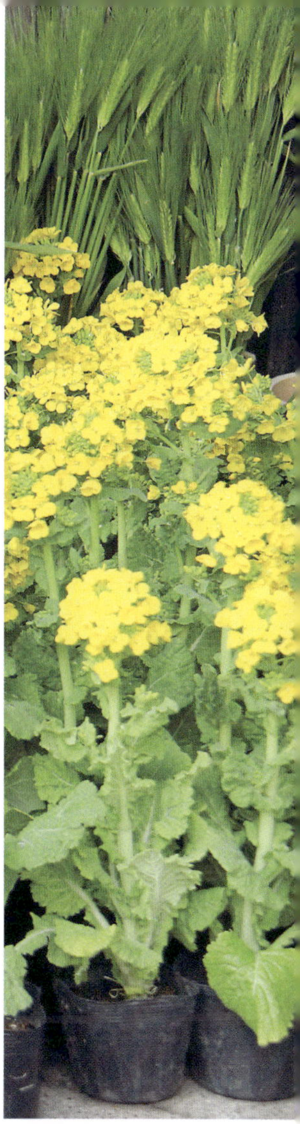
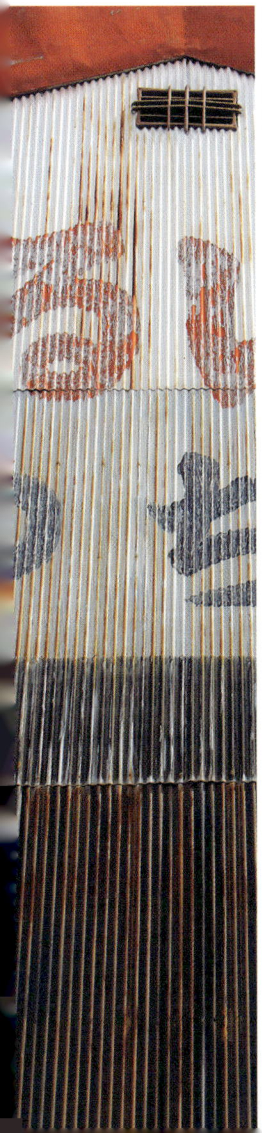
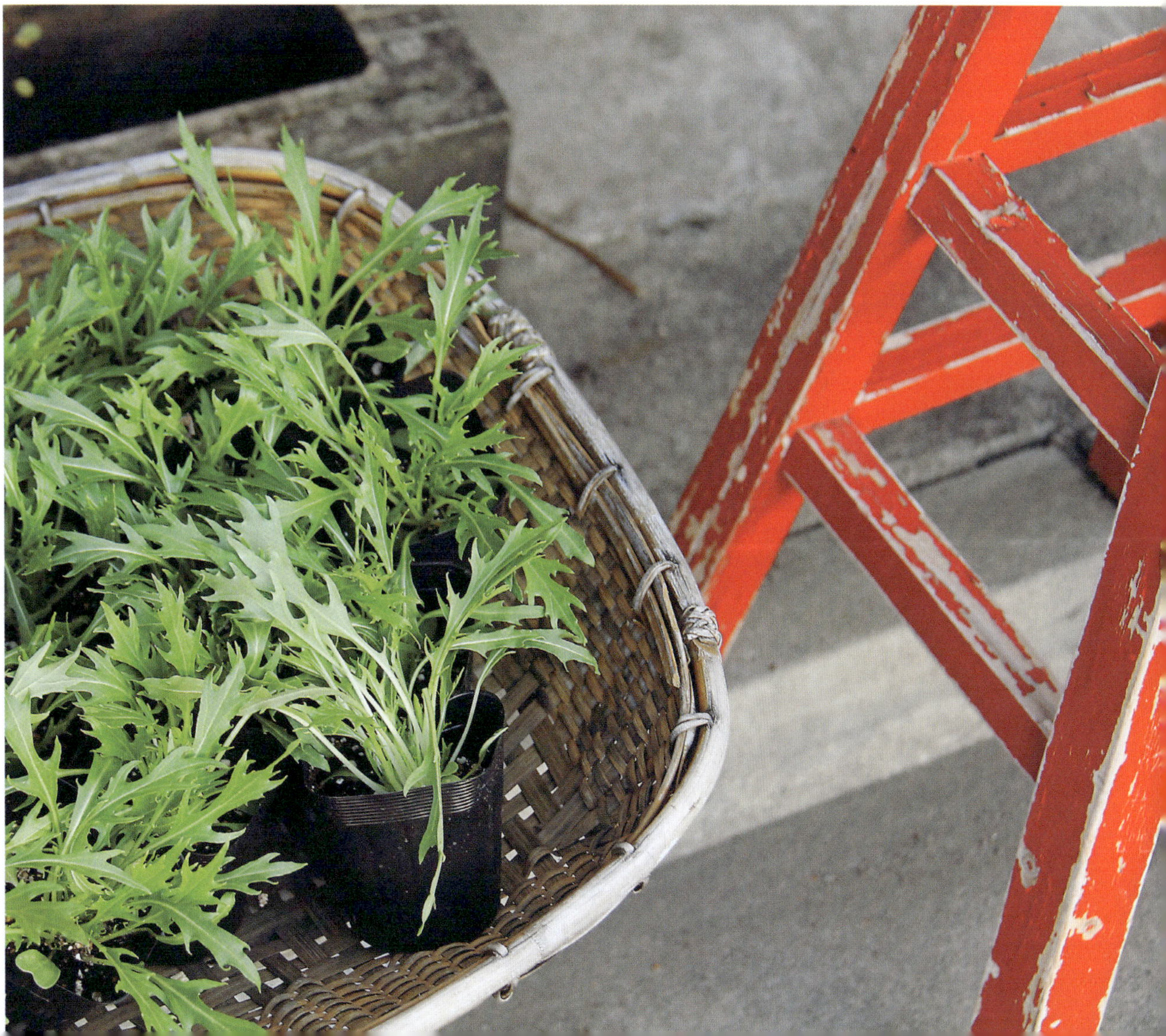

In the supermarket, Paul removed his sunglasses and I could see from the warmth in his gaze that he had a good heart: I finally felt safe and so began to relax.

Paul and I started to chat more openly, so I decided, in my own subtle way, to dig a little deeper: 'Paul ... what the f*** is going on?' Taken aback, and remaining mildly discreet, he simply replied that his boss was tied up.

Sensing that I was unlikely to relent, and with a mischievous glint in his eyes, he added, 'Well, not literally,' before turning to whisper into a refrigerated cabinet, 'although he might be ...'

Uh-huh! So there *was* a girl involved. I laughed, relieved there hadn't been a landslide.

But I was feeling a bit irked by the possibility that my host was one of those typical 'lost boys living the dream' in a ski village full of transient female passengers. I feared I was not going to like him at all. Paul and I ended up discussing life and love and generally bonding over a dish unique to Hokkaido — soup curry (see opposite).

*

Ruskin eventually called to say the coast was clear and, within minutes, my luggage was transferred into his honking four-wheel drive.

Although I had already concluded — rather presumptuously — what kind of character he was, I still made an awkward attempt to connect with him by initiating conversation.

A brief and prickly interaction ensued, with his seemingly flippant comments pushing all the wrong buttons. While he was busy raising his eyebrows, I dramatically rolled my eyes skyward in annoyance, before fixing my gaze out the passenger window for the remainder of the short drive to his home.

However, shallowness prevailed once inside his gorgeous three-storey abode, where I had my own comfy room and ensuite and access to a Western kitchen, replete with a *real* oven! In contrast to my morning, the afternoon was incredibly peaceful, tucked in on all sides by loads of powdery white stuff. I was in heaven, no matter what I thought of my host.

He left me to unpack and settle in, telling me to make myself at home while he returned to work — likely wishing I would just bugger off back to Kyoto.

By evening, still alone in the house, I started to potter around in my invisible chef's hat, concerned about having dinner ready by the time the guests arrived.

Ruskin casually wandered in some time later, and instead of jumping to it when I suggested, with some urgency, that we start preparations, he looked me in the eyes and said, in a rather defeated tone: 'Actually you and I are just going to relax with a drink and get to know each other before we do anything else.' He earned several points for the suggestion.

It turned out the situation with his female friend earlier in the day had been rather more traumatic and personal than the scenarios I'd imagined. On top of that, his day had gone from bad to worse with some concerning news from home. I apologised for walking into the middle of his nightmare and adding to it. He responded genuinely, saying that it was nice to have someone to talk to about it. And there we were, sudden and unexpected friends.

*

suupu kare

soup curry
SERVES 6–8

For a more substantial meal, serve the soup with rice and pickles (see pages 154–159) on the side. You can also serve it over cooked ramen or udon noodles.

80 ml (2½ fl oz/⅓ cup) vegetable oil
2 teaspoons sesame oil
800 g (1 lb 12 oz) boneless, skinless chicken thighs, cut into 4 cm (1½ inch) pieces
1 brown onion, thinly sliced
1 tablespoon Japanese curry powder, or other mild curry powder
1 teaspoon *shichimi togarashi* (seven-flavour spice mix), plus extra to serve
2 litres (70 fl oz/8 cups) tori dashi (page 208), or half niban dashi (page 29) and half water
½ large carrot, halved lengthways, then thickly sliced
6 thick lotus root slices
½ apple, grated
125 ml (4 fl oz/½ cup) tomato passata (puréed tomatoes)
1 garlic clove, very finely chopped
1 teaspoon finely grated fresh ginger
2 tablespoons usukuchi shoyu (light Japanese soy)
125 ml (4 fl oz/½ cup) mirin
2 Japanese (slender) eggplants (aubergines), cut into slices 1 cm (½ inch) thick, or 4 slices of regular eggplant (aubergine), each cut into slices 1 cm (½ inch) thick, then cut into quarters
200 g (7 oz) jap pumpkin (winter squash), cut into six semi-circular slices 5 mm (¼ inch) thick
150 g (5½ oz) shimeji mushrooms, broken into small clumps
1 spring onion (scallion), thinly sliced

Heat 2 tablespoons of the vegetable oil with the sesame oil in a large pot over medium–high heat. Season the chicken pieces with sea salt and freshly ground black pepper and sear, in batches, for a few minutes, or until lightly golden. Remove from the pot and set aside.

Add a little more oil to the pot if needed. Add the onion and cook, stirring occasionally, for 8 minutes, or until lightly golden.

Add the curry powder and *shichimi togarashi* and stir to combine. Cook for 30 seconds, then return the chicken to the pot. Add the dashi, carrot, lotus, apple, passata, garlic, ginger, shoyu and mirin and stir to combine.

Allow to come to the boil, then reduce the heat and simmer for 40 minutes.

Meanwhile, heat the remaining oil in a frying pan over medium–high heat. Cook the eggplant slices for 2–3 minutes on each side, or until golden. Then cook the pumpkin slices for 4–5 minutes on each side, or until golden and cooked through. Blot the vegetables with kitchen paper to remove the excess oil. Set aside.

Once the chicken has simmered for 40 minutes, add the eggplant to the soup. Cook for 15 minutes, then add the pumpkin and the mushrooms and cook for a final 5 minutes, or until the chicken and vegetables are very tender.

Serve the soup in deep bowls, with the spring onion and extra *shichimi togarashi* for sprinkling over as desired.

While there are regional differences in Japanese cuisine, there is always a very familiar thread throughout. Most dishes rely on the base flavours of shoyu, dashi, mirin and sake in varying ratios, with miso and vinegar also appearing regularly. Accents are added via only a limited number of herbs and spices (in comparison with other cuisines) — most commonly ginger, sesame, shiso, sansho and *kinome*, or the perfume of citrus such as yuzu and *sudachi*.

243　yayoi / sangatsu & uzuki / shigatsu – march & april / the 3rd & 4th months

I spent the following five days almost comatose, but in a good way. For the first time since I'd arrived in Japan I really started to unwind. I lazed around the house witnessing snowfall like I had never experienced, watching movies and writing occasionally.

When the skies were clear I ventured to the village deli and stocked up on Hokkaido camembert wrapped in a local grass, honey infused with lavender grown in a nearby field, dark chocolate and berry muesli, organic eggs and milk, smoky bacon, pickled cherries, yoghurt from a farmhouse a few minutes down the hill and spiced plum jam. I then wandered home with my bounty, peeking into the windows of small alpine restaurants offering ramen and Hokkaido crab.

I thoroughly enjoyed baking huge crusty pies, hearty stews and caramelised bread and butter puddings for the increasing number of boys who came to visit. They made me cups of tea and poured me wine — clever lads — and, after being surrounded by mostly women for several months, I was appreciative of the masculine energy. The guys who complained that the mountain locals were predominantly male were also enjoying some female company. Much laughing and many long and lovely chats ensued.

Setting aside the initial couple of hours, I adored every minute of this incredibly beautiful winter wonderland. For hours at a time, I was glued to the vision of the snow layering thickly on the slanting roof. I was truly comforted by the snow and, in an unexpected form of meditation, examined the detail and unique patterns in the individual flakes I collected as they paraded by the window on a daily basis. I was moved by the beauty, fragility and poignant message they conveyed — exquisite and fleeting, forming the perfect metaphor for freefalling with grace in a life all too short.

While it had been a rocky start, this week of peace, beauty and menfolk had facilitated a definite and much-needed shift in me. It felt good, if somewhat disconcerting. I was overbearingly emotional about leaving the mountain. I'd been once again pushed beyond my comfort zone and found that on the other side was unforeseen joy. I remain indebted to my open-minded host for his incredible hospitality and generosity when I needed it most, and for not kicking me out for being so bloody judgmental.

*

Back in Kyoto, I felt rather discombobulated, unsettled by changes and new events that now loomed on the horizon. I would soon be returning home to Sydney to briefly see my family, en route to the Melbourne Food and Wine Festival, where I was moderating a masterclass — then returning to Kyoto in a few weeks' time. My short-term lease on the luxury traditional townhouse had come to an end, and I was now bunkered down in a hotel room, conserving energy for the full-on demands that lay ahead.

It was spring and I hoped I was regenerating — slowly shedding years of crusty exterior to reveal a taut green shoot ready to stretch and blossom again. But in reality I felt stagnant, as though the cold of winter had snap-frozen my shell.

*

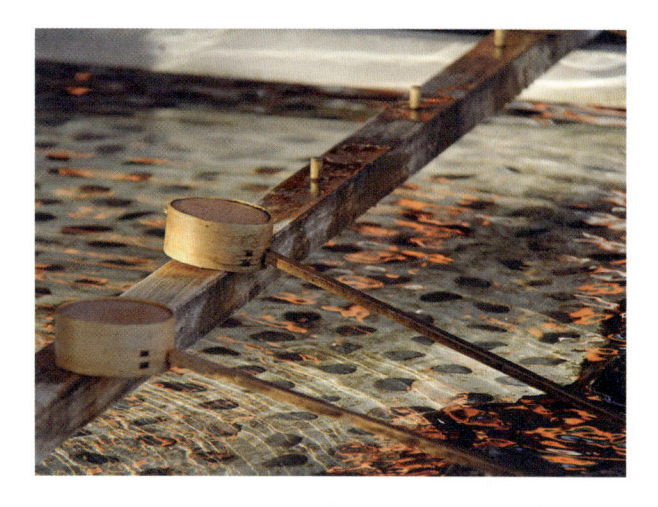

Back in Sydney, I was living in limbo as my apartment was still rented out. I felt dazed, out of place and cranky as hell. I somehow made it to Melbourne, where I was bombarded with compliments from friends and colleagues, who noticed I'd lost the deathly taint I'd sported prior to departure — and a considerable amount of weight, too.

Being thrown back into the thick of the food scene was confronting and I found the small talk excruciating. My unease was apparently noticeable, but I was somewhat reassured when several high-profile and seemingly effortlessly effervescent foodie personalities confided that they found it difficult and exhausting, too. It made me start to question why a high-profile role in food media was all so desirable in the first place. Was this still right for me? I flashed back to my crazy life pre-Japan and felt tiny pinpricks of anxiety.

There had to be a different way forward. I couldn't wait to return to Japan and was missing my simple lifestyle and diet. I craved Kyoto, where I could escape the noise and frenetic energy that invaded my senses in a crazy Western world, where it seemed impossible to slow down enough to absorb any beauty or grace.

*

I felt instantly comforted to be back on Japanese ground. Kyoto was my town, more 'home' than home in many ways, and here I was, dutifully playing tour guide to my mother and her friend.

After several days sharing a tiny one-bedroom apartment, I needed a change of scene. I jumped at an invitation to dinner at Bridget and Tad's, to sample Tad's cooking.

Our cook seemed a little bashful, but was nevertheless extremely focused. Bridget and I sat sipping sake under the *kotatsu* (low heated table), nibbling on *fuki no miso* (page 247), while Tad chopped, mixed and stirred in the kitchen directly beneath us. After a short while he appeared in the doorway with a few more dishes for our feast of very fine seasonal fare: *asupara no yaki-bitashi* (grilled asparagus dressed with dashi, shoyu and yuzu; page 247); deep-fried, crumbed baby bamboo shoots; *ebi manju* (prawn dumpling in ankake sauce; page 188); and a sublime lotus root and prawn hasami ('fried sandwich'; an exquisite version of the eggplant and pork *hasami* on page 88).

As well as teaching English at university level for a crust, Tad is completely obsessed with Japanese cuisine. In fact, it was what motivated him to move from America to Kyoto over 15 years earlier, and his local culinary knowledge is enviable. The meal was so well executed that, had I been blindfolded, I might have assumed a highly experienced Japanese chef had prepared the feast. Everything was authentic: from Tad's thoughtful plating on traditional tableware and subtle use of colour, to the humble and slightly expectant expression on his face as he presented each dish. It was a magnificent meal with great company — even if poor Tad spent most of the night either in the kitchen or running up and down the stairs listening to his audience flitting between moans of delight and raucous, sake-induced laughter.

*

zenbu zen 246

fuki no miso

bitter leaves in miso

MAKES ¾ CUP

This moreish paste, eaten like a dip with cabbage leaves or cucumber, traditionally contains the leaves from the *fuki* plant (also known as giant butterbur), a native Japanese spring vegetable that is not readily available outside Japan. *Fuki* has a naturally bitter flavour and consists of stems resembling celery stalks (commonly simmered in dashi as a side vegetable), topped with large, frill-edged leaves. New spring buds, or *fuki no tou*, are closed, papery flowers, often used in tempura.

25 g (1 oz/½ cup firmly packed) celery leaves, chopped
2–3 teaspoons fine *katsuobushi* (shaved dried, smoked bonito)
5 tablespoons saikyo miso (sweet white miso)
1 tablespoon aka miso (red miso)
1 teaspoon finely grated fresh ginger
3 teaspoons mirin
2½ tablespoons walnuts, toasted and finely chopped
200 g (7 oz) outer cabbage leaves, cut into 7 cm (2¾ inch) squares

Mix all the ingredients except the cabbage until well combined. Place in a small, non-metallic container that has a lid and smooth the surface over. Place a layer of waxed paper over the top, then cover with the lid, or at least seal tightly with several layers of plastic wrap.

Leave for a few days to mature. Stir the mixture once a day, then smooth it over again and seal well.

Serve with the cabbage leaf squares — spoon a little of the mixture onto the leaves, fold them up and eat with your fingers.

asupara no yaki-bitashi

grilled and drenched asparagus

SERVES 4 AS PART OF A MULTI-DISH MEAL

80 ml (2½ fl oz/⅓ cup) ichiban dashi (page 26)
2 teaspoons usukuchi shoyu (light Japanese soy)
2 teaspoons mirin
1 teaspoon sake
1 bunch (175 g/6 oz) asparagus, ends trimmed
2 teaspoons sesame oil
very fine strips of fresh yuzu or lemon zest, to serve (optional)

Combine the dashi, shoyu, mirin and sake in a flat, shallow container, just big enough to fit the asparagus. Set aside.

Preheat the grill (broiler) to high. Line a baking tray with foil.

Toss the asparagus with the sesame oil and place on the baking tray. Grill (broil) the asparagus, turning occasionally, for 6–10 minutes, or until the spears start to look blackened in places and are tender when pierced with the tip of a knife. The actual grilling time will depend on the thickness of your asparagus.

Immediately cut each asparagus spear in half and add to the dashi mixture, turning well to coat.

Leave to cool. Serve at room temperature in a neat bundle on a small lipped plate, garnished with zest if desired.

It's no secret the Japanese have an insatiable appetite for fine cuisine, but it appears many foreigners who choose to live here are also serious foodies with a strong appreciation for Japan's contribution to the culinary world.

Before this trip, I was naive enough to consider myself reasonably well educated on the topic. But I found myself learning a whole new language. Much of Japanese cuisine has not travelled as extensively as it might: as well as the translation stumbling block, there's the fact that many *Nihonjin* (Japanese) never leave their own island. As a result, the people are often shy and suspicious of other cultures and reluctant to share with those they have not built a relationship of trust with. I am determined, perhaps destined, to soak up as much of the unique food ethos and broader culture as possible — not only for my own interest, but in the hope I may share it with the many who may never have an opportunity to access it.

The intricacies and subtle nuances of this evolutionary cuisine and its historical and social implications are mind-boggling. How and why a certain food is placed on a specific serving dish at a certain time of the year, carried to the table and ceremoniously set before you is fascinating, inspiring and mildly intimidating.

*

A tour I'd arranged for Mum, with Japanese garden expert Mark Hovane, far exceeded my expectations when we found he was well versed in the art of the tea ceremony. When we stopped for *matcha* and *wagashi* on the verandah of a villa in the Daitokuji Temple complex, Mark explained that the view we were taking in was typical of a teahouse garden, being more *wabi sabi* than manicured.

Wabi sabi is difficult to define. In fact, attached to the Buddhist concept of impermanence, it is considered desirable not to. It is almost purposefully vague, allowing for contemplation. Not wishing to sound too cryptic, it is commonly used to describe the harmonious feeling or connection one has on experiencing 'it', in opposition to something more tangible. Words such as 'rustic' are often bandied about for foreigners who insist on a 'logical' label. My interpretation? *Wabi sabi* is something that has been withered and wizened by the elements of nature or time, or both, to reveal a more interesting, organically attractive, elegant and thought-provoking core. Even when something is missing from 'the picture', it allows an empty space on which to gaze and ponder. Although it sounds confusing, *wabi sabi* is an engaging Zen philosophy.

A vacated cicada shell still perched on a branch is a fragile and slightly exotic sign of impermanence. And a weathered fence, tainted with rivers of green, amber and blue (the result of nail rust, algae blooms and age) also holds a certain beauty for me. It's all about personal perspective and the fundamental value of *wa* (harmony).

Kyoto is the ultimate example of *wabi sabi* — looking beyond the obvious, to find an indefinable beauty that must be experienced firsthand to be truly appreciated.

When I asked Mark for his take on the concept he said, without blinking, that he believed it to mean 'finding beauty in the broken, imperfect and simple'.

He pointed out a stone lantern: one of its decorative coils had been snapped off by a devout Zen monk (who studied tea ceremony under the famous master Sen Rikyu), to fit in with the general *wabi sabi* of the teahouse and surrounds. While the act might seem to go against the flow of a naturally occurring rhythm, it brings us back to

白覩倪家甕
于殿咸人然
雀雙無感大
祭獸涯拜祖

Shrines to Inari, deity of agriculture, are found all over Japan. Situated at the base of a mountain and guarded by stone *kitsune* (fox messengers), the summit of Fushimi Inari Tashi can be reached by walking through a tunnel formed by thousands of vermilion *torii* gates. It is visually spectacular, and the atmosphere kinetic – an absolute must-do for visitors to Kyoto. It is particularly popular with rice farmers and sake brewers, who pray there at various stages of planting and harvesting.

individual interpretation. With no hard rules, the monk simply took direction from his own sense of *wabi sabi*.

*

The revolving door to my life spun once again as my final guest, Vanessa, arrived to stay. Having left her husband and kids behind, she was only too happy to take things quietly. In sync as always, we were able to just 'hang out' and enjoy Kyoto and each other, something we have perfected during 38 years of friendship. As Vanessa is also a dancer, we attended Bridget's Spring Nihon Buyoh performance where, in a touching moment, I was able to introduce my oldest friend to my newest.

We popped into one of my favourite stomping grounds: Sarasa Nishijin (an old *sento*, or bath-house), converted to a café, but still lined with the original tiles and oozing *wabi sabi*. Taking refuge from the inclement weather, we enjoyed a wonderfully warming hot chocolate, and a wedge of apple and walnut cake. I was so very happy, after all these years of travelling to Japan and merely reliving my stories with my friend, to actually be in situ, sharing it with one of the few people who allows me to just be me with no expectations. I was breathing again and not a minute too soon.

*

I had dinner lined up with a Japanese friend at a restaurant reportedly hosting one of Kyoto's rising culinary stars. Although tired, I was excited at the prospect and certainly didn't notice the 'swamp' aroma that caused Vanessa to screw up her nose on arrival. We were offered our choice of precious sake cups: glass, ceramic or silver. At the time, I had no idea that the restaurant's antique tableware was a lure for people from all over the country. The food was almost supplementary.

For about the fifth time within three weeks the meal started with tiny firefly squid. Our host poetically described their 'beautiful inner lights that glow when they swim in the sea' and I quietly hoped, while eating them, foecal tract and all, that they would provide us with some kind of virtuous energetic force, seeing as they had been snuffed out in our honour. A soup containing fresh bamboo shoots plus a helluva lot of 'famous' wakame was presented next. The seaweed had been 'scratched up' to allow it to absorb the dashi. But it had developed a gelatinous consistency not too dissimilar to raw egg whites — a texture I have not yet grown accustomed to.

I nearly choked on my own rising stomach contents when advised the next course would be my old friend the sea slug: *shiokara* (raw sea slug guts, mixed with salt to form a slimy thick, pungent sauce). My host was emphatic that this particular batch was 'only from the female reproductive organs'. Although meant to reassure me that it would be less pungent than what I'd previously experienced, it instead evoked an unsettling visual. Vanessa forced a little down, but concealed the rest under an accommodating *sakura* leaf. I dutifully finished my bowl.

Next came very fine sashimi covered by a particularly flaccid variety of rare *uni* (sea urchin). Small blobettes resembling a slightly grainy, fish-flavoured custard provided yet another textural challenge for Vanessa. Fortunately the next few dishes — an astonishingly good *gomadofu* (page 252), and tender *yakizakana* (grilled fish; page 257), put us back on track — for a while.

gomadofu

sesame 'tofu'
SERVES 6–8

While it has a tofu-like appearance and texture, hence the name, that is where the similarities end. *Gomadofu* is a mixture of ground sesame seeds and dashi, with *kuzu* starch added to set it into a slightly wobbly, tofu-like consistency.

I fell in love with it the first time I enjoyed it chilled with fresh grated wasabi and shoyu, but it became a religious experience when I first encountered it grilled as *yaki gomadofu*, with its crisp exterior, rich, creamy centre, and a luscious sesame and honey sauce over the top — pure bliss. My tip is to eat it cool in summer and hot in winter.

For this recipe it really helps to use a *suribachi* (ribbed Japanese mortar and wooden pestle) to grind the sesame seeds. The ribs in the mortar help grind the seeds and release the natural oils, and stop the seeds elusively spinning around, as they can when using a regular mortar and pestle.

75 g (2½ oz/½ cup) white sesame seeds, toasted
90 g (3¼ oz/¾ cup) *kuzu*, *katakuriko* or potato starch
750 ml (26 fl oz/3 cups) cooled kombu dashi (page 29)
1 tablespoon sake
1 tablespoon mirin
sesame oil, for greasing

CHILLED GOMADOFU
1 teaspoon finely grated fresh wasabi root or ginger, to garnish
good-quality shoyu, to serve

YAKI GOMADOFU (GRILLED GOMADOFU)
katakuriko or potato starch, for coating
sesame oil, for pan-frying
100 g (3½ oz/⅔ cup) white sesame seeds, toasted and ground
2 tablespoons ichiban dashi (page 26)
2½ teaspoons honey
2 teaspoons usukuchi shoyu (light Japanese soy)
¼ teaspoon finely grated fresh ginger
1 tablespoon boiling water
extra toasted white or black sesame seeds, lightly ground, to garnish

Using a *suribachi* (ribbed Japanese mortar and wooden pestle), grind the sesame seeds until powdery or very fine. Add the *kuzu* or starch, crushing up any lumps, and mix well. Tip the mixture into a saucepan. Use a skewer to quickly scrape out any excess mixture stuck in the mortar ridges and add it to the pan too — don't waste any of your hard work!

Mix in the dashi, sake and mirin until smooth and runny. Place over medium–high heat and stir constantly until the mixture comes almost to the boil and is just starting to thicken.

Reduce the heat to low and stir fairly constantly for about 30 minutes — the mixture will thicken quickly, but you need to keep mixing it for this length of time to cook out the starch for the best texture and flavour in the finished product. Season with a little sea salt to taste.

Very lightly oil a 20 cm (8 inch) square container with sesame oil. Working quickly — the mixture starts to set as soon as it starts to cool down! — pour the mixture into the container. The mixture should be about 2 cm (¾ inch) deep. Allow to cool slightly, then refrigerate for 3 hours, or until set.

If serving the gomadofu chilled, cut into 6–8 even squares or rectangles and serve each piece on a small plate or bowl, garnished with a tiny dollop of wasabi or ginger. Serve with a tiny jug of shoyu for drizzling over, and a small spoon to eat it with.

If making yaki gomadofu, cut into 6–8 even squares or rectangles and lightly dust all over with starch. Heat a little sesame oil in a frying pan over medium–high heat and cook the squares for 1–2 minutes on each side, or until lightly golden and warmed through.

Meanwhile, mix together the remaining ingredients (except the sesame seed garnish) and stir until smooth and thick, but still pourable.

Drain the *yaki gomadofu* briefly on kitchen paper, then serve one piece per person on small individual plates or dishes. Dollop some of the sauce over the top, letting it run down the sides a little. Sprinkle with extra sesame seeds if desired and serve with a small spoon or chopsticks.

Kyoto is rich with texture, both on a literal and metaphysical level. Layers of interest, intrigue, possibility and the unexplained promote energy, growth and discovery. Kyoto can seem shy at first, hiding itself away in mossy nooks and narrow side streets, but persistence, an open mind and heart, combined with a demonstration of respect, will open doors and suddenly clear pathways you may not otherwise have noticed were there.

255 yayoi / sangatsu & uzuki / shigatsu – march & april / the 3rd & 4th months

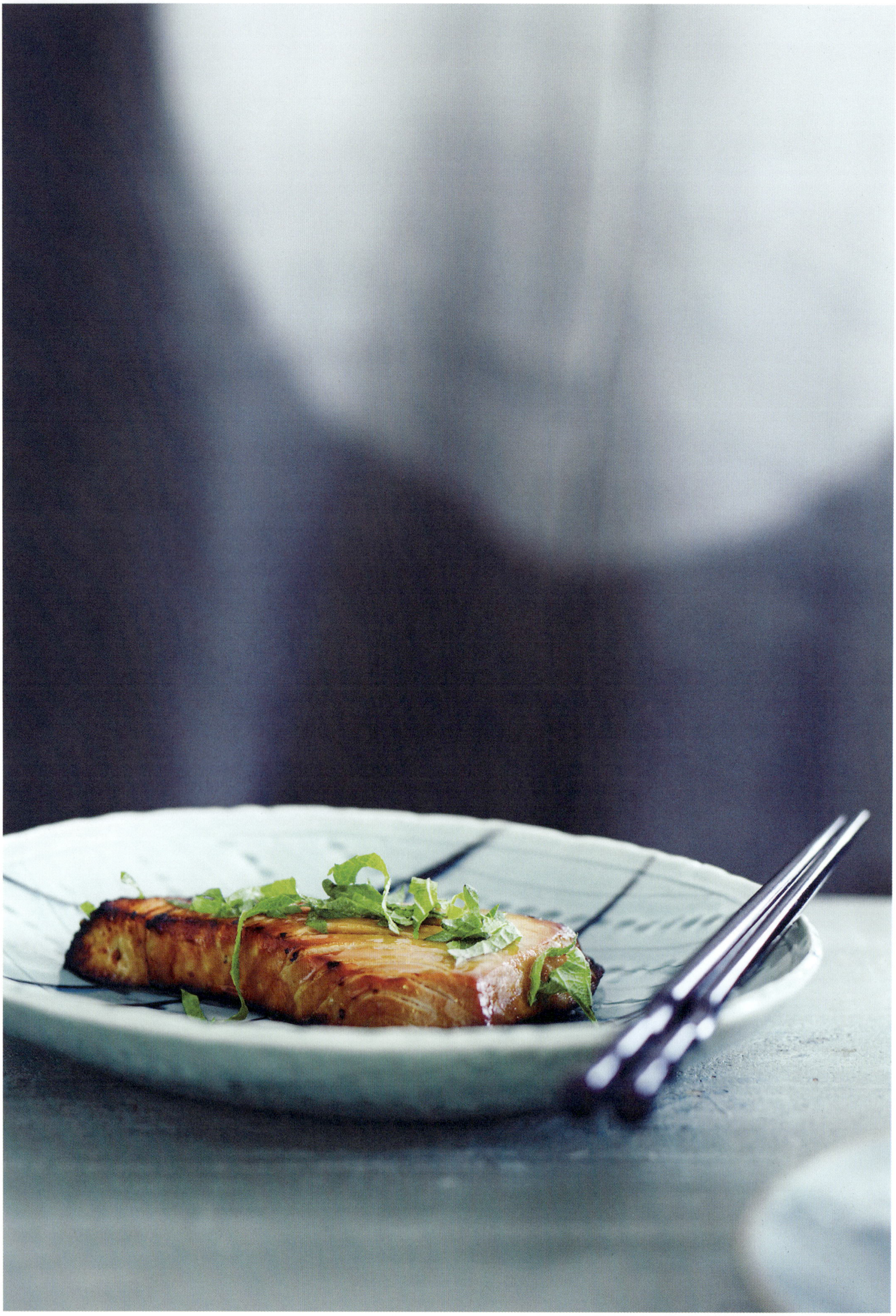

yakizakana

marinated and grilled fish

SERVES 2–4 AS A MAIN COURSE, OR UP TO 8 AS PART OF A MULTI-DISH MEAL

Literally translated as 'grilled fish', this simple dish is commonly served sprinkled with either chopped *kinome* (sansho leaves) or shiso — both fresh, aromatic herbs that marry well with oily fish.

2 x 200 g (7 oz) fish steaks from a large oily fish, such as tuna or mackerel, each about 1.5–2 cm (⅝–¾ inch) thick
2 tablespoons shoyu
1 tablespoon mirin
2½ tablespoons sake
1 teaspoon finely grated fresh ginger (optional)
finely julienned fresh *kinome* (sansho leaf) or shiso leaves, to serve
sudachi (Japanese citrus variety) or lemon wedges, to serve (optional)

Trim any bloodline from the fish. Cut each fish steak into four equal pieces.

Combine the shoyu, mirin and sake in a wide, shallow ceramic dish. If using the ginger, squeeze it between your hands to extract the juice, discarding the fibres and adding the juice to the shoyu mixture.

Add the fish pieces, turning to coat. Set aside for 10 minutes. Meanwhile, preheat the grill (broiler) to medium–high.

Place the fish on a wire rack on a foil-covered tray, then place under the grill so it is about 2 cm (¾ inch) from the heat source. Cook for 2 minutes on one side, or until starting to brown in spots on top, then turn and cook the other side until the same result occurs.

Remove from the heat and transfer to a serving plate or small individual plates. Sprinkle with the julienned *kinome* or shiso and serve with citrus wedges, if desired.

Note: You can marinate the fish in saikyo miso (sweet white miso) instead of the shoyu mixture, but refrigerate it overnight and up to 48 hours for best results. Scrape the excess miso off before grilling.

On witnessing the preparation of the next dish, Vanessa suddenly became 'very full' and advised our host she could eat no more. A live ark-shell clam was slammed onto a cutting board, then quickly sliced while it struggled to survive — a gruesome act that had me wishing I had made the call myself. But a foil of crisp, refreshing *udo* stalk — a vegetable slightly resembling overgrown white asparagus and related to the ginseng family, often eaten raw for its vaguely pine-like flavour or lightly cooked — and a variety of herbs and vegetables with a light vinaigrette rendered the dish superb beyond belief.

After sitting out that course and the next — a delightful dish of grilled *anago* (saltwater eel) in thickened dashi with *warabi* bracken — Vanessa gingerly resurfaced for the ritualistic end-of-meal offerings. We rolled ourselves home.

*

Taking a restorative morning walk through light drizzle, we became swept up in a swarm of umbrella-toting tourists. The recent showers had rendered everything more verdant and lush, with fresh-fallen pink *sakura* (cherry blossom) petals forming a pale carpet over glistening stone steps, wooden benches and thatched mossy roofs.

We spent well over a 'girlish' hour tasting *nama* (fresh) *yatsuhashi* (sweet cinnamon-scented dough; page 260), with fillings including sweet beans, chocolate, green tea and black sesame paste — before, as is imperative, sampling the crisp, dark-cooked version (sometimes dipped in chocolate).

Curiously, this is the one local specialty consistently ignored by Kyoto-ites, yet eagerly sought by tourists from other parts of Japan. If you returned to the office from a business trip or a school excursion without toting a show bag's worth of the famous confectionery your name would be mud. They are seriously good.

We reinvestigated the softer style when a specials platter displaying banana and seasonal *sakura*-centred sweets made an appearance. Vanessa had soon filled a small backpack with a selection of her newly discovered sweet bounty, ready to take home to her eagerly awaiting family. After all that heavy-duty research it was only appropriate that we stopped for a palate-cleansing matcha latte (page 264).

And, although already on a sugar high, it simply wouldn't have been right to allow my friend to return home without having tasted a *dorayaki* (pancake 'gong' with *anko* filling; page 264).

*

As far as tourists go, Kyoto is at maximum capacity during spring, particularly when the *sakura* (cherry blossoms) bloom – usually from the end of March to mid-April. People travel from all over Japan to celebrate the short-lived, frothy pink-petalled sky, under which they will picnic into the night, fuelled with sake and seasonal delicacies.

yatsuhashi

cinnamon and rice flour confectionery

MAKES 20 NAMA YATSUHASHI SQUARES AND 40 YATSUHASHI COOKIES

I sometimes stop to watch the old ladies in the streets of Kyoto as they clickety-clack with their wooden blocks, flattening and flicking their *yaki yatsuhashi* on a hot griddle — the sweet cinnamon aroma drawing in onlookers who inevitably buy once they have tasted a sample of the irresistible wares. The hot cookies are often set over a tube-shaped utensil or in moulds to curve them into bridge shapes — *yatsuhashi* translating as 'eight bridges'.

I like both the crisp, cooked version (*yaki yatsuhashi*) and the raw version, (*nama yatsuhashi*, also known as *otabe*) — a soft *mochi* (glutinous rice) dough, cut into squares or strips and eaten as is, or filled with either sweet bean paste (*anko*; see recipe on page 146), green tea, or ground sesame paste; or even chocolate or coffee, which are now also popular.

60 g (2¼ oz/⅓ cup) *mochiko* (glutinous rice flour), sifted
55 g (2 oz/⅓ cup) rice flour, sifted
75 g (2½ oz/⅓ cup) light brown sugar
1½ tablespoons very fresh ground cinnamon
100 ml (3½ fl oz) chilled water
kinako (roasted soy bean powder), for sprinkling
6 tablespoons *anko* (red bean paste) — see recipe on page 146, or you can buy it in tins from Japanese food stores

Fit a bamboo steamer on top of a saucepan filled with water. Bring to the boil over high heat.

Combine the rice flours, sugar and cinnamon in a bowl, then very gradually stir in the chilled water to form a thick paste. Cover the bowl with plastic wrap. Place the bowl in the steamer and allow to steam for 9 minutes.

Remove the bowl and mix the ingredients to bring them back together. Cover the bowl again, then place back over the steamer and cook for a further 9 minutes. Remove from the heat.

Turn the dough out onto a large sheet of baking paper. Using rubber gloves as it is very hot, knead the dough for about 10 minutes, or until it becomes smooth and elastic.

Lay another long sheet of baking paper on your work bench. Sprinkle with a little *kinako*, then place the dough on top. Using a non-stick rolling pin, start to roll out the dough, sprinkling it with a little more *kinako* as you go to stop it sticking — but don't add too much or the end result will be dry.

Roll the dough out to a 30 x 40 cm (12 x 16 inch) rectangle, about 1.5 mm (1/16 inch) thick. Use a sharp knife to cut the dough into 20 neat pieces, about 7.5 cm (3 inches) square.

To make nama yatsuhashi, fill each square with a teaspoon of the *anko* or filling of your choice and fold over into a triangle. Flatten them slightly so the filling spreads out a little. Serve immediately. (You can also store the unfilled squares, layered between sheets of baking paper, in an airtight container in the fridge for up to 2 days. Fill them just before serving.)

To make yaki yatsuhashi, preheat the oven to 170°C (325°F/Gas 3) and line a baking tray with baking paper. Cut the dough squares in half to form two rectangular strips. Place on the baking tray, then top with another layer of baking paper and a second baking tray. This will help them to stay flat as they bake.

Bake for 20–22 minutes, or until they are crisp, darker in colour and the scent of cinnamon fills your kitchen. Quickly remove from the oven and transfer to a wire rack to cool — or use a clean cloth to pick up each hot cookie and mould it over the handle of a wooden spoon (or another thin tubular utensil) to give it a lightly arched shape along its length. You need to watch these cookies as there is a fine line between cooked and burnt! If your oven temperature is out, you may need to adjust the cooking time.

When completely cool, store them in a well-sealed, airtight container.

Tip: Stir chopped *nama yatsuhashi* through ice cream for a chewy, creamy taste sensation. The baked cookies also make an excellent wafer to garnish ice cream.

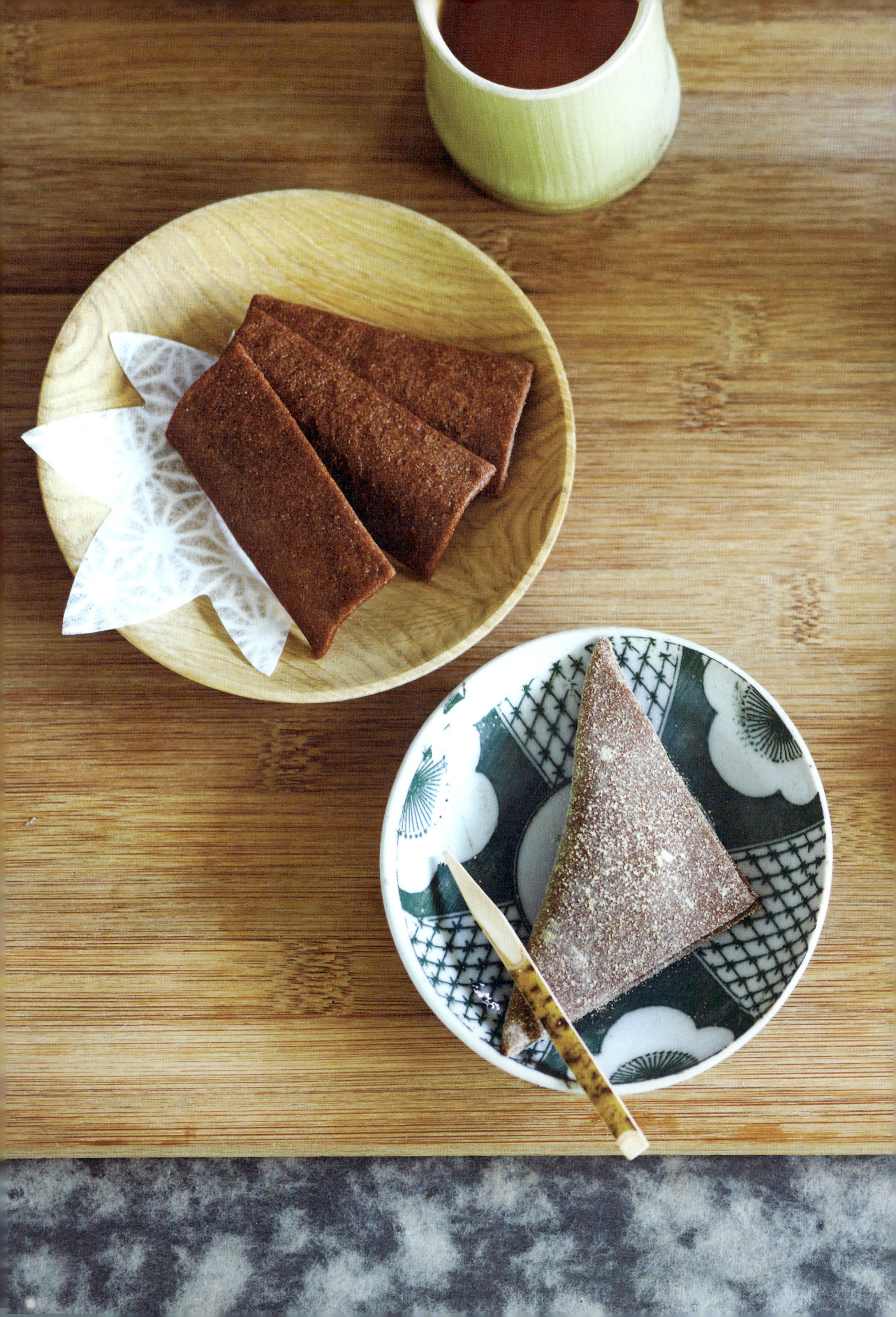

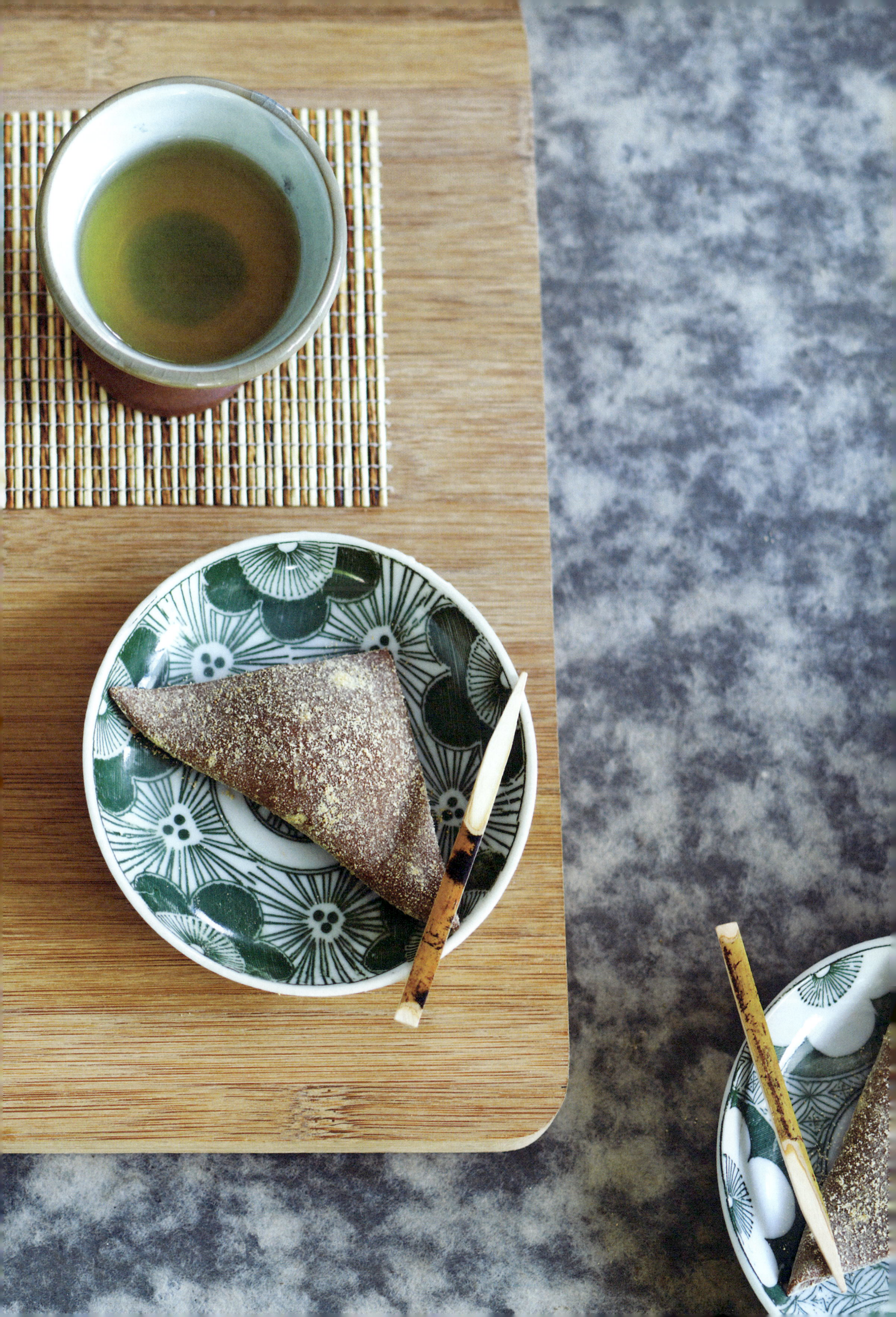

matcha latte

green tea 'latte'
SERVES 1

1 teaspoon matcha (green tea powder), plus extra for sprinkling (optional)
2 tablespoons boiling water
1 teaspoon *kuromitsu* (see page 182), honey or caster (superfine) sugar, or to taste
170 ml (5½ fl oz/⅔ cup) hot milk
whipped cream (optional)

Place the matcha in a small ceramic bowl. Use a Japanese bamboo tea whisk or tiny balloon whisk to mix in the boiling water. Whisk for a couple of minutes, or until foamy on the surface.

Briskly whisk in your sweetener, then gradually whisk in the hot milk until foamy on top — you will achieve a better result with a bamboo tea whisk.

You can drink the tea immediately from the bowl, or pour it into a mug and top with whipped cream and an extra sprinkling of matcha if desired.

In summer, serve it over ice in a tall glass.

dorayaki

'gong' cakes
MAKES 6

This sweet, bean-filled cake has, like many foods in ancient cultures, been named or inspired by legend or folklore. The story goes that after hiding out in a small village, an absent-minded samurai left behind his *dora* (gong). A resourceful local farmer found it an appropriate cooking vessel, and these pancake-like treats were born.

Dorayaki traditionally (and most commonly) consist of red bean paste sandwiched between two flattish round cakes. However, they are now found with a variety of modern fillings. Fresh cream mixed with the beans, or a layered effect of matcha cream and red bean paste, is the latest trend; strawberries and cream, thick custard (including chocolate, coffee and matcha/green tea flavours) or chestnut, black sesame and sweet potato pastes are also popular.

Like most traditional Japanese sweets, this dish is not overly *amai* (sweet) — and unless you opt for the cream or custard versions, not particularly rich — so it makes an appropriate sweet for this subtle, elegant cuisine.

It is also a great afternoon treat with a cup of green tea, especially when served fresh.

Oishii!

2 eggs
2 tablespoons caster (superfine) sugar
2 tablespoons honey, warmed until runny
1 tablespoon mirin
1 teaspoon bicarbonate of soda (baking soda)
150 g (5½ oz/1 cup) plain (all-purpose) flour, sifted
vegetable oil, for cooking
6 tablespoons *anko* (sweet red bean paste; see page 146)
 — or use 4 tablespoons *anko*, lightly combined with
 3 tablespoons whipped cream

Using a small balloon whisk, beat the eggs, sugar, honey and mirin for a few minutes until pale and fluffy. Dissolve the bicarbonate of soda in 60 ml (2 fl oz/¼ cup) water, then stir it into the egg mixture. Add the sifted flour and mix to combine well, but don't overbeat. Cover and leave to rest for 30 minutes.

The mixture will have thickened slightly, so add a tablespoon or two of cold water and mix lightly to ensure you have a pouring custard consistency.

Heat a flat griddle or large cast-iron frying pan over medium–low heat; this is important for achieving an even, deep-gold colour. Dip some folded kitchen paper in a tiny bit of oil and rub it evenly over the top. Use a clean piece of kitchen paper to wipe off any excess — only a very thin film of oil is needed.

Working very close to the base of the pan, pour in 1½ tablespoons of the batter in one spot and allow it to spread out naturally to a 9 cm (3½ inch) diameter. Continue this all around the pan, but make sure there is enough space between each for the pancakes to spread. Cook for 4 minutes, or until a deep, even gold underneath. Flip the pancakes over and cook for another 20–30 seconds.

Remove to a wire rack with the just-cooked-side facing down. Cover with a lightly dampened tea towel (dish towel) to stop the pancakes drying out while you cook the remaining batter.

Place about 1 tablespoon of *anko* or anko cream in the centre of one of the rounds. Press down lightly with the back of a spoon to spread the *anko* very slightly, leaving 1 cm (½ inch) free around the outside edge. Press another cake round on top and cup it between your hands, pushing down with your fingertips and heel of your palm to press the outside edges together, forming a slightly domed shape on both sides.

You can either serve immediately with green tea, or wrap them individually in plastic wrap and store in an airtight container at room temperature (for plain *anko*) or in the fridge (if containing cream). They are best eaten that day.

You can also freeze the individually wrapped (plain *anko*) cakes in a zip-lock bag for up to 2 months. Thaw at room temperature before serving.

Variation: For matcha cream, place 1 teaspoon matcha (green tea powder) in a bowl with 1½ tablespoons icing (confectioners') sugar and 80 ml (2½ fl oz/⅓ cup) whipping cream. Beat until the cream is firmly whipped and the colour is an even green. You can add extra tea and sugar depending on your taste. Fill the pancakes with half *anko* and half matcha cream, or use the matcha cream in place of the *anko*.

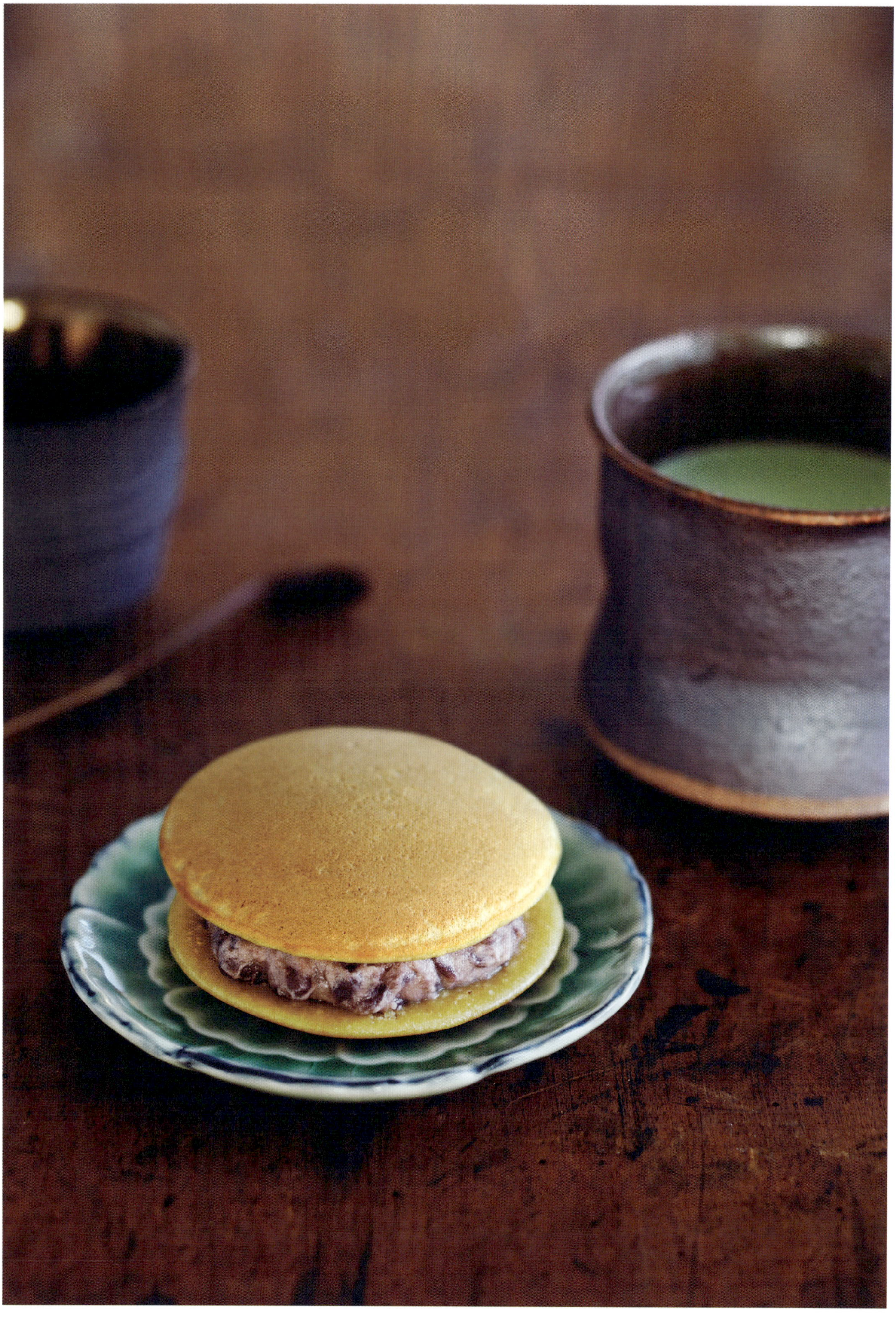

267 yayoi / sangatsu & uzuki / shigatsu – march & april / the 3rd & 4th months

I finally had Kyoto to myself. With time to reflect, it was interesting to note that, like me, all of my guests had responded to different aspects of the town's makeup, as though they were entangled in a complex human relationship. As with an introduction to a new friend or lover, although it shouldn't have mattered, their approval of my choice of Kyoto was reassuring. As nutty as it may sound, I am convinced that Kyoto has the ability to communicate and enrich through some form of paranormal energy.

I'd come to realise that even the food had a personality of its own. A visiting friend's teenage son shared with me that he loved Japan but didn't see the point of some of the food. I explained that what he thought was 'celery cooked in water' was in fact the stem of a rare spring vegetable that had been respectfully simmered to perfection in a light dashi, skilfully retaining its crisp texture and allowing the natural flavours to shine through — and that was the point. Challenging me further, he continued on to say he really didn't like Japanese food, because there was no 'centre' to it — at home you could have a big steak with vegetables and various garnishes, but in Japan 'all the food was garnish'.

I had to laugh because, to a degree, it's true. But what a pleasurable way to sustain ourselves: an abundance of elegant, flavoursome, nurturing garniture. Small and perfect 'bits' wins over a slab of 'meat and three veg' for me any day.

In my final week in Japan, I visited the last of the flowering blossoms in the Kitano Tenmangu Shrine and, although there were a good number of people by my side, I once again had the feeling of being alone. I breathed deep, ingesting the atmosphere into my molecules, wishing it to enforce my new mantra of 'not returning to a life that no longer served me'. A decrepit monk shuffled in on his walking stick to investigate the changing garden. As he stooped down, the afternoon light bathed his fragile outline in an uncanny aura and I wondered how many more seasons he would see out.

It was extremely difficult to bid farewell to Kyoto and newly formed friendships. My new-found 'family' had shared so very much with me. I was completely lovesick and knew, in my heart, that I would be back.

And, just eight months later — I was. A different Jane. Having had the time to reflect and process events, I was finally ready to embrace Kyoto more intimately.

I'd returned to Australia to find major changes taking place around me. A continuing series of curious events led to an extension on my manuscript delivery date and my thoughts instantly returned to Kyoto.

I spent a further three months in the same apartment in Kyoto, culling and rewriting and experiencing a whole new level of unveil. Without effort, I met the most amazing new people who provided me with invaluable information on Kyoto, its culture, subcultures and of course cuisine, and allowed me to not only peel off one thick layer of the proverbial onion, but to find the 'golden ticket'.

Go-en was working overtime because I had finally liberated myself by releasing the grip on my life as it was and, being there to bunker down, I had no expectations. Everything genuinely came to me without being sought. I was frequently contacted out of the blue and I cosmically bumped into Kyoto experts, who in turn introduced me to local characters full of scintillating knowledge and history — all connected to food culture in some unique way.

I took my time to pore over everything. I declined invitations that would have inevitably been fun, interesting or educational, in preference for rest or 'me' time when I needed it. I was relaxed and happy to the point of sheer, unadulterated joy — something all too rare in our busy lives — and the doors just kept on opening. It was like learning the magic words to a cryptic puzzle. I experienced incredible new foods, places and blossoming friendships. It was only by returning that I realised how much of the last trip was merely a comedown from preceding events and a much-needed part of the journey, if only to gain perspective. I was now able to put into practice the invaluable lessons I had learnt during round one. I am indebted to Kyoto and her people for giving me the enormously generous gift of discovering both self and community.

I now understand that what we regard as 'Zen' is about mindfully riding the ebb and flow, not being completely blissed out all the time — which is a state I had naively anticipated achieving by merely plonking myself in Kyoto. It's about appreciating the beauty in the simple things in life, whether that be time with your family, sitting on a park bench breathing in the fresh air, noting the sweet crunch in an apple, or indeed going to work so you can enjoy life's essentials.

The fact I am on this Earth and able to do any of those things is something worth appreciating. While that might sound pretty basic — perhaps bleeding obvious — the reality is that it is too easy to shift the centre one way or another. Balance is a juggling act, but one I am now all the better equipped for. I challenge myself to listen to my body, heart and mind equally, and acknowledge that I am always learning. I am human. I will trip up every now and again.

Being a perfectionist will see you through certain situations, and possibly serve you more than well on occasion, but it is not sustainable long-term without turning yourself inside out.

My hard-edged shell — fashioned from chronic overload and excess stimulation — had, when cracked, allowed me to appreciate my inner workings in the delicate light that shone through the breaks; my very own *wabi sabi*.

Zenbu Zen
('Everything's Zen')

*

無病息災

I left Kyoto the day before the devastating earthquake and tsunami of March 2011. I hope this book inspires you to visit Japan, which will support the Japanese people in continuing to rebuild their lives with grace and dignity. Thank you to all who volunteer their time and energy on the long road ahead.

Even after 27 years spent pacing between my two 'homes', I have really only just begun to scratch the surface of Japan's incredible culture.

Something tells me I will be back again soon.

This book is dedicated to my brother Adam — mainly because I won't hear the end of it otherwise, but also because of his great generosity.

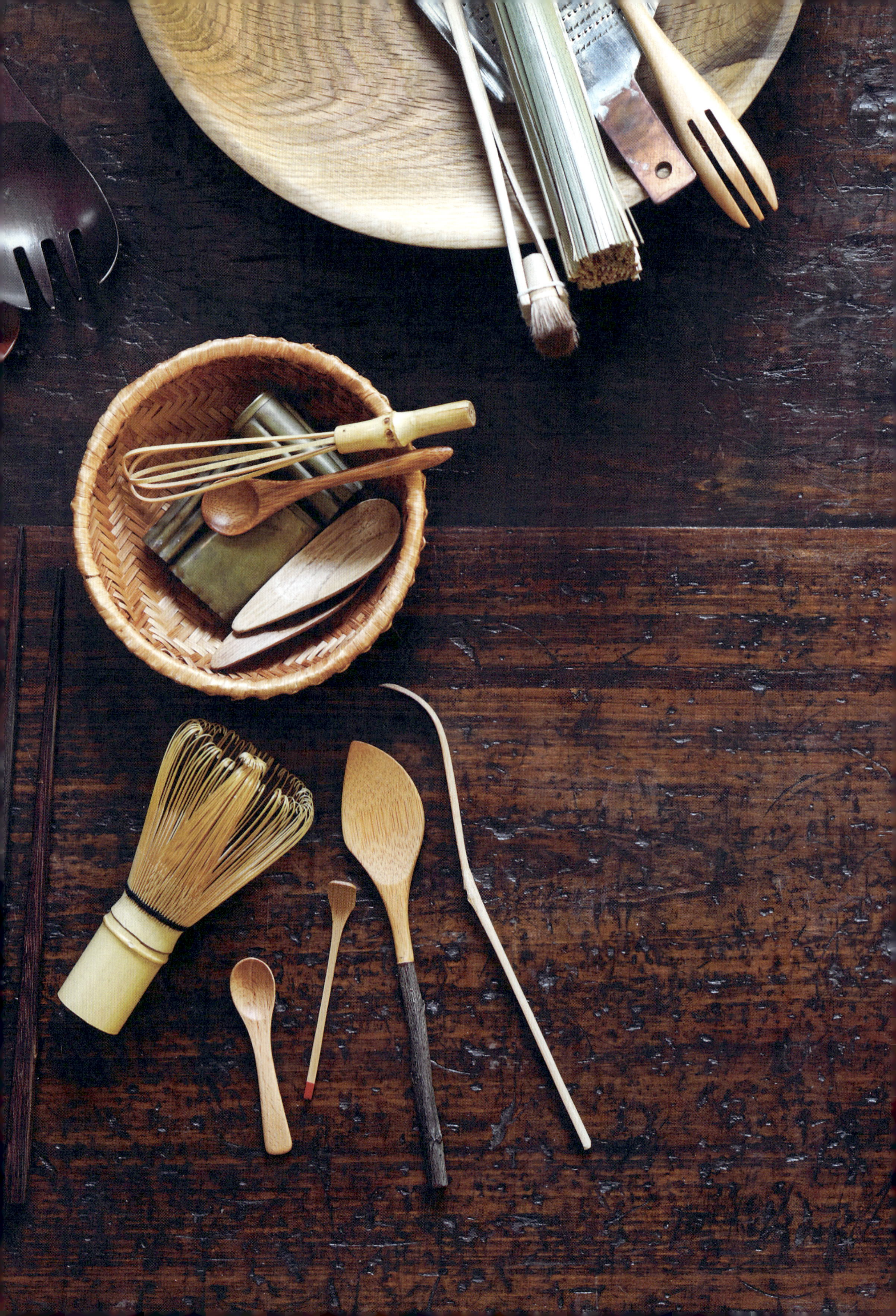

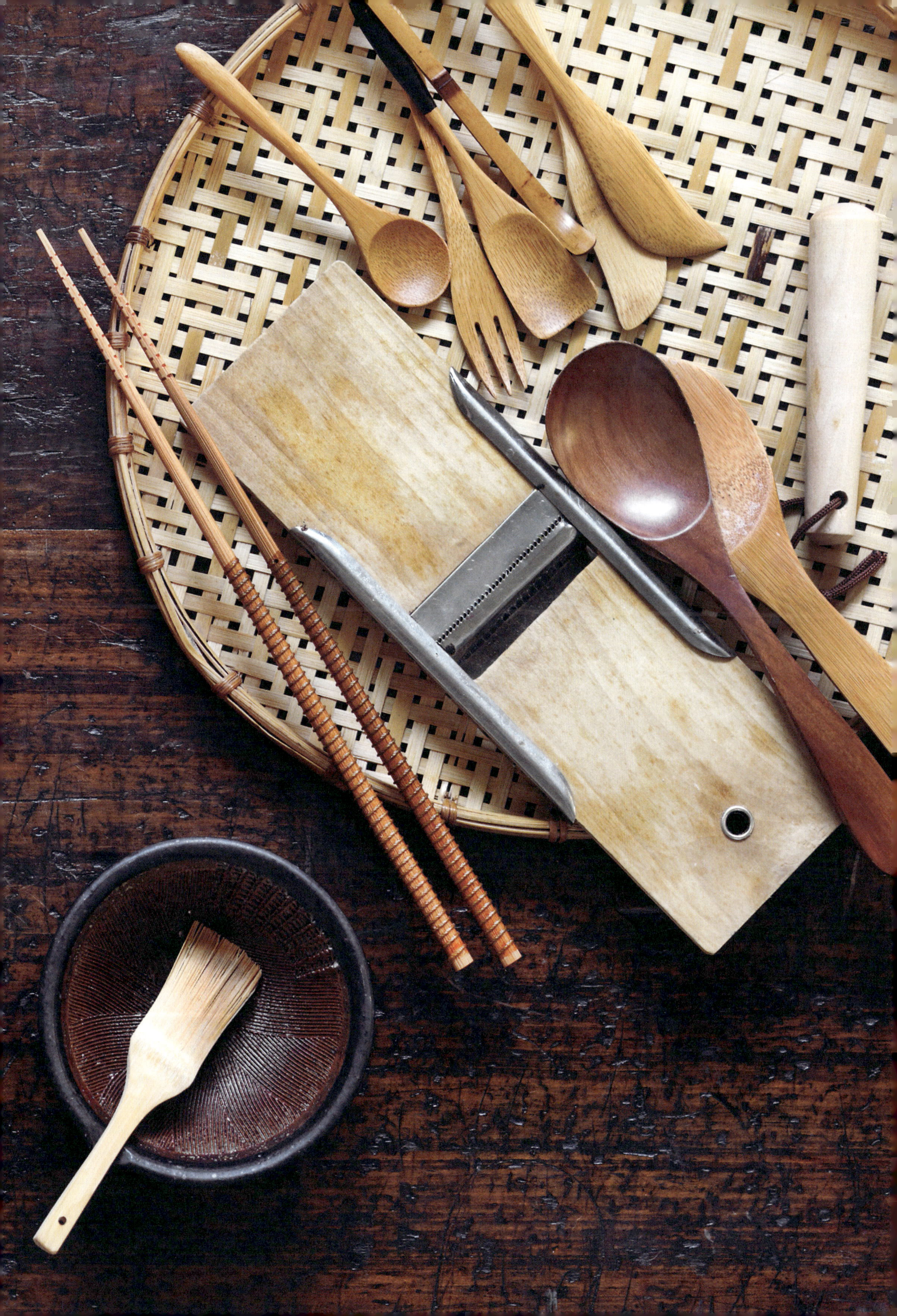

thank you

arigato gozaimashita

Universe — I trusted and you rocked! Jumping into the void scared the hell out of me, but has brought me more happiness and reward than I knew was possible.

A rather large and woolly blanket thank you to Matt Handbury, Sally, Chris, Laura, Deb, Shannon and all the other good folk at Murdoch Books who madly run around sticking pages together and getting them onto shelves.

To Carla G and Katri H — your respectful editing, feedback and very kind words meant the world to me.

Thank you Vicky, Belinda and Ellie for your top-notch recipe testing — I couldn't have done it without you.

Cath Muscat and Olivia Andrews — it's always great to meet new galpals, but hey, you guys are freakin' talented too. I can't thank you enough. Stunning work.

Thank you also to Simon B.

Thank you Katy Holder for the gorgeous Kanji/Shodo. Good thing your face didn't get eaten by a horse, eh?

Reuben Crossman — you are a lifesaver. I can't possibly thank you enough for all the painstaking hours sorting through thousands of my images, your highly considered design and your incredible effort to bring it all together. You know I think you are brilliant, that's been said many times … but you are also an excellent chauffeur and I owe ya! Thank you for your friendship and support and beautiful work. We'll always have 'the budgie'.

To my family, friends and my beautiful Gerardo — without your love, support and patience I wouldn't be able to do what I do.

To my Japan-based friends — you welcomed me so openly, invited me into your homes and lives, trusted, shared with and taught me so much: Bridget and Tad, Mark H, Ricky and Mitsuko, Michiko and Paul, Liz W, Elsbeth, Peter H, Kathy I, Kiyomi, Michael Baxter, Ruskin, Paul, Kozaemon-san, Myong Hee and Bob, Mayumi and Terry, Misako, Kikuko, Yukari, Kya and Ries, Ikeda-san, Yutaka-san, Kuroda-san, Hasegawa-san, the Sekigawa family, Mari Fujii, the Taura family, Akemi and the Kameoka ladies, John Ashburne, Chris Rowthorn, Sally, Albie and Eric from EDK, Michael from Deep Kyoto and also to Curtis Hawes for introducing me to his stunning 'Gion House'.

To all others who have travelled here to share in snippets of my Kyoto journey — thank you for joining me in my favourite place in the world.

Ness — you made it (and made me so happy)! Lindy-san 'raku raku'. Finky — it was a blast!

A special thank you to Kay Scarlett for always believing, encouraging and deciphering the essence of my stream-of-consciousness ramblings …

And finally — thank you Kyoto! Always in my heart. xx

275 arigato gozaimashita – thank you

zenbu zen 276

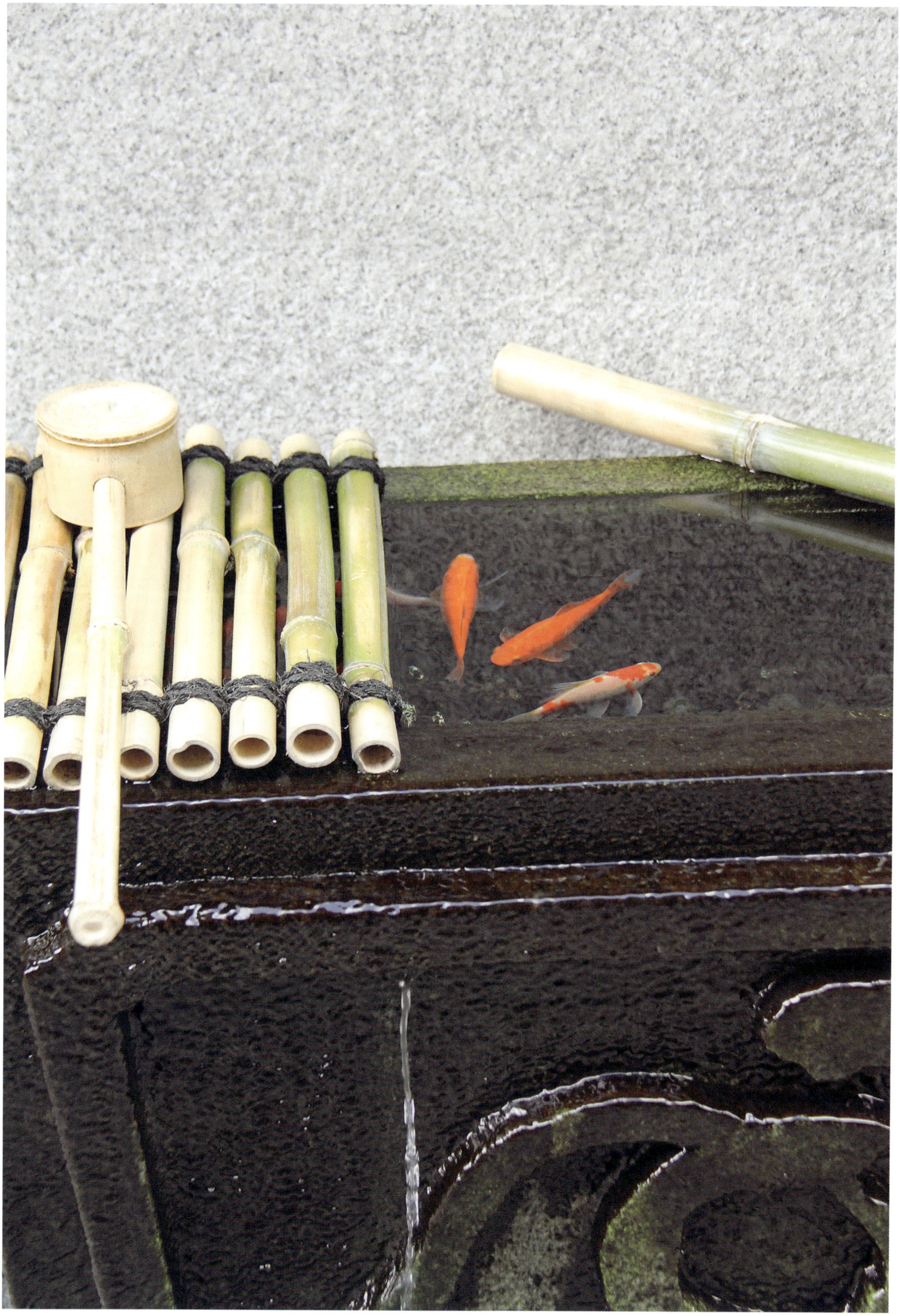

glossary

Some fresh Japanese ingredients are not readily available outside Japan, so I have included alternative ingredient suggestions wherever possible. Most dried or preserved Japanese ingredients are available from Asian grocers or markets, gourmet stores and several large supermarket chains. Try to seek out Japanese specialty food stores for the best selection.

Please visit my blog — eatspeakjl.blogspot.com — for additional information on Japanese food and culture.

azuki bean (or adzuki bean): A dried red bean used in Japanese confectionery — such as *yokan* (page 146) and *dorayaki* (page 264) — and in savoury *sekihan*, a dish of rice and beans (representing the colours of the Japanese flag), served at celebratory occasions. Azuki beans reportedly promote healthy skin and fight fluid retention.

burdock root (gobo/gobou): A long, thin root vegetable with brown skin and creamy flesh. A member of the daisy family, it resembles salsify and has a flavour not unlike jerusalem artichoke. Very high in fibre, burdock root is available fresh during the cooler months and is great in simmered dishes; finely shaved burdock root fries well in tempura-like dishes such as *kakiage* (page 165). The root is naturally bitter and oxidises quickly, so should be soaked in lightly vinegared water before cooking. Frozen shredded burdock root is readily available in Asian stores.

daikon: A large white radish, believed to ease colds and congestion and aid digestion. It is used raw in dressings and salads, and is a popular vegetable for simmering in winter dishes. I also like it roasted and in stir-fries.

donabe: A Japanese lidded ceramic or cast-iron cooking vessel, often shortened to *nabe* (which is also the name for the hotpot dishes cooked in it). It makes for great table presentation, but a regular heavy-based casserole dish or deep-sided saucepan can usually be used instead.

edamame: Bright green soy beans, usually purchased in their bristly pods. Wonderfully nutty when fresh, they are more commonly sold frozen in packets. In their dried form, soy beans are called *daizu*.

furikake: Dry seasonings that are sprinkled over dishes such as *ochazuke* (page 176) for added flavour; it might include nori flakes, toasted sesame seeds, dried shiso, *katsuobushi* (shaved dried, smoked bonito) or similar.

ginko (or ginnan): The nut-like inner seed of the ginko tree (or gingko tree). Rarely available fresh outside Japan; substitute with the tinned or cryovac product.

Japanese drop-lid (otoshibuta): A round lid, made of lightweight wood, that floats on the surface of simmering dishes to help keep soft ingredients submerged without crushing them, and stops too much liquid evaporating. A cartouche (a round of baking paper) can be used instead.

karashi (hot Japanese mustard): A spicy mustard similar to hot English mustard, with which it can be substituted.

katakuriko: The starch of the dog-toothed violet — a preferred thickening agent for delicate sauces and simmered dishes due to its undetectable flavour. It also acts well as a coating for fried foods, rendering them particularly crisp. A cheaper alternative, potato starch or potato flour, can be easily substituted for most recipes.

kinako: The finely ground powder of roasted dried soy beans (*daizu*). It has a malty, nutty flavour and is used predominantly in confectionery and desserts

kinome: The tiny, slightly astringent leaves of the numbing Japanese sansho plant. The pretty sprigs are commonly used as a garnish, and the flavour is a cross between pepper, citrus and menthol.

konnyaku: A starchy, high-fibre jelly, used to bulk out foods. Made from the starch of the *konjak*, or devil's tongue root, it has very few calories and, being bland, absorbs the flavour of whatever it is cooked with. The mottled, greyish jelly comes in both block form and noodle-like strands and is believed to cleanse the body. Sometimes it is available as *aka konnyaku*, coloured red and flavoured with mild chilli powder.

kurosato: Dark, unrefined cane sugar from Okinawa, with a malty, smoky molasses-like sweetness.

kuzu (or kudzu): Starch from the *kuzu* plant, which makes an excellent thickening agent for clear sauces and Japanese confectionery as it does not become cloudy. It is usually sold as little 'pebbles' which dissolve easily in liquid. Arrowroot can be substituted.

matcha (or maccha): green tea powder; commonly used as a drink in tea ceremonies, and for flavouring Japanese confectionery.

mirin: A sweet, pale-golden rice liquor used to add sweetness to sauces and dressings.

miso: A high-sodium paste made from fermented soy beans, used to flavour soups and sauces and to preserve foods. Available in a variety of grades, colours and flavours, depending on the particular blend of ingredients used (see page 46).

mitsuba: Japanese trefoil (literally 'three-leaf') — a parsley-like herb with a fresh, clean flavour, generally used as a garnish and to flavour soups, hotpots and salads.

mizuna: Feathery dark green leaves used fresh in salads; mizuna can also be cooked and eaten as a vegetable, particularly in hotpots (*nabe*) or *ohitashi* (page 79).

panko: Large, crisp, white breadcrumbs available from Japanese food stores and most supermarkets. There are instructions for homemade panko on page 43.

ponzu: A liquid sauce or dressing flavoured with soy sauce, citrus and *katsuobushi*. Freshly made is superior for flavour, but it is also sold ready-made in bottles.

sake: See pages 184–185. You can buy cheap, inferior cooking sake, but I prefer to use proper drinking sake as the flavour is more clean, crisp and delicious. Commonly used alongside or instead of mirin in many Japanese dishes.

sansho: Japanese pepper. Ground sansho (or sansho powder) is the ground form of the dried peppercorns, and has a slightly numbing effect similar to the Chinese

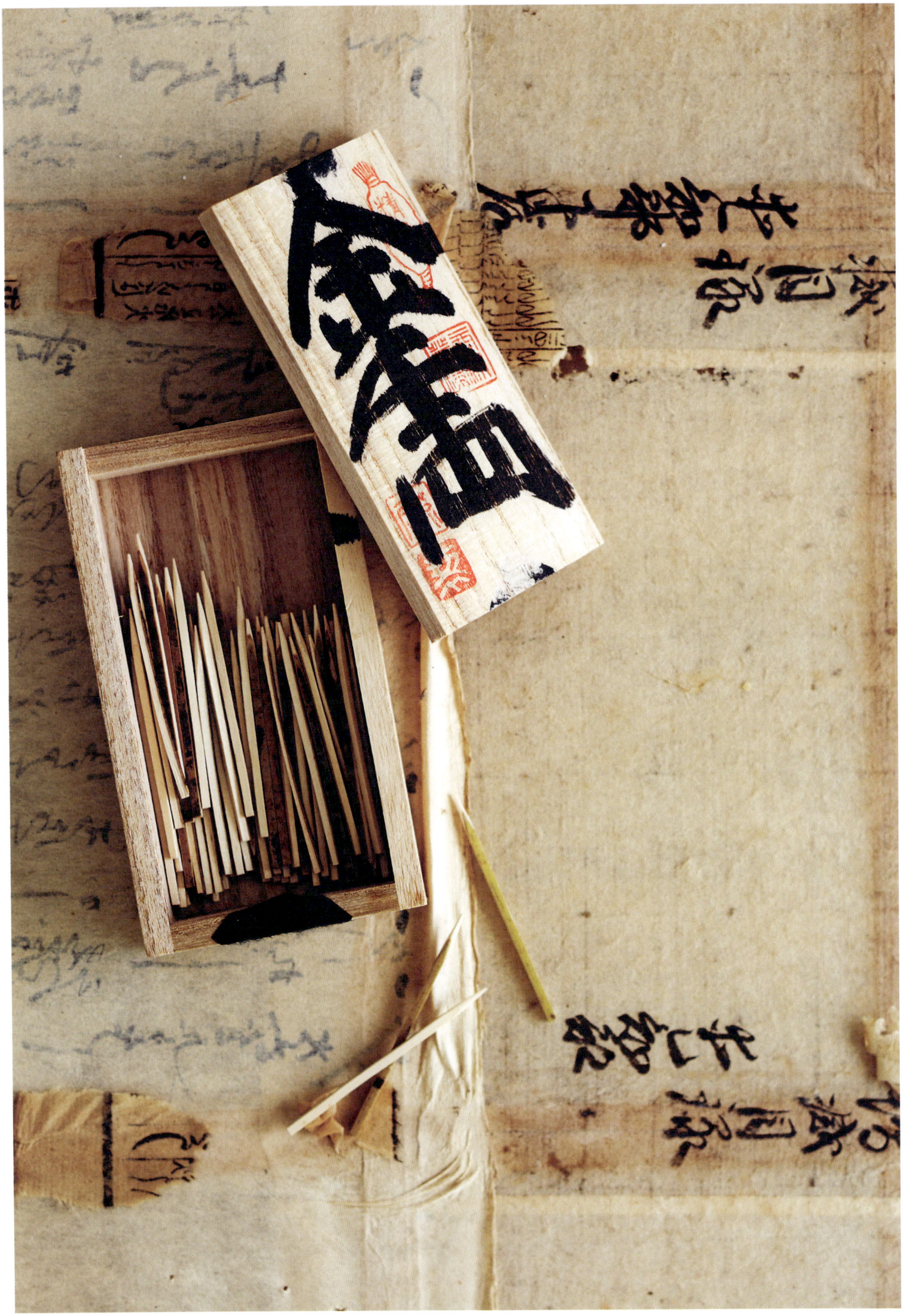

sichuan pepper to which it is related. Sansho peppercorns are sometimes used fresh or brined. Look for *kinome*, the plant's fresh fragrant leaves in season.

seaweed: An edible sea vegetable widely used in Japanese cooking to add flavour and nutrients; varieties include kombu, wakame, hijiki and nori. Kombu is most commonly used to make dashi (pages 26 and 29) and *tsukudani* (pages 113–115).

seri: A leafy herb with a sharper flavour than the parsley-like *mitsuba*, used in dishes where *mitsuba* is too subtle to add an obvious accent. It is more readily available in winter in Japan.

shichimi togarashi: A seven-flavour spice mix, typically containing *togarashi* (chilli pepper), sesame seeds, yuzu peel, ground sansho, hemp seeds, nori and ginger. It is often sprinkled over noodle soups, *nabe* (hotpots) and fried foods for extra flavour, aroma and bite.

shiso: Known in the West as perilla; a bushy green herb with large, broad, serrated green or reddish-purple leaves. Related to mint, it has a fresh fragrance and flavour, with hints of aniseed and citrus. Best used at the end of cooking, or as a garnish or in salads. The tiny flowers are edible and used as a garnish in season.

shoyu: The Japanese word for soy sauce. The Japanese commonly use two main varieties: usukuchi shoyu, a 'light' Japanese soy, is thin and has a fresh flavour; it is a little saltier than koikuchi shoyu — a darker, thicker, slightly sweeter soy, with a more complex flavour.

suribachi: A ribbed Japanese mortar and wooden pestle — an essential yet inexpensive utensil for authentic Japanese cooking. Compared to a regular smooth mortar and pestle, it provides extra 'grip' when grinding slippery ingredients such as sesame seeds, and is much less labour intensive.

umeboshi: Japanese pickled plums; easily obtainable at Japanese grocers and good supermarkets. They can be eaten just as they are, as a salty snack with drinks, or soaked in water to remove some of the salt, then added to dressings and other dishes for a subtle plum flavour. They are usually flavoured and coloured red with shiso leaves.

wasabi: Also known as Japanese horseradish, this pungent and peppery root, when very finely grated, is an essential accompaniment to sashimi and sushi, as its astringent properties help kill bacteria and parasites on the raw fish. Try to find fresh wasabi, as the commercial paste is far inferior. If fresh is not available, use the powdered version to make a paste.

yuzu: An addictively fragrant Japanese citrus. The fresh zest is commonly used as an aromatic or garnish; dried and ground, it is added to soups and hotpots as a condiment. The juice is used in dressings and sauces, or used to finish soups/hotpots. It is best fresh in season (winter), but bottled is more readily available.

index

A
ankake sauce 81, 88
anko 128, 146
Arashiyama 37, 174
artworks 57–8, 128–9, 205
asparagus, grilled and drenched 247
asupara no yaki-bitashi 245, 247
Australia 15, 268
    food culture 143–4
awabi modoki 229, 230
azuki/adzuki beans 278

B
bainiku (pickled plum purée) 173
bamboo 175
    bamboo shoot rice 92, 93
    simmered bamboo shoots and wakame 35
bancha (green tea) 122
beauty in simplicity 7, 15, 248, 269
beef
    simmered beef and burdock 176–7
    simmered beef tendon, cheek and konnyaku 119, 124
    sweet potato and beef mince croquettes 63
beef, *see also* wagyu
betsu onaka (two stomachs) 81
birthday party 96–7
bitter leaves in miso 247
bonito 25
bracken starch dumpling 182
breakfasts 24, 48, 56, 113, 203
Buddhism 16, 57, 110, 234
    earthly desires 57
    blessing 129
    monks 16, 58, 162, 168, 178, 228
    temples 16, 18, 98, 107, 128, 186
    vegetarian cuisine 129, 161–3, 228
burdock 69, 177
    burdock root salad 66
    fresh, preparing 66
    gobo (root) 24, 96, 228, 278
    simmered beef and burdock 176
buri to daikon no nimono 119, 125
butabara kushiyaki 80, 171, 173
butaniku no kakuni 141

C
cabbage with yuzu dressing 41
carrots 24
    daikon and red carrot pickle 98, 104
celery pickled in miso 158
chawan mushi 213, 214
cherry blossom 15, 56, 259, 268

chicken 92
    fried chicken 69, 71
    'parent and child' rice bowl 208–9
    stock 208–9
Chinese New Year 196
Chinese spinach 198
chopsticks 48, 112
    rules of use 48
Christmas 92
Christmas cakes 56
chrysanthemum leaves 79
    'drenched' chrysanthemum leaf salad 79
cinnamon and rice flour confectionery 260–1
Coming of Age Day 132
croquettes
    cream 58, 62
    sweet potato and beef mince 63
cucumber pickled in miso 158
cucumber pickles 41
curry
    curry powder 63
    soup curry 241
custard cups, steamed savoury 214–15

D
daikon 58, 157, 278
    daikon dressing 65
    daikon and red carrot pickle 98, 104
    daikon salad 96
    pickled daikon 155
    simmered daikon with yuzu miso sauce 91
daikon graters 65
Daitokuji Temple 248
daizu 201
daizu no gomoku-ni 48, 198, 199
dashi 25
    dried kelp 29
    no. 1 (*ichiban dashi*) 25, 26
    no. 2 (*niban dashi*) 25, 29
    shiitake 29
    tori (chicken) 208–209
donabe 278
dorayaki 258, 264
dressings *see* sauces and dressings
dried fish 28
dried kelp dashi 29
duck and leek hotpot 76

E
ebi manju 187, 188, 245
ebiimo (potato) 96, 112
Ebisu Festival 130

edamame 201, 278
eggplant
   fried 'sandwiches' 88
   grilled eggplant with sansho miso 53

F
fish 25, 80
   dried fish 28
   fish paste cakes 152
   marinated and grilled fish 257
   rice gruel with snapper and yuzu 218–19
   simmered Japanese yellowtail and daikon 125
fish markets 149
flea markets 68–9
Flower Lantern Festival 56–7
food halls 48, 69
fried foods 42, 45, 69, 228
fried 'sandwiches' 88
fuki (bitter leaf) 112, 247
fuki no miso 247
furikake (seasonings) 176, 278
furofuki daikon 91
Fushimi Inari Shrine 128, 250
futomaki zushi 196

G
garland chrysanthemum 79
garlic 167, 228
garlic pickled in miso 159
geisha *(or geiko)* 220, 221
giant bees 185, 187
ginger tea 87, 204
Ginjo (sake) 184
ginko/gingko nuts 69, 278
Gion 57, 213, 220–1
gobo sarada 66
go-en (connections) 129–30, 131, 170, 174, 268
The Golden Pavilion 174
gomadofu 51, 73, 251, 252
gong cakes 264–5
green tea 'latte' 264
gyuuniku to gobo no nimono 176
gyuusuji to konnyaku no miso-ni 119, 124

H
haafu 48
half-moon shapes 157
hasami-age 88
Hatsumode (first shrine visit) 107, 110
Heian Jingu Shrine 72, 73, 107
heshiko (fermented mackerel) 118–19
Higashiyama 22, 24, 37
Hokkaido 24, 234, 235

Honjozo (sake) 184
hotate batayaki 34
houjicha to kinako aisu 225

I
ice cream
   roasted tea and *kinako* 225
   yuzu and saikyo miso 220, 224
ichiban dashi 26

J
Japanese cuisine 58, 73, 248, 268
   base flavours 242
   herbs and spices 242
   importance of dashi 25, 242
   traditional 118, 143–4, 229
Japanese drop-lid 278
Japanese yellowtail, simmered, and daikon 125
Jizo 186
Junmai (sake) 184
Jyoruri-Ji Temple 128

K
kaiseki cuisine 96, 162–3, 168, 187, 213
kakiage 165, 185
Kamakura 228
Kameoka 143
kamo-negi nabe 73, 76
Kanazawa 187
kara-age 69, 71
karashi (mustard) 30, 278
katakuriko 278–9
katsu (cutlets) 39
katsudon 208
katsuo dashi 25
katsuobushi 25, 176
kinako 279
kinako shiro torafuru 203
kinako and white chocolate truffles 203
kinome 279
Kitayama 37, 38–9
kohaku namasu 98, 104
komatsuna (mustard spinach) 79
kombu 25, 112
kombu dashi 29
kombu no tsukudani 112, 115
kombu preserves 115
konnyaku 112, 279
konnyaku gobo 24
korokke (croquettes) 58
koshu (aged sake) 185
koto 168, 170

283 index

Kozaemon family brewery 184–5, 187
Kumano Jinja 38
kuriimu korokke 62
Kurodani Temple 98
kuromitsu 182
kurosato 279
kuzu/kudzu 279
kyabetsu to yuzu-ae 41
kyo-ebiimo (potato/yam cross) 96
Kyoto 15, 16, 22, 37, 38–9, 58, 203, 255, 269
   cuisine 97, 268
   gentleness of 132, 220, 245
   light 60
   location 37
   population 171–2
   'prawn potato' 96
   snow 207, 226
   Station 69
kyo-yasai (Kyoto vegetables) 96
kyuuri miso zuke 158–9

L
leeks 73, 167
   duck and leek hotpot 76
   pencil-thin leeks with mustard miso dressing 87
lily bulbs 112
lotus 88, 104
lunisolar calendar 16

M
maiko (apprentice geisha) 220, 221
Manganji Temple 24
markets 58, 149
matcha cream 265
matcha latte 258, 264
matcha/maccha 279
meditation 49, 57, 168
   on snow 244
minchi korokke 63
mindfulness 15, 269
mirin 279
miso 279
miso butaniku no nabe 136–7
miso pastes 46
miso pork hotpot 136–7
miso shiru 39, 46
miso soup 39, 46
miso zuke 38, 158
miso-katsu 174
mitsuba 279
mizuna 279
Mizunami 174
mochi (rice cakes) 110, 144

mock abalone of tofu-stuffed shiitake 230
Mount Kurama 198
mushrooms 185, 198
   wagyu with king brown mushrooms 65
mustard miso dressing 87

N
nabe 25, 136
nagaimo (yam) 51
nagaimo yoromushi 228
nama fu (wheat gluten) 81
nama yuba (soy milk skin) 80, 81, 84–5, 112
Nama zake (sake) 184
namako (sea slug) 168, 251
Nanzenji Temple 49
narazuke (pickle) 221
natto 92
negi no karashi sumiso-ae 87
New Year 110, 120
   cuisine 98
   prayers 69
   ritual cleaning 97–8
New Year's Eve 95, 102, 107, 196
New Year's soup 105
niban dashi 29
nigari 116
Nigorizake (sake) 184
Nishi Otani mausoleum 97–8
Nishiki-koji 149
nori preserves 113
   nori no tsukudani 112, 113
nure senbei (rice crackers) 30

O
oboro dofu 112, 116
ochazuke 174, 176
octopus, tender simmered 122
oden (winter hotpot) 96, 149
ohitashi 79
okara 73, 85, 140
okara itame 140
oyakodon 208–9
ozoni 105, 110

P
panko breadcrumbs 43, 279
pantry 'essentials' 24–5
'parent and child' rice bowl 208–9
The Philosopher's Path 16, 49, 56
pickle stands 38, 154
pickles 38, 154, 176
   pickled daikon 155
   pickled plum purée 173

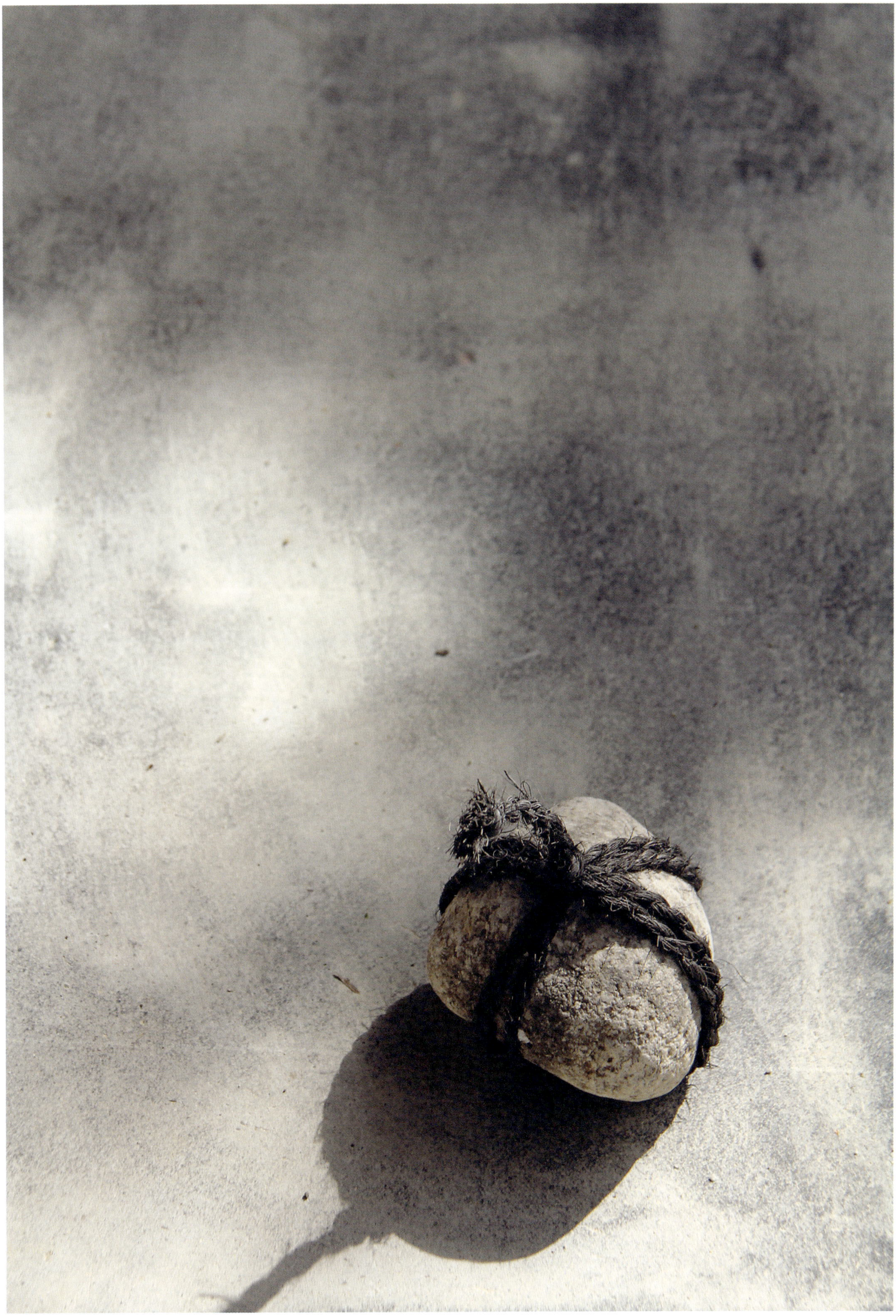

plantain lily 198
ponzu 279
pork 45, 48, 56
   fried crumbed pork cutlets 42–3
   grilled pork belly skewers 173
   hearty pork, vegetable and miso soup 181
   miso pork hotpot 136–7
   slow simmered pork belly in shoyu and black sugar 141
pork belly 141
Portuguese influences 45, 73
prawn and taro dumpling 188–9, 245
priest run 22
pumpkins 58

R
red bean confectionery 146–7
renkon (lotus root) 24, 80
restaurants 39, 72–3, 80–1
   antique tableware 251
   katsu 39–40
   in mountains 185–6
   smoking in 80
   superior 96–7
   tofu 49–50, 112
   Touzentei 213
rice 144, 149
   'parent and child' rice bowl 208–9
   rice crackers 30, 33
   rice gruel with snapper and yuzu 218–19, 220
   rice with tea 176
ryokan 193, 213

S
sado (*chado*) 15
sake 24, 26, 56, 95, 96, 162, 279
sake brewing 184–5, 187
salads
   burdock root salad 66
   daikon salad 96
   'drenched' chrysanthemum leaf salad 79
sansho 279, 281
Sanzen-in Temple 220–1
sardines 196
   dried 28
sashimi 80
satsuma-age 149, 152
sauces and dressings
   ankake sauce 88
   bainiku (pickled plum purée) 173
   daikon dressing 65
   gobo sarada dressing 66

   kuromitso (black sugar sauce) 182
   miso mustard dressing 87
   tempura-style dipping sauce 165
   tonkatsu sauce 42, 43
   wakame *ankake* sauce 214
   'white' tofu dressing 164
   yuzu dressing 41
   yuzu miso sauce 91
scallops, seared, with butter and shoyu 34
sea slugs 168, 251
seafood 48, 80, 96–7
   see also fish
seasonality 16, 48, 228
seaweed 281
self-reflection 16, 170
Sen Rikyu 229
senbei (rice crackers) 30, 33
Senbon Dori 133
seri 281
sesame 'tofu' 252
set soy milk 116
setsubun 196
shiatsu 170, 233
shichimi togarashi 51, 73, 281
shiitake mushrooms 115
   mock abalone of tofu-stuffed shiitake 230
   shiitake mushroom dashi 29
   vegetarian starter 230
Shinto wedding 72
Shintoism 16, 107, 110
shira-ae 164, 228
shiso 30, 281
shochu ('flu tonic') 187
shogacha 87, 204
shojin ryori cuisine 167, 228–9
shopping 24–5, 56, 118, 133, 244
shoyu 281
shrine visits 107, 110
shungiku no ohitashi 73, 79
side dishes 113
soba noodles 100, 101
   year-crossing soba noodles 98, 100–1
soup
   rice gruel 218
   soup curry 241
   steamed savoury custard cups 214–15
soy beans 112, 143, 201
   for 'protection' 196, 198
   simmered soy beans and vegetables 198, 199
soy milk 73, 82
   to make 84–5
   set 116

soy milk skin 73, 80, 82, 83, 84–5
soy sauce 281
steamed buns 56
stock, chicken 208–9
stock, *see also* dashi
supermarkets 24, 38
suribachi (mortar and pestle) 41, 281
sushi 96
suupu kare 241
sweet potato and beef mince croquettes 63

T
tai to tamago okayu 218–19
Takashimaya Department Store 48
Takayama 192
takenoko gohan 92, 93
tako no yawarakani 119, 122
takuan 155
tea ceremony 15, 48, 149, 161–2, 248
tempura 45, 73, 81
tofu 85, 116
   grilled tofu with sansho miso 53
   koyadofu 229
   mock abalone of tofu-stuffed shiitake 230
   simmered tofu 52
   stir-fried tofu lees and vegetables 140
   tofu pickled in miso 159
   'white' tofu dressing 164
Tokyo 15, 58, 170
tonjiru 174, 181
tonkatsu 42–3
tonkatsu sauce 42, 43
Tooji 58
tori to gobo no kara-age 71
toshikoshi soba 98, 100–1
tsukemono (pickles) 149, 154
tsukudani (side dishes) 113
tsunami 221, 233, 235

U
udo (vegetable) 258
umami (fifth taste) 26, 198
umeboshi 173, 176, 281

V
vegetable fritters 165
vegetables 58, 96, 143, 198
vegetarian cuisine 161–3, 228

W
wabi sabi 248, 251, 269
wagashi (sweets) 48, 149, 161
wagyu 48, 58, 80, 149
wagyu with king brown mushrooms 65
wakame 251
   simmered bamboo shoots and wakame 35
   wakame *ankake* sauce 214
wakatake nimono 24, 35
warabi mochi 174, 182
wasabi 80, 281

Y
yaki wagyu to enringi 65
yakidofu no kinome dengaku 51, 53
yakizakana 251, 257
yatsuhashi 258, 260
year-crossing soba noodles 98, 100–1
yellowtail 125
yokan 144, 146
yuba chips 80, 84
yuba (soy milk skin) 73, 84, 149
yudofu 49, 51, 52
yuzo to miso aisu 224
yuzu 30, 281
   dried rind 24
yuzu dressing 41
yuzu miso sauce 91
yuzu and saikyo miso ice cream 221, 224

Z
zaru soba 101
Zen 9, 102, 149, 248, 269
Zen garden 49
zenzai 129

Published in 2012 by Murdoch Books Pty Limited

Murdoch Books Australia
Pier 8/9
23 Hickson Road
Millers Point NSW 2000
Phone: +61 (0) 2 8220 2000
Fax: +61 (0) 2 8220 2558
www.murdochbooks.com.au
info@murdochbooks.com.au

Murdoch Books UK Limited
Erico House, 6th Floor
93–99 Upper Richmond Road
Putney, London SW15 2TG
Phone: +44 (0) 20 8785 5995
Fax: +44 (0) 20 8785 5985
www.murdochbooks.co.uk
info@murdochbooks.co.uk

For Corporate Orders and Custom Publishing contact
Noel Hammond, National Business Development Manager
Murdoch Books Australia

Publisher: Sally Webb
Art Direction and Design: Reuben Crossman
Project Manager: Laura Wilson
Editors: Katri Hilden and Carla Grosetti
Food Photography: Cath Muscat
Lifestyle Photography: Jane Lawson
Additional food styling and merchandising: Simon Bajada
Home Economist: Olivia Andrews
Production Manager: Karen Small

Text © Jane Lawson 2012
The moral right of the author has been asserted.
Design © Murdoch Books Pty Limited
Food photography © Cath Muscat 2012
Lifestyle photography © Jane Lawson 2012

All rights reserved. No part of this publication may be reproduced, stored in a retrieval system or transmitted in any form or by any means, electronic, mechanical, photocopying, recording or otherwise, without the prior written permission of the publisher.

A cataloguing-in-publication entry is available from the catalogue of the National Library of Australia at www.nla.gov.au.

A catalogue record for this book is available from the British Library.

Printed by 1010 Printing International Limited, China

The Publisher and stylist would like to thank Edo Arts, www.edoarts.com; chefs armoury, www.chefsarmoury.com; made in japan melbourne, www.mij.com.au; kami papers, www.kami.com.au; Ridgeline Pottery www.benrichardson.com.au; and japan city, Bondi junction for lending equipment for use and photography.

IMPORTANT: Those who might be at risk from the effects of salmonella poisoning (the elderly, pregnant women, young children and those suffering from immune deficiency diseases) should consult their doctor with any concerns about eating raw eggs.

OVEN GUIDE: You may find cooking times vary depending on the oven you are using. For fan-forced ovens, as a general rule, set the oven temperature to 20°C (35°F) lower than indicated in the recipe.

We have used 20 ml (4 teaspoon) tablespoon measures. If you are using a 15 ml (3 teaspoon) tablespoon, add an extra teaspoon of the ingredient for each tablespoon specified.

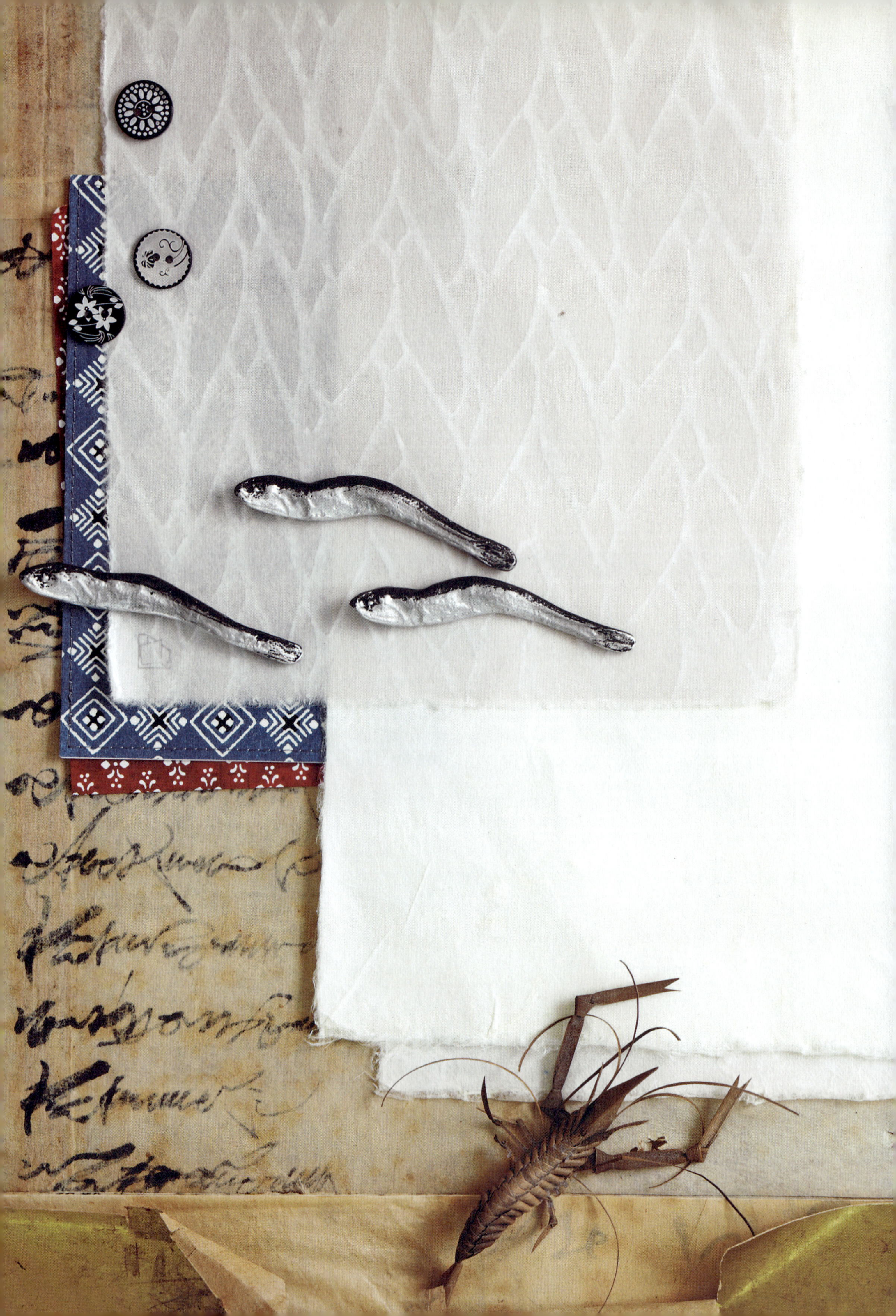